The Economics of the Great Depression

For my lovely wife Monica

The Economics of the Great Depression

A Twenty-First Century Look Back at the Economics of the Interwar Era

Randall E. Parker

Professor of Economics, East Carolina University, Greenville, North Carolina, USA

Edward Elgar

Cheltenham, UK • Northampton, MA, USA

Published by
Edward Elgar Publishing Limited
Glensanda House
Montpellier Parade
Cheltenham
Glos GL50 1UA
UK

Edward Elgar Publishing, Inc.
William Pratt House
9 Dewey Court
Northampton
Massachusetts 01060
USA

A catalogue record for this book is available from the British Library

Library of Congress Cataloging in Publication Data

Parker, Randall E., 1960-
  The economics of the great depression : a twenty-first century look back at the economics of the interwar era / Randall E. Parker.
      p. cm.
  Includes bibliographical references and index.
  1. United States—Economic conditions—1918-1945. 2. Depressions—1929—United States. I. Title.
  HC106.3.P33468 2007
  330.973'0917—dc22

                              2006037995

ISBN 978 1 84542 127 4

Printed and bound in Great Britain by the MPG Books Group

Contents

Acknowledgements   vi
Foreword by Victor Zarnowitz   vii
Preface   x

An Overview of the Great Depression   1
Peter Temin   29
Ben Bernanke   52
James Hamilton   68
Robert Lucas   88
Lee Ohanian   102
Christina Romer   124
Barry Eichengreen   138
Stephen Cecchetti   155
James Butkiewicz   177
Michael Bordo   191
Charles Calomiris   210
Allan Meltzer   224

References   242
Index   256

Acknowledgements

I would like to thank several individuals who were responsible for the completion of this book:

My wife Monica for her love, friendship and unquestioned support.

Richard and Paula Parker, my father and mother. They made me know the value of work, and I have never wanted for anything a day in my life.

My brother Rick, who threatened me with bodily harm if I did not finish my Ph.D. Threats such as these from an older brother have a certain incentive effect. My sister-in-law Ginger deserves a special thanks too as she and my brother gave to me freely when I was in graduate school, and they really did not have a lot to spare.

My entire family. I have never walked alone. May we all lead contemplative lives.

Victor Zarnowitz, you have made this world a better place to live.

Gucharan S. Laumas, who told me to play the hand I was dealt and take my happiness as it comes. I have never received better advice.

James Fackler and W. Douglas McMillin, thanks for all you have done for me. There are debts here that I am not sure I can repay.

Philip A. Rothman, valued colleague, world-class time series econometrician, and great friend.

Craig Landry and Mohammad Jahan-Parvar, you know fellas, this may be the beginning of a beautiful friendship.

The economists who agreed to speak with me for this book. Thanks for your kind attention.

Foreword

Victor Zarnowitz
Senior Fellow and Economic Counselor
The Conference Board

Randall Parker's 2002 collection of interviews with eleven economists born between 1905 and 1919, *Reflections on the Great Depression*, demonstrates how strong was the impact on each of them of the general economic declines of the 1930s. Whether in America, Europe, or Asia, contemporary witnesses and/or future students of the subject soon learned that this depression was unique in its severity, duration and global diffusion. These insights guided some to choose economics in general and business cycles in particular as their principal subjects of study and career.

In fact, the Great Depression ranks high among the topics most widely and intensively explored in literature on macroeconomic theory and history. Yet progress in understanding the sources and extent of this critical episode has been unusually slow. Even now, more than 60 years later, some of the related issues are much debated, yet not fully resolved. This only added to the lure and challenge of the subject, while revealing its unexpected complexity.

The short period of barely 21 years between the two World Wars witnessed an unprecedented confluence of political, financial and economic disasters: without doubt, the worst phase of modern history. The Great Depression, though far from being the whole, was a central part of this nexus of adverse causes, contents, and consequences. The interwar generation of economists and historians on the whole lacked the information and perspective, tools and models, to comprehend these extraordinary developments. Only lately did the requisite instruments, data, and knowledge become available to the profession.

The present volume draws on these resources by combining the results of twelve comprehensive interviews the author conducted with the equal number of economists who studied and tried to explain the Great Depression in great detail and partly new ways. Whereas the first volume concentrated on personal recollections of older economists, this one discusses the current state of accumulated professional knowledge about all aspects of the Great Depression. Its title is correspondingly broad and ambitious: *The Economics of the Great Depression: A Twenty-First Century Look Back at the Economics of the*

Interwar Era.

Personal reflections would be expected to differ much from scientific findings, and they do. This explains any of the apparent conflicts between the opinions and statements in the two books, despite the fact that they target the same long-gone era. But all the interviewees are highly professional economists who dealt with the broad but, I think, for them sufficiently well-defined subject of business cycles. And this helps to explain the elements of complementarity that also coexist in Randy Parker's two volumes.

The generally well-known senior economists of *Reflections* were still young and learning in the fateful 1930s, and probably just exposed to standard economics. They were struggling with how to reconcile the views on the efficiency of competitive markets with the reality of high and growing joblessness and poverty that they saw all around them at the time. It was only considerably later, at least not before the early post-World War II years, that they came up with ideas about the role of money and credit in business cycles, monetary and fiscal policies, banking and other institutions, the gold standard and other exchange rate regimes, to name a few. But, to a large extent, it was the Great Depression that gave impetus to their thinking about these matters. As a result, much was accomplished by these economists, in the area of business cycles and elsewhere.

Yet these efforts were far from enough for a full understanding of the Great Depression. A great deal more and different work was left to do by the younger generation of economists interviewed in *The Economics of the Great Depression*. This includes the elaborations of several hypotheses, some of them older and others new, about which factors account for the initial downturn and which for the extent and spread of the Great Depression. The monetary hypothesis has a relatively long and rich development. The downturn that led to the worst contraction ever is linked to the collapse of the money supply and the financial system. The Federal Reserve is responsible for failing to prevent or contain these catastrophes. Another old hypothesis is that of debt deflation, and a new related one is that of the impact of bank panics on the allocation of funds from lenders to borrowers (the nonmonetary/financial hypothesis). The length, depth, and international spread of the Depression are now much better understood thanks to the revival of research on the structure and operation of the gold standard in the interwar period. The orthodox commitment to the gold standard came back after World War I in the worst imaginable way and under the worst conditions. The center of the trouble was in Western Europe as much as in the United States.

A basic question asked in the past, and now newly raised, was how to reconcile people's desires to go on producing, exchanging, and consuming with the massive idleness induced by the Depression. This led to the highly controversial yet also interesting and hence instructive "real business cycle" hypothesis.

Inevitably, reading the "Reflections" is much easier than reading the "Economics" of the Great Depression, but it is also less informative. Taken together, the two books will give anyone who peruses them a wealth of information about, not just the interwar period and its mostly woeful legacy, but also about business cycles in the past and present more generally. My own taste goes more to statistics and econometrics, but tables and charts about the Great Depression can readily be found in the literature covered amply in Randy Parker's two volumes.

Enjoy the journey as we continue in our search for understanding of this most important historical economic epoch.

Preface

Understanding the Great Depression is the Holy Grail of macroeconomics as Ben Bernanke (1995) has correctly claimed. Every generation of economists tries to wrap their hands around this prized chalice. My first book, *Reflections on the Great Depression*, contained interviews with 11 of the top economists who lived through the Depression and was an account of what we have learned from the interwar generation of economists and their crack at trying to explain the Great Depression. A historian friend of mine once told me that many times a generation has to pass before there is an honest evaluation of a particular historical epoch. Often the participants in real time have a genuine stake in how the episode is interpreted. Critical and disinterested evaluations only come about when those who lived through the time have come and gone, at least from active scholarship. This is probably true. We are now at that point in our evaluation of the economics of the interwar era. The purpose of this book is to provide an account of what we have learned from the post-World War II generation of economists and their crack at trying to explain the Great Depression.

A new set of eyes, theoretical advances, more sophisticated statistical and econometric techniques, time, and the fact that we still do not have a complete set of answers (and almost certainly never will) all have a way of pulling each generation of economists toward a fresh look at the Great Depression. It was said by Eichengreen and Temin (1997) that "the modern literature can be regarded as having substantially solved the riddle of the Great Depression." The rest is down to details and filling in the minor colors of the landscape in a grand painting. I believe that most of the economics profession, and certainly most economic historians, would say this is true. And yet, the next step in this evolution has only begun. This book stops at a time when a new paradigm has just been introduced to this literature. Proponents of real business cycle analysis and dynamic stochastic general equilibrium (DSGE) modeling have indicated they view the economics of the Great Depression as a totally open question. A full understanding of the economic events of the interwar era can not be provided by current explanations, as these explanations do little to shed light on what really occurred. We need to start again from the ground up. Some find this position maddening. Others think it absurd. Perhaps and perhaps not, but one thing is for sure. The next generation of economists, the ones after the post-World War II generation, are now just beginning to have their crack at trying to explain the Great Depression. Wherever it may wind up and whatever we may learn when it is all said and done, the DSGE research agenda has done us all a great service by continuing to shine the scholarly light on this literature. I look forward to where it may lead.

Thirty years from now when another new generation of economists takes their fresh look at the Great Depression, maybe someone reading this book will realize that the next book in this series on the evolution of the economic literature on the Great Depression will then be ready to be written. For those who have not appreciated the two works I have put together, you will be happy to know it will not be me. But whoever it may be, I hope they learn as much as I did, have as much fun in doing the project as I did, and get to meet some incredibly interesting people. Be ready; scholars tend to speak more plainly in person than how they write, as the interviews in this book will reveal. When they say things compactly and with precision, in a way that helps make a whole strand of the literature crystal clear and helps to summarize dozens upon dozens of scholarly papers and books, that is a moment not to be missed.

For the here and now, when the discussions in this book are scholarly in tone, maybe the reader will learn something from these interviews or at least have what was already known reinforced in their mind. When they are humorous and the conversation becomes lighter, maybe the reader will share in some of the fun I had putting this book together. As I said in *Reflections on the Great Depression*, my sincere hope is that these interviews give you a healthy dose of the former and a happy dose of the latter. It was really worth the trip.

Randall E. Parker

An Overview of the Great Depression

Modern macroeconomics emerged from the economic catastrophe that was the Great Depression. The Depression produced the economists who began and nurtured the economic literature on the Great Depression in particular, and the development of modern macroeconomics in general. The interwar generation had their crack at trying to explain the economics of the Great Depression. This book contains interviews with 12 of the leading economists of the post-World War II generation who have made significant advances in our understanding of the economics of the Great Depression: Peter Temin, Ben Bernanke, James Hamilton, Robert Lucas, Lee Ohanian, Christina Romer, Barry Eichengreen, Stephen Cecchetti, James Butkiewicz, Michael Bordo, Charles Calomiris and Allan Meltzer. The purpose of this book is to provide an account of what we have learned from the post-World War II generation of economists and their crack at trying to explain the Great Depression. We will turn our attention to these individuals in the interviews that follow. Before we do, however, it is important to provide some historical and theoretical background for the interviews.

This chapter provides an overview of selected events and economic explanations of the interwar era, so that the reader can put the substance of the interviews into proper context. What follows is not intended to be a detailed and exhaustive review of the literature on the Great Depression, or of any one theory in particular. Rather, I will attempt to describe what I consider to be the "big picture" events and topics of interest. In doing so, I hope to highlight the content and importance of the questions and answers contained in the 12 interviews. For the reader who wishes more extensive analysis and detail, references to additional materials are also included.

THE 1920s

The Great Depression, and the economic catastrophe that it was, is perhaps properly scaled in reference to the decade that preceded it, the 1920s. By conventional macroeconomic measures, this was a decade of brisk economic growth in the United States. Perhaps the moniker "the roaring twenties" summarizes this period most succinctly. The disruptions and shocking nature of World War I had been survived and it was felt the United States was entering a "new era." In January 1920, the Federal Reserve seasonally adjusted index of industrial production, a standard measure of aggregate economic activity, stood at 81 (1935–39 = 100). When the index peaked in July 1929 it was at 114, for a growth rate of 40.6 percent over this period. Similar rates of growth over the 1920–29 period equal to 47.3 percent and 42.4 percent are computed using annual real gross national product data from Balke and Gordon (1986) and Romer (1988a), respectively. Further computations using the Balke and Gordon (1986) data indicate an average annual growth rate of real GNP over the 1920–29 period equal to 4.6 percent. In addition, the relative international economic strength of this country was clearly displayed by the fact that nearly one-half of world industrial output in 1925–29 was produced in the United States (Bernanke, 1983a).

The decade of the 1920s also saw major innovations in the consumption behavior of households. The development of installment credit over this period led to substantial growth in the consumer durables market (Bernanke, 1983a; Olney, 1991, 1999). Purchases of automobiles, refrigerators, radios and other such durable goods all experienced explosive growth during the 1920s as small borrowers, particularly households and unincorporated businesses, utilized their access to available credit (Persons, 1930; Soule, 1947; Bernanke, 1983a; Olney, 1991, 1999).

Economic growth during this period was mitigated only somewhat by three recessions. According to the National Bureau of Economic Research (NBER) business cycle chronology, two of these recessions were from May 1923 through July 1924 and October 1926 through November 1927. Both of these recessions were very mild and unremarkable. In contrast, the 1920s began with a recession lasting 18 months from the peak in January 1920 until the trough of July 1921. Original estimates of real GNP from the Commerce Department showed that real GNP fell 8 percent between 1919 and 1920 and another 7 percent between 1920 and 1921 (Romer, 1988a). The behavior of prices contributed to the naming of this recession "the Depression of 1921," as the implicit price deflator for GNP fell 16 percent and the Bureau of Labor Statistics wholesale price index fell 46 percent between 1920 and 1921. However, Romer (1988a) has argued that the so-called "post-war depression" was not as severe as once thought. While the deflation from war-time prices was substantial, revised estimates of real GNP show falls in output of only 1 percent between 1919 and 1920 and 2 percent between 1920 and 1921. Romer (1988a) also argues that the behaviors of output and prices are inconsistent with the conventional explanation of the Depression of 1921 being primarily driven by a decline in aggregate demand. Rather, the deflation and the mild recession are better understood as resulting from a decline in aggregate demand together with a series of positive supply shocks, particularly in the production of agricultural goods, and significant decreases in the prices of imported primary commodities. Overall, the upshot is that the growth path of output was hardly impeded by the three minor downturns, so that the decade of the 1920s can properly be viewed economically as a very healthy period.

Friedman and Schwartz (1963) label the 1920s "the high tide of the Reserve System." As they explain, the Federal Reserve became increasingly confident in the tools of policy and in its knowledge of how to use them properly. The synchronous movements of economic activity and explicit policy actions by the Federal Reserve did not go unnoticed. Taking the next step and concluding there was cause and effect, the Federal Reserve began in the 1920s to use monetary policy as an implement to stabilize business cycle fluctuations. "In retrospect, we can see that this was a major step toward the assumption by government of explicit continuous responsibility for economic stability. As the decade wore on, the System took – and perhaps even more was given – credit for the generally stable conditions that prevailed, and high hopes were placed in the potency of monetary policy as then administered" (Friedman and Schwartz, 1963).

The giving/taking of credit to/by the Federal Reserve has particular value pertaining to the recession of 1920–21. Although suggesting the Federal Reserve probably tightened too much, too late, Friedman and Schwartz (1963) call this episode "the first real trial of the new system of monetary control introduced by the Federal Reserve Act." It is clear from the history of the time that the Federal Reserve felt as though it had successfully passed this test. The data showed that the economy had quickly recovered and brisk growth followed the recession of 1920–21 for the remainder of the decade.

Moreover, Eichengreen (1992) suggests that the episode of 1920–21 led the Federal Reserve System to believe that the economy could be successfully deflated or "liquidated" without paying a severe penalty in terms of reduced output. This conclusion, however, proved to be mistaken at the onset of the Depression. As argued by Eichengreen (1992), the Federal Reserve did not appreciate the extent to which the successful deflation could be attributed to the unique circumstances that prevailed during 1920–21. The European economies were still devastated after World War I, so the demand for United States' exports remained strong many years after the War. Moreover, the gold standard was not in operation at the time. Therefore, European countries were not forced to match the deflation initiated in the United States by the Federal Reserve (explained below pertaining to the gold standard hypothesis).

The implication is that the Federal Reserve thought that deflation could be generated with little effect on real economic activity. Therefore, the Federal Reserve was not vigorous in fighting the Great Depression in its initial stages. It viewed the early years of the Depression as another opportunity to successfully liquidate the economy, especially after the perceived speculative excesses of the 1920s. However, the state of the economic world in 1929 was not a duplicate of 1920–21 as pointed out by Temin (1989), Eichengreen

(1992) and Eichengreen and Temin (1997). By 1929, the European economies had recovered and the interwar gold exchange standard was a vehicle for the international transmission of deflation. Deflation in 1929 would not operate as it did in 1920–21. The Federal Reserve failed, among other things, to understand the economic implications of this change in the international standing of the United States' economy and the functioning of the interwar gold exchange standard. The result was that the Depression was permitted to spiral out of control and was made much worse than it otherwise would have been had the Federal Reserve not considered it to be a repeat of the 1920–21 recession.

THE BEGINNINGS OF THE GREAT DEPRESSION

In 1927, in the eyes of many contemporary observers, the seeds of the Great Depression were planted when the Federal Reserve eased policy to assist the Bank of England through a time of trial they were experiencing in maintaining the gold standard. By January 1928 those seeds began to germinate as the Federal Reserve became contractionary in response to perceived speculative excesses that many blamed on the aforementioned monetary easing. It is around this time that two of the most prominent explanations for the depth, length, and worldwide spread of the Depression first came to be manifest. Without any doubt, the economics profession – with the exception perhaps, at least for now, of the real business cycle modelers – would come to a firm consensus around the idea that the economic events of 1928–33 cannot be properly understood without a solid linkage to both the behavior of the supply of money together with Federal Reserve actions on the one hand and the flawed structure of the interwar gold standard on the other. I shall have more to say about these below.

It is well documented that many public officials, such as President Herbert Hoover and members of the Federal Reserve System in the latter 1920s, were intent on ending what they perceived to be the speculative excesses that were driving the stock market boom. Moreover, as explained by Hamilton (1987), despite plentiful denials to the contrary, the Federal Reserve assumed the role of "arbiter of security prices." Although there continues to be debate as to whether or not the stock market was overvalued at the time (White, 1990; DeLong and Schleifer, 1991; McGrattan and Prescott, 2004), the main point is that the Federal Reserve believed there to be a speculative bubble in equity values. Hamilton (1987) describes how the Federal Reserve, intending to "pop" the bubble, embarked on a highly contractionary monetary policy in January 1928. Between December 1927 and July 1928 the Federal Reserve conducted $393 million of open market sales of securities so that only $80 million remained in the Open Market account. Buying rates on bankers' acceptances were raised from 3 percent in January 1928 to 4.5 percent by July, reducing Federal Reserve holdings of such bills by $193 million, leaving a total of only $185 million of these bills on balance. Further, the discount rate was increased from 3.5 percent to 5 percent, the highest level since the recession of 1920–21. "In short, in terms of the magnitudes consciously controlled by the Fed, it would be difficult to design a more contractionary policy than that initiated in January 1928" (Hamilton, 1987).

The pressure did not stop there, however. The death of Federal Reserve Bank President Benjamin Strong and the subsequent control of policy ascribed to Adolph Miller of the Federal Reserve Board insured that the fall in the stock market was going to be made a reality. Miller, as a vast many did back then, firmly believed in the real bills doctrine, the idea that loans should only be made for productive purposes to accommodate the needs of the business community and should be self-liquidating. The real bills doctrine made monetary policy passive and endogenous with respect to the level of business activity. Any credit that was extended that was not backed by "real bills" was considered speculative and thus inflationary (Meltzer, 2003). The speculative excesses of the stock market were hurting the economy, causing inflation that would inevitably have to be followed by deflation, and the Federal Reserve continued attempting to put an end to this perceived harm (Cecchetti, 1998). The amount of Federal Reserve credit that was being extended to market participants in the form of broker loans became an issue in 1929. The Federal Reserve adamantly discouraged lending that was collateralized by equities. The intentions of the Board of Governors of the Federal Reserve were made clear in a letter dated February 2, 1929, sent to Federal Reserve banks. In part the letter read:

> The board has no disposition to assume authority to interfere with the loan practices of member banks so long as they do not involve the Federal reserve banks. It has, however, a grave responsibility whenever there is evidence that member banks are maintaining speculative security loans with the aid of Federal reserve credit. When such is the case the Federal reserve bank becomes either a contributing or a sustaining factor in the current volume of speculative security credit. This is not in harmony with the intent of the Federal Reserve Act, nor is it conducive to the wholesome operation of the banking and credit system of the country. (Board of Governors of the Federal Reserve, 1929: 93–94, quoted from Cecchetti, 1998)

The deflationary pressure to stock prices had been applied. It was now a question of when the market would break. Although the effects were not immediate, the wait was not long. Nor was the impact restricted to the US. Eichengreen (2004) points out that the initial downturn in the US was intensified as US exports began falling in 1929 as a result of an even greater monetary tightening in Latin America and Europe in response to the Federal

Reserve's monetary stringency in 1928–29. The gold standard required countries to raise interest rates to stem gold loss to the US. Thus the gold standard has a role in explaining the onset of the Depression as well its depth and worldwide spread.

THE ECONOMY STUMBLES

The NBER business cycle chronology dates the start of the Great Depression in August 1929. For this reason many have said that the Depression started on Main Street and not Wall Street. Be that as it may, the stock market plummeted in October of 1929. The bursting of the speculative bubble had been achieved and the economy was now headed in an ominous direction. The Federal Reserve's seasonally adjusted index of industrial production stood at 114 (1935–39 = 100) in August 1929. By October it had fallen to 110 for a decline of 3.5 percent (annualized percentage decline = 14.7 percent). After the crash, the incipient recession intensified, with the industrial production index falling from 110 in October to 100 in December 1929, or 9 percent (annualized percentage decline = 41 percent). In 1930, the index fell further from 100 in January to 79 in December, or an additional 21 percent.

While popular history treats the crash and the Depression as one and the same event, economists know that they were not. But there is no doubt that the crash was one of the things that got the ball rolling. Several authors have offered explanations for the linkage between the crash and the recession of 1929–30. Mishkin (1978) argues that the crash and an increase in liabilities led to a deterioration of households' balance sheets. The reduced liquidity led consumers to defer consumption of durable goods and housing and thus contributed to a fall in consumption. Temin (1976a) suggests that the fall in stock prices had a negative wealth effect on consumption, but attributes only a minor role to this given that stocks were not a large fraction of total wealth; the stock market in 1929, although falling dramatically, remained above the value it had achieved in early 1928, and the propensity to consume from wealth was small during this period. Romer (1990) provides evidence suggesting that if the stock market were thought to be a predictor of future economic activity, then the crash can rightly be viewed as a source of increased consumer uncertainty that depressed spending on consumer durables and accelerated the decline that had begun in August 1929. Flacco and Parker (1992) confirm Romer's findings using different data and alternative estimation techniques.

Looking back on the behavior of the economy during the year of 1930, industrial production declined 21 percent, the consumer price index fell 2.6 percent, the supply of high-powered money (that is, liabilities of the Federal Reserve consisting of currency in circulation and bank reserves; also called the monetary base) fell 2.8 percent, the nominal supply of M1 (the product of the monetary base multiplied by the money multiplier) dipped 3.5 percent and the ex post real interest rate turned out to be 11.3 percent, the highest it had been since the recession of 1920–21 (Hamilton, 1987). In spite of this, when put into historical context, there was no reason to view the downturn of 1929–30 as historically unprecedented. Its magnitude was comparable to that of many recessions that had previously occurred. Perhaps there was justifiable optimism in December 1930 that the economy might even shake off the negative movement and embark on the path to recovery, rather like what had occurred after the recession of 1920–21 (Bernanke, 1983a). As we know, the bottom would not come for another 27 months.

THE ECONOMY CRUMBLES

During 1931, there was a "change in the character of the contraction" (Friedman and Schwartz, 1963). In November and December 1930, the first of a series of banking panics now accompanied the downward spasms of the business cycle. Although bank failures had occurred throughout the 1920s, the magnitude of the failures that occurred in the early 1930s was of a different order altogether (Bernanke, 1983a). The absence of any type of deposit insurance resulted in the contagion of the panics being spread to sound financial institutions and not just those on the margin, although the importance of this contagion in pre–1933 panics is questioned by the evidence presented in Calomiris and Mason (2003b). Regional unit banking in the US, after the McFadden Act of 1927 forbad nationwide banking, also made banking panics particularly harsh in certain geographical, especially agricultural, areas (Wicker, 1996). Moreover, institutional arrangements that had existed in the private banking system designed to provide liquidity to fight bank runs before 1913 were not exercised after the creation of the Federal Reserve System, although counter-evidence is provided by Calomiris and Mason (1997). For example, during the panic of 1907, the effects of the financial upheaval had been contained through a combination of lending activities by private banks, called clearing houses, and the suspension of deposit convertibility into currency. While these countermeasures did not prevent bank runs and the financial panic, they lessened their economic effect to a significant extent, as the economy quickly recovered in 1908. The aftermath of the panic of 1907 and the desire to have a central authority to combat the contagion of financial disruptions was one of the factors that led to the establishment of the Federal Reserve System. After the creation of the Federal Reserve, clearing house lending and suspension of deposit convertibility by private banks were not undertaken. Believing the Federal Reserve to be the "lender of last resort," it was apparently thought that the responsibility to fight bank runs was the domain of the central bank (Friedman and Schwartz, 1963; Bernanke, 1983a).

Unfortunately, when the banking panics came in waves and the financial system was collapsing, being the "lender of last resort" was a responsibility that the Federal Reserve either could not or would not assume.

The economic effects of the banking panics were devastating. Aside from the obvious impact of the closing of failed banks and the subsequent loss of deposits by bank customers, the growth rate of the money supply accelerated its downward spiral. Although the economy had flattened out after the first wave of bank failures in November–December 1930, with the industrial production index steadying from 79 in December 1930 to 80 in May 1931, the remainder of 1931 brought a series of shocks from which the economy was not to recover for some time.

In May, the failure of Austria's largest bank, the Kredit-anstalt, touched off financial panics in Europe. In September 1931, having had enough of the distress associated with the international transmission of economic depression, Britain abandoned its participation in the gold standard. The US, however, stuck it out and steadfastly maintained its ties to gold. As pointed out by Kindleberger (1986) and Hamilton (1988), important macroeconomic measures such as the money supply, prices and output all experienced accelerated declines in the period after Britain abandoned gold and the US defended the dollar. Preservation of the exchange rate came at a heavy price in terms of continued and worsening domestic instability. Further, just as the United States' economy appeared to be trying to begin recovery, the second wave of bank failures hit the financial system in June 1931 and did not abate until December. In addition, the Hoover administration in December 1931, adhering to its principles of limited government, embarked on a campaign to balance the federal budget. Tax increases resulted in June 1932, just as the economy was to hit the first low point of its so-called "double bottom" (Hoover, 1952).

The results of these events are now evident. Between January and December 1931 the industrial production index declined from 78 to 66, or 15.4 percent, the consumer price index fell 9.4 percent, the nominal supply of M1 dipped 5.7 percent, the ex post real interest rate remained at 11.3 percent, and although the supply of high-powered money actually increased 5.5 percent, the currency–deposit and reserve–deposit ratios began their upward ascent, and thus the money multiplier started its downward plunge (Hamilton, 1987). If the economy had flattened out in the spring of 1931, then by December output, the money supply, and the price level were all on negative growth paths that were dragging the economy deeper into depression.

The economic difficulties were far from over. The economy displayed some evidence of recovery in late summer/early fall of 1932 after a series of very large open market purchases executed by the Federal Reserve in spring and early summer 1932. However, in December 1932 the third, and largest, wave of banking panics hit the financial markets and the collapse of the economy arrived with the business cycle hitting bottom in March 1933.

Industrial production between January 1932 and March 1933 fell an additional 15.6 percent. For the combined years of 1932 and 1933, the consumer price index fell a cumulative 16.2 percent, the nominal supply of M1 dropped 21.6 percent, the nominal M2 money supply fell 34.7 percent, and although the supply of high-powered money increased 8.4 percent, the currency–deposit and reserve–deposit ratios accelerated their upward ascent. Thus the money multiplier continued on a downward plunge that was not arrested until March 1933. Similar behaviors for real GDP, prices, money supplies and other key macroeconomic variables occurred in many European economies as well (Temin, 1989; Snowdon, 2002).

An examination of the macroeconomic data in August 1929 compared to March 1933 provides a stark contrast. The unemployment rate of 3 percent in August 1929 was at 25 percent in March 1933. The industrial production index of 114 in August 1929 was at 54 in March 1933, or a 52.6 percent decrease. Given, as mentioned above, that the United States produced one-half of world industrial production in 1925–29, the United States accounted for one-fourth of the fall in world industrial output. The money supply had fallen 35 percent, prices plummeted by about 33 percent, and more than one-third of banks in the United States were either closed or taken over by other banks. The "new era" ushered in by "the roaring twenties" was over. Roosevelt took office in March 1933 – thereafter the 20th Amendment moved all subsequent inaugurations to January to eliminate this type of prolonged interregnum of inaction from November 1932 to March 1933 – a nationwide bank holiday was declared from March 6 until March 13, and the United States abandoned the international gold standard in April 1933. Recovery commenced immediately and the economy began its long path back to the pre-1929 secular growth trend.

CONTEMPORARY EXPLANATIONS

The economics profession during the 1930s, although not universally, was at a loss to explain the Depression. The most prominent conventional explanations were of two types. First, some observers at the time firmly grounded their explanations on the two pillars of classical macroeconomic thought, Say's Law and the belief in the self-equilibrating powers of the market. Many argued that it was simply a question of time before wages and prices adjusted fully enough for the economy to return to full employment and achieve the realization of the putative axiom that "supply creates its own demand." Second, the Austrian school of thought argued that the Depression was the inevitable result of the credit boom/overinvestment cycle during the 1920s that had led to an imbalance in the structure of production between long-lived and short-lived goods (Hayek, 1967; Eichengreen and Mitchener, 2004). The best remedy for the situation was to let the Depression run its course so that the economy could be purified from the negative effects of the false expansion. Government intervention was viewed by the Austrian school as a mechanism that would simply prolong the agony and make any subsequent depression worse than it would ordinarily be.

The Hoover administration and the Federal Reserve Board also contained several so-called "liquidationists." These individuals basically believed that economic agents should be forced to re-arrange their spending proclivities and alter their alleged profligate use of resources. If it took mass bankruptcies to produce this result and wipe the slate clean so that everyone could have a fresh start, then so be it. The liquidationists viewed the events of the Depression as an economic penance for the speculative excesses of the 1920s. Thus, the Depression was the price that was being paid for the misdeeds of the previous decade. This is perhaps best exemplified in the well-known quotation of Treasury Secretary Andrew Mellon, who advised President Hoover to "Liquidate labor, liquidate stocks, liquidate the farmers, liquidate real estate." Mellon continued, "It will purge the rottenness out of the system. High costs of living and high living will come down. People will work harder, live a more moral life. Values will be adjusted, and enterprising people will pick up the wrecks from less competent people" (Hoover, 1952). Hoover apparently followed this advice as the Depression wore on. He continued to reassure the public that if the principles of orthodox finance were faithfully followed, recovery would surely be the result. The thought back then among many Federal Reserve governors and others was that deflation was the inevitable consequence of speculative inflation and therefore deflationary economic contractions were a natural consequence of the path of business activity (Calomiris and Wheelock, 1998; Meltzer, 2003).

The business press at the time was not immune from such liquidationist prescriptions either. The *Commercial and Financial Chronicle*, in an August 3, 1929 editorial entitled "Is not group speculating conspiracy, fostering sham prosperity?", complained of the economy being replete with profligate spending including:

> (a) The luxurious diversification of diet advantageous to dairy men ... and fruit growers ...; (b) luxurious dressing ... more silk and rayon ...; (c) free spending for automobiles and their accessories, gasoline, house furnishings and equipment, radios, travel, amusements and sports; (d) the displacement from the farms by tractors and autos of produce-consuming horses and mules to a number aggregating 3,700,000 for the period 1918–1928 ... (e) the frills of education to thousands for whom places might better be reserved at bench or counter or on the farm. (Quoted from Nelson, 1991)

Persons, in a paper which appeared in the November 1930 *Quarterly Journal of Economics*, demonstrates that some academic economists also held similar liquidationist views.

Although certainly not universal, the descriptions above suggest that no small part of the conventional wisdom at the time believed the Depression to be a penitence for past sins. In addition, it was thought that the economy would be restored to full employment equilibrium once wages and prices adjusted sufficiently. Say's Law will ensure the economy will return to health, and supply will create its own demand sufficient to return to prosperity, if we simply let the system work its way through. Many contemporaries would also insist on adding adherence to the gold standard to the list of orthodox principles that, if steadfastly maintained, would extricate the economy from its current malaise. In his memoirs published in 1952, 20 years after his election defeat, Herbert Hoover continued to steadfastly maintain that if Roosevelt and the New Dealers had stuck to the policies his administration put in place, the economy would have made a full recovery within 18 months after the election of 1932.

There were dissenting voices to the conventional wisdom of the time. In particular, there was a movement in Congress to change the charter of the Federal Reserve System. Congressmen James Strong of Kansas and T. Alan Goldsborough of Maryland both sponsored legislation that would have mandated the Federal Reserve to adopt a price level target. The Goldsborough bill of 1932 (following similar legislative efforts Goldsborough had begun as early as 1922), which passed the House 289–60 (Krooss, 1969), directed the Federal Reserve to use all available means to return wholesale commodity prices to the level that existed before the deflation and then to keep them there. Strong's bill of 1926 had similar objectives of mandating price stability as the key goal for monetary policy. The fact that this legislation may not be consistent with maintenance of the gold standard was not lost on Congressman Goldsborough, as Section 3 of the legislation gave the Federal Reserve the authority to raise the official price of gold if the gold reserve minimums were threatened. The Goldsborough bill was dead on arrival when it got to the Senate. Carter Glass, a Senator from Virginia, was a staunch supporter of the real bills doctrine, was the watchdog of monetary legislation in the Senate, played a major role in drafting the Federal Reserve Act, and was not going to permit this bill to see the light of day (see the conversations with James Butkiewicz and Allan Meltzer in this book). Meltzer (2003) claims the defeat of the 1926 Strong bill was a missed opportunity to avoid the Depression completely. Knowing what we know now, it is impossible to see how this could be otherwise. The defeat of the Goldsborough bill in the summer of 1932 was a blown chance to get out of the Depression sooner than we did.

MODERN EXPLANATIONS

This section describes the main hypotheses that have been presented in the literature attempting to explain the causes for the depth, protracted length, and worldwide propagation of the Great Depression.

Modern explanations of the Great Depression have settled into several different categories. One major branch of the literature focuses its attention on the US as the main source of economic calamity which was then spread throughout the world primarily by the gold standard (the monetary hypothesis). Another major branch of the literature takes a much more worldly approach, insisting that a more accurate viewing of the Depression is most properly done in an international context, eschewing a US-centric approach (the gold standard hypothesis). Other major branches have made contributions that augment, expand and complement existing approaches (the nonmonetary/financial approach and its relation to the monetary hypothesis), while still other branches are taking the literature in completely different and new directions (the real business cycle hypothesis). Regardless of which approach is taken, the literature today has moved toward what Ben Bernanke labeled "the comparative approach." That is, much of the research on the Depression – while not universally nor should we expect or desire it to be – is conducted by examining a battery of countries and comparing what we learn from each (a partial listing would include Choudhri and Kochin (1980); Eichengreen and Sachs, 1985; Hamilton, 1988; Temin, 1989; Bernanke and James, 1991; Eichengreen, 1992; Bernanke, 1995; Bernanke and Mihov, 2000; *Review of Economic Dynamics*, volume 5, 2002; Balderston, 2003; Cole and Ohanian, 2004b; and Eichengreen, 2004).

It should be noted that I do not include a section covering the nonmonetary/nonfinancial theories of the Great Depression. These theories, including Temin's (1976a) focus on autonomous consumption decline, the collapse of housing construction contained in Anderson and Butkiewicz (1980) and the issues of land use control discussed in Field (1992), the effects of the stock market crash (discussed above), the uncertainty hypothesis of Romer (1990), the default/installment credit structure that led to the collapse of durables spending in the early stages of the Depression discussed in the excellent paper by Olney (1999), and the Smoot–Hawley Tariff Act of 1930, are all worthy of mention and can rightly be apportioned some of the responsibility for initiating and propagating the Depression. However, any theory of the Depression must be able to account for the protracted nonneutralities associated with the punishing deflation imposed on the United States and the world during that era. While there are still many important topics relating to nonmonetary/nonfinancial theories of the Depression that are worthy of our attention (see the conversation with Peter Temin in this book), my reading of the empirical results of the economic literature indicates that they do not have the explanatory power of the other theories mentioned above to account for the depths to which the world economy plunged.

The Monetary Hypothesis

In reviewing the economic history of the Depression above, it was mentioned that the supply of money fell by 35 percent, prices dropped by about 33 percent, and one-third of all banks vanished. Milton Friedman and Anna Schwartz, in their 1963 book *A Monetary History of the United States, 1867–1960*, call this massive drop in the supply of money "the Great Contraction."

Friedman and Schwartz (1963) discuss and painstakingly document the synchronous movements of the real economy with the disruptions that occurred in the financial sector. They point out that the series of bank failures that occurred beginning in October 1930 worsened economic conditions in two ways. First, bank shareholder wealth was reduced as banks failed. Second, and most importantly, the bank failures were exogenous shocks and led to the drastic decline in the money supply. The persistent deflation of the 1930s follows directly from this "great contraction."

However, this raises an important question: where was the Federal Reserve while the money supply and the financial system were collapsing? If the Federal Reserve was created in 1913 primarily to be the "lender of last resort" for troubled financial institutions, it was failing miserably. Friedman and Schwartz pin the blame squarely on the Federal Reserve and the failure of monetary policy to offset the contractions in the money supply. As the money multiplier continued on its downward path, the monetary base, rather than being aggressively increased, simply progressed slightly upwards on a gently positive sloping time path. As banks were failing in waves, was the Federal Reserve attempting to contain the panics by aggressively lending to banks scrambling for liquidity? The unfortunate answer is "no." When the panics were occurring, was there discussion of suspending deposit convertibility or suspension of the gold standard, both of which had been successfully employed in the past? Again the unfortunate answer is "no." Did the Federal Reserve consider the fact that it had an abundant supply of free gold, and therefore that monetary expansion was feasible? Once again the unfortunate answer is "no." The argument can be summarized by the following quotation:

> At all times throughout the 1929–33 contraction, alternative policies were available to the System by which it could have kept the stock of money from falling, and indeed could have increased it at almost any desired rate. Those policies did not involve radical innovations. They involved measures of a kind the System had taken in earlier years, of a kind explicitly contemplated by the founders of the System to meet precisely the kind of banking crisis that developed in late 1930 and persisted thereafter. They involved measures that

were actually proposed and very likely would have been adopted under a slightly different bureaucratic structure or distribution of power, or even if the men in power had had somewhat different personalities. Until late 1931 – and we believe not even then – the alternative policies involved no conflict with the maintenance of the gold standard. Until September 1931, the problem that recurrently troubled the System was how to keep the gold inflows under control, not the reverse. (Friedman and Schwartz, 1963)

The inescapable conclusion, also discussed in Hsieh and Romer (2004), is that it was a failure of the policies of the Federal Reserve System in responding to the crises of the time that made the Depression as bad as it was. If monetary policy had responded differently – and according to Bordo, Choudhri and Schwartz (2002) and Hsieh and Romer (2004) the Federal Reserve had the ability to do so – the economic events of 1929–33 need not have been as they occurred. This assertion is supported by the results of Fackler and Parker (1994). Using counterfactual historical simulations, they show that if the Federal Reserve had kept the M1 money supply growing along its pre-October 1929 trend of 3.3 percent annually, most of the Depression would have been averted. McCallum (1990) also reaches similar conclusions employing a monetary base feedback policy in his counterfactual simulations, as do Bordo, Choudhri and Schwartz (1995) using similar estimation techniques. Christiano, Motto and Rostagno (2003) construct a dynamic stochastic general equilibrium model of the US with a banking sector and financial frictions and fit it to data from the 1920s and 1930s. They confirm that different monetary policies during the Depression would have moderated the economic collapse.

Friedman and Schwartz trace the seeds of these regrettable events to the death of Federal Reserve Bank of New York President Benjamin Strong in 1928. Strong's death altered the locus of power in the Federal Reserve System and left it without effective leadership. Friedman and Schwartz maintain that Strong had the personality, confidence and reputation in the financial community to lead monetary policy and sway policy makers to his point of view. Friedman and Schwartz believe that Strong would not have permitted the financial panics and liquidity crises to persist and affect the real economy. Instead, after Governor Strong died, the conduct of open market operations changed from a five-man committee dominated by the New York Federal Reserve to a 12-man committee of Federal Reserve Bank governors. Decisiveness in leadership was replaced by inaction and drift. Others reject this point, claiming the policies of the Federal Reserve in the 1930s were not inconsistent with the policies pursued in the decade of the 1920s (Wicker, 1965; Wheelock, 1987; Temin, 1989).

Meltzer (1976) also points out errors made by the Federal Reserve. His argument is that the Federal Reserve failed to distinguish between nominal and real interest rates. That is, while nominal rates were falling, the Federal Reserve did virtually nothing, since it construed this to be a sign of an "easy" credit market. However, in the face of deflation, real rates were rising and there was in fact a "tight" credit market. Failure to make this distinction led money to be a contributing factor to the initial decline of 1929 and beyond. Meltzer (2003) adds a laundry list of further errors made by the Federal Reserve including a reliance on the real bills doctrine in addition to the belief that deflation was the inevitable consequence of inflation, a purging of speculative excesses, a reliance on interest rates to indicate monetary tightness or ease, the failure to act as lender of last resort, and the inability or unwillingness to simply follow the rules of the gold standard.

Cecchetti (1992) and Nelson (1991) bolster the monetary hypothesis by demonstrating that the deflation during the Depression was anticipated at short horizons, once it was under way. The result, using the Fisher equation, is that high ex ante real interest rates were the transmission mechanism that led from falling prices to falling output. In addition, Cecchetti (1998) and Cecchetti and Karras (1994) argue that if the lower bound of the nominal interest rate is reached, then continued deflation renders the opportunity cost of holding money negative. In this instance the nature of money changes. Now the rate of deflation places a floor on the real, after-tax return nonmoney assets must provide to make them attractive to hold. If they cannot exceed the rate on money holdings, then agents will move their assets into cash and the result will be negative net investment and a decapitalization of the economy.

The monetary hypothesis, however, is not without its detractors. As we shall see in the interviews, for example, the research agenda of Harold Cole and Lee Ohanian finds only a limited role for money and financial factors in explaining the Depression. Moreover, Peter Temin claims that simply saying monetary policy was a mistake does not explain history, what actually happened and why individuals behaved as they did. Moreover, expecting the Federal Reserve to have aggressively increased the monetary base by whatever amount was necessary to stop the decline in the money supply is hindsight. A course of action for monetary policy such as this was well beyond the scope of discussion among policy makers and was far outside the dominant thinking prevailing at the time which was the gold standard mentalité.

Bernanke (1983a) argues that the monetary hypothesis: (i) is not a complete explanation of the link between the financial sector and aggregate output in the 1930s; (ii) does not explain protracted non-neutrality; and (iii) is quantitatively insufficient to explain the depth of the decline in output. Bernanke (1983a) not only resurrected and sharpened Fisher's (1933) debt deflation hypothesis, but also made further contributions to what has come to be known as the nonmonetary/financial hypothesis.

The Nonmonetary/Financial Hypothesis

Bernanke (1983a), building on the monetary hypothesis of Friedman and

Schwartz (1963), presents an alternative interpretation of the way in which the financial crises may have affected output. The argument involves both the effects of debt deflation and the impact that bank panics had on the ability of financial markets to efficiently allocate funds from lenders to borrowers. These nonmonetary/financial theories hold that events in financial markets other than shocks to the money supply can help to account for the paths of output and prices during the Great Depression.

Fisher (1933) asserted that the dominant forces that account for "great" depressions are (nominal) over-indebtedness and deflation. Specifically, he argued that real debt burdens were substantially increased when there were dramatic declines in the price level and nominal incomes. The combination of deflation, falling nominal income and increasing real debt burdens led to debtor insolvency, lowered aggregate demand, and thereby contributed to a continuing decline in the price level and thus further increases in the real burden of debt.

Bernanke (1983a), in what is now called the "credit view," provided additional details to help explain Fisher's debt deflation hypothesis. He argued that in normal circumstances, an initial decline in prices merely reallocates wealth from debtors to creditors, such as banks. Usually, such wealth redistributions are minor in magnitude and have no first-order impact on the economy. However, in the face of large shocks, deflation in the prices of assets forfeited to banks by debtor bankruptcies leads to a decline in the nominal value of assets on bank balance sheets. For a given value of bank liabilities, also denominated in nominal terms, this deterioration in bank assets threatens insolvency. As banks reallocate away from loans to safer government securities, some borrowers, particularly small ones, are unable to obtain funds, often at any price. Further, if this reallocation is long-lived, the shortage of credit for these borrowers helps to explain the persistence of the downturn. As the disappearance of bank financing forces lower expenditure plans, aggregate demand declines, which again contributes to the downward deflationary spiral. For debt deflation to be operative, it is necessary to demonstrate that there was a substantial build-up of debt prior to the onset of the Depression and that the deflation of the 1930s was at least partially unanticipated at medium- and long-term horizons at the time that the debt was being incurred. Both of these conditions appear to have been in place (Hamilton, 1992; Evans and Wachtel, 1993; Fackler and Parker, 2005).

In addition, the financial panics which occurred hindered the credit allocation mechanism. Bernanke (1983a) explains that the process of credit intermediation requires substantial information gathering and non-trivial market-making activities. The financial disruptions of 1930–33 are correctly viewed as substantial impediments to the performance of these services and thus impaired the efficient allocation of credit between lenders and borrowers. That is, financial panics and debtor and business bankruptcies resulted in an increase in the real cost of credit intermediation. As the cost of credit intermediation increased, sources of credit for many borrowers (especially households, farmers and small firms) became expensive or even unobtainable at any price. This tightening of credit put downward pressure on aggregate demand and helped turn the recession of 1929–30 into the Great Depression.

I would also like to make special mention of the behavior of expectations. As the Depression deepened and 1930 turned into 1931, there was another reason for a "change in the character of the contraction" in 1931. Although Friedman and Schwartz attribute this "change" to the bank panics that occurred, a change also took place because of the emergence of pessimistic expectations (please see my interview with James Tobin in *Reflections on the Great Depression*). If it was thought that the early stages of the Depression were symptomatic of a recession that was not different in kind from similar episodes in our economic history, and that recovery was a real possibility, the public need not have had pessimistic expectations. Instead the public may have anticipated things would get better. However, after the British left the gold standard, expectations changed in a very pessimistic way. The public may very well have believed that the business cycle downturn was not going to be reversed, but rather was going to get worse than it was. When households and business investors begin to make plans based on the economy getting worse instead of making plans based on anticipations of recovery, the depressing economic effects on consumption and investment of this switch in expectations are common knowledge in the modern macroeconomic literature. For the literature on the Great Depression, the empirical research conducted on the expectations hypothesis focuses almost exclusively on uncertainty (which is not the same thing as pessimistic/optimistic expectations) and its contribution to the onset of the Depression (Romer, 1990; Flacco and Parker, 1992). Although Keynes (1936) writes extensively about the state of expectations and their economic influence, the literature is silent regarding the empirical validity of the expectations hypothesis in 1931–33. Yet, in spite of this, the continued shocks that the United States' economy received demonstrated that the business cycle downturn of 1931–33 was of a different kind than had previously been known. Once the public believed this to be so and made their plans accordingly, the results had to be economically devastating. There is no formal empirical confirmation and I have not segregated the expectations hypothesis as a separate hypothesis in the overview. However, the logic of the above argument compels me to be of the opinion that the expectations hypothesis provides an impressive addition to the monetary hypothesis and the nonmonetary/financial hypothesis in accounting for the economic experiences of the United States during the Great Depression.

The Gold Standard Hypothesis

Research on the operation of the interwar gold standard has deepened our understanding of the Depression and its international character. The way and manner in which the interwar gold exchange standard was structured and operated provide a convincing explanation of the international transmission of deflation and depression that occurred in the 1920s and 1930s.

The story has its beginning in the 1870–1914 period. During this time the gold standard functioned as a pegged exchange rate system where certain rules were observed. Namely, it was necessary for countries to permit their money supplies to be altered in response to gold flows in order for the price-specie-flow mechanism to function properly. It operated successfully because countries that were gaining gold allowed their money supply to increase and raise the domestic price level to restore equilibrium and maintain the fixed exchange rate of their currency. Countries that were losing gold were obligated to permit their money supply to decrease and generate a decline in their domestic price level to restore equilibrium and maintain the fixed exchange rate of their currency. Eichengreen (1992) discusses and extensively documents that the gold standard of this period functioned as smoothly as it did because of the international commitment countries had to the gold standard and the level of international cooperation exhibited during this time. "What rendered the commitment to the gold standard credible, then, was that the commitment was international, not merely national. That commitment was activated through international cooperation" (Eichengreen, 1992).

The gold standard was suspended when the hostilities of World War I broke out. By the end of 1928, major countries such as the United States, the United Kingdom, France and Germany had re-established ties to a functioning fixed exchange rate gold standard. However, Eichengreen (1992) points out that the world in which the gold standard functioned before World War I was not the same world in which the gold standard was being re-established. A credible commitment to the gold standard, as Hamilton (1988) explains, required that a country maintain fiscal soundness and political objectives that insured the monetary authority could pursue a monetary policy consistent with long-run price stability and continuous convertibility of the currency. Successful operation required these conditions to be in place before re-establishment of the gold standard was operational. However, many governments during the interwar period went back on the gold standard in the opposite set of circumstances. They re-established ties to the gold standard because they were incapable, due to the political chaos generated after World War I, of fiscal soundness and did not have political objectives conducive to reforming monetary policy such that it could insure long-run price stability. "By this criterion, returning to the gold standard could not have come at a worse time or for poorer reasons" (Hamilton, 1988). Kindleberger (1986) stresses the fact that the pre-World War I gold standard functioned as well as it did because of the unquestioned leadership exercised by Great Britain. After World War I and the relative decline of Britain, the United States did not exhibit the same strength of leadership Britain had shown before. The upshot is that it was an unsuitable environment in which to re-establish the gold standard after World War I and the interwar gold exchange standard was destined to drift in a state of malperformance as no one took responsibility for its proper functioning. However, the problems did not end there.

The interwar gold exchange standard operated with four structural/technical flaws that almost certainly doomed it to failure (Eichengreen, 1986; Temin, 1989; Bernanke and James, 1991; Kitson, 2003). The first, and most damaging, was an asymmetry in the response of gold-gaining countries and gold-losing countries that resulted in a deflationary bias that was to drag the world deeper into deflation and depression. If a country was losing gold reserves, it was required to decrease its money supply to maintain its commitment to the gold standard. Given that a minimum gold reserve had to be maintained and that countries became concerned when the gold reserve fell within 10 percent of this minimum, little gold could be lost before the necessity of monetary contraction, and thus deflation, became a reality. Moreover, with a fractional gold reserve ratio of 40 percent, the result was a decline in the domestic money supply equal to 2.5 times the gold outflow. On the other hand, there was no such constraint on countries that experienced gold inflows. Gold reserves were accumulated without the binding requirement that the domestic money supply be expanded. Thus the price-specie-flow mechanism ceased to function and the equilibrating forces of the pre-World War I gold standard were absent during the interwar period. If a country attracting gold reserves were to embark on a contractionary path, the result would be the further extraction of gold reserves from other countries on the gold standard and the imposition of deflation on their economies as well, as they were forced to contract their money supplies. "As it happened, both of the two major gold surplus countries – France and the United States, who at the time together held close to 60 percent of the world's monetary gold – took deflationary paths in 1928–1929" (Bernanke and James, 1991).

Second, countries that did not have reserve currencies could hold their minimum reserves in the form of both gold and convertible foreign exchange reserves. If the threat of devaluation of a reserve currency appeared likely, a country holding foreign exchange reserves could divest itself of the foreign exchange, as holding it became a more risky proposition. Further, the convertible reserves were usually only fractionally backed by gold. Thus, if countries were to prefer gold holdings as opposed to foreign exchange reserves for whatever reason, the result would be a contraction in the world money supply as reserves were destroyed in the movement to gold. This effect can be thought of as equivalent to the effect on the domestic money supply in a fractional reserve banking system of a shift in the public's money holdings toward currency and away from bank deposits.

Third, the powers of many European central banks were restricted or excluded outright. In particular, as discussed by Eichengreen (1986), the Bank of France was prohibited from engaging in open market operations. Given that France was one of the countries amassing gold reserves, this restriction largely prevented it from adhering to the rules of the gold standard. The proper response would have been to expand its supply of money and inflate so as not to continue to attract gold reserves and impose deflation on the rest of the world. This was not done. France continued to accumulate gold until 1932 and did not leave the gold standard until 1936.

Lastly, the gold standard was re-established at parities that were unilaterally determined by each individual country. When France returned to the gold standard in 1926, it returned at a parity rate that is believed to have undervalued the franc. When Britain returned to the gold standard in 1925, it returned at a parity rate that is believed to have overvalued the pound. In this situation, the only sustainable equilibrium required the French to inflate their economy in response to the gold inflows. However, given its legacy of inflation during the 1921–26 period, France steadfastly resisted inflation (Eichengreen, 1986). The maintenance of the gold standard and the resistance to inflation were now inconsistent policy objectives. The Bank of France's inability to conduct open market operations only made matters worse. The accumulation of gold and the exporting of deflation to the world was the result.

Taken together, the flaws described above made the interwar gold standard dysfunctional and in the end unsustainable. Looking back, we observe that the record of departure from the gold standard and subsequent recovery was different for many different countries. For some countries recovery came sooner. For some it came later. It is in this timing of departure from the gold standard that recent research has produced a remarkable empirical finding. From the work of Choudri and Kochin (1980), Eichengreen and Sachs (1985), Temin (1989), and Bernanke and James (1991), we now know that the sooner a country abandoned the gold standard, the quicker recovery commenced. Spain, which never restored its participation in the gold standard, missed the ravages of the Depression altogether. Britain left the gold standard in September 1931, and started to recover. Sweden left the gold standard at the same time as Britain, and started to recover. The United States left in March 1933, and recovery commenced. France, Holland, and Poland continued to have their economies struggle after the United States' recovery began as they continued to adhere to the gold standard until 1936. Only after they left did recovery start; departure from the gold standard freed a country from the ravages of deflation.

Temin (1989) and Eichengreen (1992) argue that it was the unbending commitment to the gold standard that generated deflation and depression worldwide. They emphasize that the gold standard required fiscal and monetary authorities around the world to submit their economies to internal adjustment and economic instability in the face of international shocks. Given how the gold standard tied countries together, if the gold parity was to be defended and devaluation was not an option, unilateral monetary actions by any one country were pointless. The end result is that Temin (1989) and Eichengreen (1992) reject Friedman and Schwartz's (1963) claim that the Depression was caused by a series of policy failures on the part of the Federal Reserve. Actions taken in the United States, according to Temin (1989) and Eichengreen (1992), cannot be properly understood in isolation with respect to the rest of the world. If the commitment to the gold standard was to be maintained, monetary and fiscal authorities worldwide had little choice in responding to the crises of the Depression. Why did the Federal Reserve continue a policy of inaction during the banking panics? Because the commitment to the gold standard, what Temin (1989) has labeled "The Midas Touch," gave them no choice but to let the banks fail. Monetary expansion and the injection of liquidity would lower interest rates and lead to a gold outflow. Continued deflation due to gold outflows would begin to call into question the monetary authority's commitment to the gold standard. "Defending gold parity might require the authorities to sit idly by as the banking system crumbled, as the Federal Reserve did at the end of 1931 and again at the beginning of 1933" (Eichengreen, 1992). Thus, if the adherence to the gold standard were to be maintained, the money supply, and thus Federal Reserve actions, was endogenous with respect to the balance of payments and defense of the exchange value of the dollar.

Eichengreen (1992) concludes further, leaving out many of the details here, that what had made the pre-World War I gold standard so successful was absent during the interwar period: credible commitment to the gold standard activated through international cooperation in its implementation and management. Had these important ingredients of the pre-World War I gold standard been present during the interwar period, twentieth-century economic history might have been very different.

The Real Business Cycle Hypothesis

Lucas and Rapping (1969, 1972) were the first efforts directed toward trying to see if the disaster that was the Great Depression could be understood within a modeling framework of rational household and firm behavior. That is, as stated in Lucas (1981), was there a way of taking the interwar observations on wages, prices and hours worked per adult and "reconciling these observations with intelligent behavior on agents' parts[?]" The Great Depression was (and in many ways remains) a great puzzle as there were millions of the world's citizens who wanted to consume more housing, food and clothing and producers by the hundreds of thousands who wanted to manufacture more housing, food and clothing and yet the two sides could not get together. Why? What was preventing these economically improving, mutually beneficial exchanges from taking place? What was it that prevented people from working and producing more? This is the central question of the real business cycle approach to the Great Depression and the answers are formulated from the construction and estimation of dynamic stochastic general equilibrium (DSGE) models. Using the neoclassical model of capital accumulation and growth theory for the analytical foundation, the idea is that business cycles evolve over time and economic fluctuations are more properly viewed dynamically and not simply within an analytical framework that treats them as a collection of static points in time. An excellent overview of the real business cycle approach to understanding macroeconomic fluctuations is provided by Plosser (1989).

As the name implies, real business cycle theory looks to "real" factors, as opposed to nominal factors like money supply or price changes, as the main forces driving the business cycle. Downward economic fluctuations can be understood as resulting from the general equilibrium responses of utility-maximizing households and profit-maximizing firms to negative shocks imposed on these economic agents such as reductions in total factor productivity, preference changes, or laws and other institutional barriers that prevent increased work effort or growth in entrepreneurial activity. Of course, shocks can also be positive in nature and thereby encourage economic growth. While still in its infancy, the research agenda linking the real business cycle approach and the economic experiences of the Great Depression is heavily influenced by Nobel laureate Edward Prescott and is clearly being driven by the work of Harold Cole and Lee Ohanian of the University of California at Los Angeles (UCLA).

Cole and Ohanian (1999) is the first attempt to assess how much of the massive decline and weak recovery from 1929 to 1939 can be accounted for by neoclassical growth theory. Cole and Ohanian (1999) identify several different economic shocks such as technology shocks, fiscal policy shocks, trade shocks, and monetary shocks and then ask if these shocks can account for the decline and recovery of the US economy from 1929 to 1939. While technology, fiscal policy and monetary shocks do account for a share of the 1929 to 1933 decline, and trade and financial intermediation shocks do not, none of them do a good job of reconciling the rapid recovery predicted by the neoclassical growth model with the actual anemic recovery from 1933 to 1939. Cole and Ohanian (1999) conjecture, but do not confirm empirically, that most of the difference between what is predicted and what actually occurred during the recovery can be accounted for by the National Industrial Recovery Act (NIRA) policies implemented by President Roosevelt. In a companion paper in the *Federal Reserve Bank of Minneapolis Quarterly Review*, Prescott (1999) states that the key to understanding the Depression is explaining why market hours worked per adult fell to 72 percent of their 1929 level in 1934 and remained at 79 percent of their 1929 level in 1939. Prescott claims "[i]n the 1930s, labor market institutions and industrial policy actions changed normal market hours. I think these institutions and actions are what caused the Great Depression."

Cole and Ohanian (2000) investigate whether the transmission of deflation can account for the Depression using DSGE models. They argue that the debt deflation transmission mechanism of Fisher (1933) and Bernanke (1983a) and the surprise deflation theory of Lucas and Rapping (1969) are invalid candidates since they do not consistently explain both the Depression and the recession of 1920–21. They examine the high and inflexible wage and banking shock hypotheses in the empirical work conducted. However, the results indicate that neither the high and inflexible wage nor the banking shock hypotheses account for much of the downward path of the economy from 1929 to 1933. Examination of the data after correcting for compositional issues in labor market and wage characteristics shows that wages were high in only one sector of the economy and wages were below trend in most of the others during this period. Moreover, the banking shock is minor in magnitude, output had a small elasticity with respect to shocks in the financial sector and furthermore, the ratio of bank deposits-to-output increased substantially during this period, rather than falling as it should have if the banking shock story is valid. They conclude by noting total factor productivity increased "[a]bout 5 percent relative to trend in 1921, but fell about 14 percent below trend between 1929 and 1933." The upshot is they suspect some negative shock to productivity contributed to the initial downturn and propagation of the Great Depression.

Cole and Ohanian (2004b) is an international continuation of the search for the negative productivity shocks that they suspect sent the world economy into a tailspin. As mentioned previously, this paper is one example of the more recent comparative approach that includes cross-country data sets used in estimation. Cole and Ohanian (2004b) is structured as an international econometric horse race between monetary/deflation shocks versus productivity shocks in accounting for the behavior of 17 economies from 1929 to 1933 for which they have data. If deflation is thought to be the main propagator of the Depression, the correlation in the data between deflation and output change should be close to one. It is not. As computed by Cole and Ohanian (2004b), the deflation/output change correlations are negative or slightly positive in three of the four years between 1929 and 1933. If deflation is thought to be the main propagator of the Depression, the countries with the largest deflations should have had the biggest depressions. They apparently did not. The major conclusion is that at most monetary/deflation shocks account for one-third, while productivity shocks account for two-thirds, of the fall in output over the 1929–33 period. This paper, together with Ohanian (2001), begins the task of trying to uncover the sources of the productivity shocks that apparently bear such responsibility for the Depression. The influences of changes in capacity utilization, the quality of factor inputs, the composition of production, labor hoarding practices and increasing returns, either individually or in combination, all fail to account for a significant share of the fall in total factor productivity from 1929 to 1933. The fall in total factor productivity may have come about from changes in organizational capital in the beginning of the Depression that persisted, or from the destruction of relationship/lending capital as discussed by Bernanke (1983a), or through the imposition of inefficient government policies early in the Depression. As of this writing, the research effort continues to try and identify the sources of productivity shocks in the Great Depression era. At this moment, they remain largely unknown for the US during the 1929–33 period but some progress has been made for the 1933–39 period using DSGE models (Cole and Ohanian, 2004a, discussed below). Additionally, internationally-oriented applications of the DSGE modeling approach for the Great Depression can be found in Cole and Ohanian (2002) for the UK, Amaral and MacGee (2002) for the US and Canada, Beaudry and Portier (2002) for France, Fisher and Hornstein (2002) for Germany, and Perri and Quadrini (2002) for Italy.

The real business cycle hypothesis has not been accepted uncritically. Many dismiss the real business cycle approach on the grounds that it is an application of general equilibrium modeling to what was obviously a disequilibrium phenomenon. Others object to viewing, in any terms, a 25 percent unemployment rate as a Pareto-efficient outcome resulting from a utility-maximizing household, labor/leisure intertemporal substitution decision. And there are many others, for example Gertler (2000), Bordo, Erceg and Evans (2000a), and most of the interviews contained in this book (with the obvious exception of Lee Ohanian), who have great difficulty with the inadequacies of the types of models used in the estimation of wage flexibility and banking/financial shocks and the methodology employed by Cole and Ohanian (2000) in attempting to assess the consistency and validity of different transmission mechanisms for the recession of 1920–21compared to the Great Depression of 1929–33. The list goes on. It is obvious that there is substantial resistance in the profession, as there should be, to any new approach that attempts to overturn or dismiss much of what we thought we already knew about the Great Depression. Harold Cole and Lee Ohanian are not the first people in this literature to face such resistance (think Friedman and Schwartz (1963), Peter Temin (1976a, 1989), and Barry Eichengreen (1992)), nor will they be the last. But, in the end, be they right or wrong or in between, they deserve to be heard. Once you read the interview with Lee Ohanian you will see that he and Harold Cole are likely to have something to say for many years to come.

RECOVERY AND THE NEW DEAL

March 1933 was the rock bottom of the Depression and the inauguration of Franklin D. Roosevelt represented a sharp break with the status quo (Eggertsson, 2005). Upon his taking office, a bank holiday was declared, the United States left the interwar gold exchange standard the following month, and the government commenced with several measures designed to resurrect the financial system. These measures included: (i) the intensified activity of the Reconstruction Finance Corporation which set about funneling large sums of liquidity to banks and other intermediaries; (ii) the creation of deposit insurance which effectively stopped the runs on banks that were so prevalent before the bank holiday; (iii) the Securities Exchange Act of 1934 which established margin requirements for bank loans used to purchase stocks and bonds and increased information requirements to potential investors; and (iv) the Glass–Steagall Act which strictly separated commercial banking and investment banking. Although delivering some immediate relief to financial markets, lenders continued to be reluctant to extend credit after the events of 1929–33, and the recovery of financial markets was slow and incomplete. Bernanke (1983a) estimates that the United States' financial system did not begin to shed the inefficiencies under which it was operating until the end of 1935.

Policies designed to promote different economic institutions were enacted as part of the New Deal. The National Industrial Recovery Act (NIRA) was passed on June 6, 1933 and was designed to raise prices and wages. In addition, the Act mandated the formation of planning boards in critical sectors of the economy. The boards were charged with setting output goals for their respective sector and the usual result was a *restriction* of production. In effect, the NIRA was a license for industries to form cartels and was struck down as unconstitutional in 1935 (see the discussion of Cole and Ohanian (2004a) below). The Agricultural Adjustment Act of 1933 was similar legislation designed to *reduce* output and raise prices in the farming sector. In 1936 it too was ruled unconstitutional.

Other policies intended to provide relief directly to people who were destitute and out of work were rapidly enacted. The Civilian Conservation Corps, the Tennessee Valley Authority, the Public Works Administration and the Federal Emergency Relief Administration were set up shortly after Roosevelt took office and provided jobs for the unemployed and grants to states for direct relief. The Civil Works Administration, created in 1933–34, and the Works Progress Administration, created in 1935, were also designed to provide work relief to the jobless. The Social Security Act and the National Labor Relations Act (also called the Wagner Act) were also passed in 1935. There surely are other programs that have been left out of the above list, but the intent was the same. In the words of Roosevelt himself, addressing

Congress in 1938:

> Government has a final responsibility for the well-being of its citizenship. If private co-operative endeavor fails to provide work for the willing hands and relief for the unfortunate, those suffering hardship from no fault of their own have a right to call upon the Government for aid; and a government worthy of its name must make fitting response. (Quoted from Polenberg, 2000)

The Depression had shown the inaccuracies of classifying the 1920s as a "new era." Rather, the "new era," as summarized by Roosevelt's words above and initiated in government's involvement in the economy, began in March 1933.

The NBER business cycle chronology shows continuous growth from March 1933 until May 1937, at which time a 13-month recession hit the economy. The business cycle rebounded in June 1938 and continued on its upward march to and through the beginning of the United States' involvement in World War II. The recovery that started in 1933 was a welcome economic reversal with real GNP experiencing annual rates of growth around 10 percent between 1933 and December 1941, excluding the recession of 1937–38 (Romer, 1993). However, as reported by Romer (1993), real GNP did not return to its pre-Depression level until 1937 and real GNP did not catch up to its pre-Depression secular trend until 1942. Indeed, the unemployment rate, peaking at 25 percent in March 1933, continued to dwell around 15 percent in late 1941. It is in this sense that most economists attribute the ending of the Depression to the onset of World War II. The War brought complete recovery as the unemployment rate quickly plummeted after December 1941 to its historical nadir during the War of below 2 percent.

The questions remain, however, if the War completed the recovery, what initiated it, what sustained it through the end of 1941 and most importantly, why was the recovery so anemic? Should we point to the relief programs of the New Deal and the leadership of Roosevelt? Certainly they had psychological/expectational effects on consumers and investors and made Roosevelt's commitment to reflation policies credible, as argued by Eggertsson (2005). These actions helped to heal the suffering experienced during that time. However, as shown by Brown (1956), Peppers (1973), and Raynold, McMillin and Beard (1991), fiscal policy contributed little to the recovery, and certainly could have done much more.

Once again we return to the financial system for answers. The abandonment of the gold standard, the impact this had on the money supply, and the deliverance from the economic effects of deflation would have to be singled out as the most important contributor to the recovery. Romer (1993) stresses that Eichengreen and Sachs (1985, 1986) have it right. Recovery did not come before the decision to abandon the old gold parity was made operational. Once this became reality, devaluation of the currency permitted expansion in the money supply and inflation which, rather than promoting a policy of beggar-thy-neighbor, allowed countries to escape the deflationary vortex of economic decline. As discussed in connection with the gold standard hypothesis, the simultaneity of leaving the gold standard and recovery is a robust empirical result that reflects more than simple temporal coincidence.

Romer (1993) reports an increase in the monetary base in the United States of 52 percent between April 1933 and April 1937. The M1 money supply virtually matched this increase in the monetary base, with 49 percent growth over the same period. The sources of this increase were two-fold. First, aside from the immediate monetary expansion permitted by devaluation, as Graham and Whittlesey (1940) and Romer (1993) explain, monetary expansion continued into 1934 and beyond as gold flowed to the United States from Europe due to the increasing political unrest and heightened probability of hostilities that began the progression to World War II. Second, the increase in the money supply matched the increase in the monetary base and the Treasury chose not to sterilize the gold inflows. This is evidence that the monetary expansion resulted from policy decisions and not endogenous changes in the money multiplier. The new regime was freed from the constraints of the gold standard and the policy makers were intent on taking actions of a different nature than what had been done between 1929 and 1933.

The Depression had turned a corner and the economy was emerging from the abyss in 1933. However, it still had a long way to go to reach full recovery. Friedman and Schwartz (1963) comment that "the most notable feature of the revival after 1933 was not its rapidity but its incompleteness." They claim that monetary policy and the Federal Reserve were passive after 1933. The monetary authorities did nothing to stop the fall from 1929 to 1933 and did little to promote the recovery. The Federal Reserve made no effort to increase the stock of high-powered money through the use of either open market operations or rediscounting; Federal Reserve credit outstanding remained "almost perfectly constant from 1934 to mid-1940" (Friedman and Schwartz, 1963). As we have seen above, it was the Treasury that was generating increases in the monetary base at the time by issuing gold certificates equal to the amount of gold reserve inflow and depositing them at the Federal Reserve. When the government spent the money, the Treasury swapped the gold certificates for Federal Reserve notes and this expanded the monetary base (Johnson, 1939; Romer, 1993).

Moreover, in regard to the incompleteness of the recovery, as Cole and Ohanian (1999) point out, the actual recovery was far weaker than what would be predicted by neoclassical growth theory. Why was this so? Cole and Ohanian (2004a), following earlier work by Weinstein (1980, 1981) and Bernstein (1987), show that the NIRA codes bear much of the responsibility for the weak recovery. Employing a multisector dynamic stochastic general equilibrium model that embeds a model of the NIRA codes and their impact of limiting competition and increasing labor bargaining power, Cole and

Ohanian (2004a) find that the NIRA codes are responsible for about 60 percent of the difference between actual and trend output from 1934 to 1939. Thus the New Deal programs associated with the National Industrial Recovery Act can correctly be apportioned much of the responsibility for the persistence of the Great Depression.

A TWENTY-FIRST CENTURY LOOK BACK AT THE ECONOMICS OF THE INTERWAR ERA

This "Overview of the Great Depression" will serve as the background for the following interviews. It is 74 years since 1933 and much intellectual effort has been expended trying to sort out the economics of the Great Depression. What have we learned and where do we stand in 2007? Let's find out. The questions start now ...

Peter Temin

Peter Temin graduated summa cum laude from Swarthmore College in 1959 and received his Ph.D. from MIT in 1964. He is currently Elisha Gray II Professor of Economics at MIT. Certainly on any scorecard listing those who have made the greatest contributions to our understanding of the Great Depression, Peter Temin would be at the top of the list. His criticisms of the Friedman and Schwartz hypothesis have been many and are ongoing (as this interview reveals). His book *Lessons from the Great Depression*, together with the work of Eichengreen and Sachs (1985) and Eichengreen (1992) among others, helped to send the economic literature on the Great Depression down the gold standard path. His knowledge of the economics and politics of the interwar era, both in the US and internationally, is vast. It took me two months to prepare for this interview. I needed it. I spoke with Peter Temin in his office, January 4, 2005, on the campus of MIT.

Are we any closer to learning how economic policies and economic policy leadership come to be changed? This seems to be an important question that both you and Eichengreen are focusing on recently. You've said in your 1991 paper that "Sargent described the effects of regime changes. We need a theory of their causes." And further, "Possession of theories that comprehend the reaction of economies to massive and novel economic shocks will reduce the probability of another Great Depression." Are we there yet?
We're not there yet, but the best guess at the moment certainly is the way to get a change in policy is to get a change in leadership. This is what Kuhn (1962) said about scientific revolutions a long time ago saying that maybe the people who use the old paradigm don't change their minds, they simply die out. New people come in. In the Depression, talking about the United States, Hoover maintained actually while he was in office, and long after he was in office, that his policies were the correct policies to undertake and it was only Roosevelt coming in who took a fresh view.

Hoover continued to maintain that in his memoirs.
Yes, that is right, written in the 1950s.

If only we had stayed with it, recovery would have come 18 months earlier or

something like that.
Exactly. Exactly. While it didn't come 18 months earlier it came very quickly after Hoover left office.

Can you briefly tell me how you got involved in the literature on the Great Depression?
I got involved in it as a young scholar teaching economic history. Friedman and Schwartz's *A Monetary History of the United States*, with a long, long discussion of the Great Depression, came out in 1963. It was very early in my teaching career and I naturally wanted to teach it. It is an important good book. But I was not convinced by it, at least for the Great Depression. So I set to work to try and figure what I thought really was going on. And so probably the most constant thread of my research for the past 40 years has been that I keep coming back to the Great Depression like a sore tooth to see what can be done.

In your 1976 book you write "After 1931 the story becomes so complex and the interactions so numerous it is no longer possible to envisage separate movements in different parts of the world. Worldwide influences such as harvest failures tied different economies together to some extent before the Depression was well under way. And as the Depression continued and deepened, its impact spread across countries through commodity and capital markets. A worldwide prospective, as opposed to a national one, is needed to analyze the events after 1931." I can hear the gold standard agenda coming out here. It's also in your May 1976 AER *paper. Can you please talk about what led you to take up that line of inquiry which, I think has done so much to advance our understanding?*
That's a good question and I'm not at all sure I know the answers. I'll have to go back a long way. It's certainly true that 1931 is a turning point in the Great Depression and it certainly becomes worldwide at that point if not before. At this time, 2005, I would attribute the spread largely to the currency crisis that happened during the summer of 1931, but I'm not sure I was thinking of that in the 1970s. So, I assume what I was doing was taking note of the worldwide impact, about which not much was written at that point. Looking at it and thinking how complicated it was, I was at that time very much impressed by the role of Germany. That we needed to look at Europe and America was clear in my mind. And I suppose I had begun to read about changes in other continents and other areas by then.

And the gold standard was linking them together.
Yes, but in the 1970s I really didn't think about the linking together. The quote that you read I think is a fair representation of my views at that time in which I was convinced they were linked together. But at that point I didn't have the mechanism that linked them together. And even now, by the way just to

continue this, the gold standard is not enough to link all these people together because the gold standard was a phenomenon of Europe and America. Other countries had tried, and the Japanese with exquisite bad timing went back on to gold in 1930 and then immediately went off it in 1931. Even outposts of Europe like Spain were sort of on the gold standard, but not really. When you get to South America some countries were, some countries weren't. Asia and Africa had countries that typically were not on the gold standard, but some colonies were. So then the other factors that I mentioned, capital flows, commodity effects through agricultural prices which were the exports of a lot of these countries, whose prices collapsed during the Great Depression. The effects through the agricultural market were as important as the gold standard in having this be a truly worldwide spread.

I guess maybe I should ask it differently. What happened between 1976 and 1989 to make you write your book Lessons from the Great Depression *in 1989? Anything that you can put your finger on?*
Yes. The set of articles written by Eichengreen and Sachs (1985, 1986) in which they said the gold standard was key to the Great Depression. I mean it is really their innovation. I've been a publicist for this (*Temin smiles broadly*), but I do need to give them credit for having seen that the thing that generally ties this together is the gold standard.

Do you not think that Olney's 1999 paper together with Romer (1990) and Mishkin (1978) go a long way toward explaining consumption behavior and thus largely explain what was thought to be autonomous?
Well ... I'm sorry that people are not still working on this very much because I think the question of consumption is still open. There are still unexplained shifts in consumption.

Actually, this has been brought up now in the real business cycle literature. Cole and Ohanian (1999) are now talking about this some more.
Yes, OK. The real business cycle people have their own agenda and (*Temin chuckles*) I think they are largely nuts. But I'm glad to see people looking at this. That's good.

OK, but there's still something that needs to be looked at?
There's a lot that needs to be looked at in that area. I think Mishkin (1978) and Romer (1990) were very interesting and provocative and clearly part of the story. But there is a bigger story as well.

And Olney's paper, you like her presentation?
Yes, Olney's paper is a nice paper.

OK, this one is a bit of a longer question. Do you agree with Michael Kitson (2003) that the causes of the Great Depression are one thing but the extent of the Great Depression is due to the operation of the gold standard? I guess here he means its spread and its extent.

Well I tried in the 1989 book to disentangle these aspects instead of wanting to talk about the origin, the spread and the recovery together. The gold standard is very important in the spread. It's also important in the origin. It is the set of policies that were used to preserve the gold standard. It is the policies that led the Reichsbank in Germany and the Federal Reserve Bank in the United States to try to move against speculation. Whenever you hear that term your ears should prick up as to what it is that is called speculation because it is a very loaded term. It was these actions, I think more than anything else, that precipitated the original downturn. Now, these things were in turn the effect of dislocations that followed from the First World War. So one could say that the origin of the Great Depression came from the First World War and the dislocations there, and so that's not the gold standard. Even if you take that point, one has to give the gold standard a supporting role because in the early 1920s there were a lot of problems of adjustment to the new conditions and a lot of economic distress. But while there were problems within individual countries it wasn't a worldwide depression partly because there were flexible exchange rates. Once we were in the mid-1920s, the main industrial nations went back on to the gold standard. Then the ability of countries to adapt to these new changes was severely impaired. So to that extent that made it harder to have a soft landing into the new situation and more likely that there would be a hard landing.

Kitson (2003) lays out four principles of the gold standard and I'd like to quickly go over them. "First, it assumes the 'law of one price' – that the process of global competition will ensure that a basket of goods will cost the same in all countries." Secondly, it assumes the demand for money is stable. Third, it assumes that monetary authorities do not intervene to prevent increased gold reserves adding to the money supply or being sterilized. "Fourth, it assumes that the burden of adjustment would be borne by prices and not by quantities. This is the pre-Keynesian assumption that the economy tends toward full employment – an assumption that is so obviously inappropriate to the interwar period." Do you agree with those different assumptions?

Well, yes. I mean it's too strong. It may be that people who adopt the gold standard believe in all that, but you don't have to believe in all that (*Temin chuckles*) to favor the gold standard. There is another definition by Ken Dam (1982) which says that more briefly. But there is a very important point at the end of that which Kitson makes which is exactly right. The adjustments need to be made by internal means, deflation rather than devaluation, and the assumption that this was an easy thing to do does rest on price flexibility. I think the people from the 1930s were willing to have the quantity effects too, to have an upward sloping aggregate supply curve as opposed to a vertical supply curve as well. So that's not a necessary thing, but I'm sure that to the extent they thought prices were flexible it made it easier to do that.

You say in your book Lessons from the Great Depression *that gold standard countries were supposed to live with the exchange rates bequeathed to them and adjust internally, as we just discussed. The world changed after the War. The gold standard could not accommodate these changes. Moreover given the maldistribution of gold, the gold standard asymmetry, and the fact that the burden of adjustment fell fully on debtor countries, the gold standard was doomed. In fact, the attempt to preserve it is what produced the Great Depression. Would you agree with Michael Kitson that the gold standard was simply structurally flawed and could not have survived even with coordination and cooperation?*
Well that's a very large question. Let me break it up into a bunch of different questions.

Please do.
First is the question as to whether it was fixed rates that led to all the problems or whether it was fixed rates at pre-war parity that led to them. That's a question on which people are still writing and people have written about, for England in particular. My sense is that if there had been an adjustment of rates things would have been easier but that it still would have required a large adjustment. The problem with knowing whether that would have avoided the Great Depression is we don't really have a good theory of how a bad recession turned into a great depression. That goes back to your initial question about changes in regime. So what we can do is say perhaps it would have reduced the probability of the Great Depression. But we can't say how much. So that's one thing about the nature of the gold standard. The other question is, even with the gold standard with different rates or the gold standard as it was, if there had been cooperation would it have worked? Well, I think that we, looking back, could design a set of cooperative activities which could have avoided the Great Depression. However, those actions, I think, could not have been done at the time. In other words, I think this is basically an ahistorical exercise. The United States might have loaned massively to Germany. It did with the Dawes plan and then the Young plan. So the United States would certainly feel that at the time they came into their crisis they could have loaned a great deal. But at that point they were very nervous. This is where you have to bring in not simply the ideas of people, in other words, whether they were willing to cooperate and do all this much, but also the politics of it. As Thomas Ferguson and I have written (Ferguson and Temin, 2003), German politics were really rather wild

by 1931. Brüning seems to have gotten himself involved in trying to make statements for domestic consumption that he did not want to have overheard internationally. Of course, that's always hard to do, particularly hard to do in the modern world. He scared people who were lending and the example of that which we discuss in our paper is the French. The French were lending to Germany and wanted very much to continue and stabilize it. But they were so put off by the statements of Brüning in the spring and early summer of 1931 that they just pulled out. So, while one could say a massive loan from country x to country y would have calmed down investors and so forth, I don't think that's a historically relevant point because in the historical context you just can't see people making these kinds of loans.

So there's a realpolitik *disconnect then?*
That's right. Ed Prescott wrote a paper a couple of years ago, among others, saying if the Fed in the United States had massively increased the money supply that would have avoided the Great Depression in the United States and that might be right. If we have a model and we put it through, it goes through. But the size of the monetary movement is just way out of the historical ballpark. So, yes, as an exercise that's fine to say it could have been done. But it doesn't really help us understand what actually happened.

We're going to get to that here shortly.
(*Temin chuckles*) OK.

I've actually published a paper like that myself (both laugh gently). *But nevertheless, if I could try to sum up, if you'll indulge me, we can break it down later if you want. One of the major un-doings was the shock from World War I and the Depression should be viewed in the context of the overall second Thirty Years War trying to re-establish the status quo ante in a changed world leading to contraction and a sustained downturn. World War I was the shock and the propagating mechanism was the gold standard. The resumption of the gold standard announced the continuation of the policy regime that existed before the War. But more than this, it was the fundamental adherence to the gold standard mentality, that it was a prerequisite for prosperity, that actions outside of it were not in the realm of discussion and were not taken seriously and that deflation was the prescription and the only way to cope with falling demand. This mentality and the universal commitment to this system, and thus the difficulty for any one country to take independent action, determined the depth and severity of the Depression and drove the world economy into the ground. Does this about sum it up?*
Yes. I think that's quite a good summary.

All right then, we'll move on. I've always scratched my head when people have said the Depression would have been corrected if only prices and also wages had been more flexible and we had more deflation. This strikes me as being fundamentally wrong, just like Hoover's statements about his policies, that if Roosevelt had stuck with them, recovery would have come 18 months after the election of 1932, and as you point out in your book (Temin, 1989) when Brüning says he fell 100 meters from the goal. What do you think about that? What if wages had been more flexible, would that have helped and so forth?

Well, clearly if prices had been more flexible then we could have had a deflation instead of depression and then an adjustment in prices and that would have been fine. But, in the historical context of the interwar period, it's hard to think that prices could be as flexible as they would need to be to make this thing work. First of all there are all the distributional effects as different prices change at different rates. So, the economic model where all prices fall by half, if that worked that would be fine but I have the feeling that there would be these changes, differences in rates, that would affect distribution variables. The second issue is financial institutions which are set up for stable prices. This goes back to Fisher's old debt deflation ideas and the question is could the Fed have avoided having a very high real interest rate? There really are two questions here. The first one is the institutions, the financial institutions, and could they have kept themselves out of trouble? In other words could we have avoided the various problems of the summer of 1931? I think it would have been very hard with the very sharp deflation going on. The second part of this is monetary policy because with very rapid deflation the real interest rate then rises quite dramatically and that all by itself would cause a Great Depression. Now, all of these things, of course, depend on expectations because if prices are falling there's the famous overshooting argument of Dornbusch (1976) where the exchange rate changes in the twinkling of an eye and then slowly returns to normal. Now, if prices could have fallen in the twinkling of an eye, so that this didn't affect anybody's expectations, that people's expectations then were *after* the fall as prices rose back up in a kind of overshooting thing to some equilibrium, then perhaps some of these issues would come into play. But in the way that it happened in the 1930s, some prices, like agricultural prices, fell rapidly while industrial prices fell much more slowly. This gave rise to expectations and then it's not just the ex post real interest rate that was high, but also the ex ante real interest rate was high, causing problems. So I think the question is much more complicated than it appears and it would require quite a complex analysis with a lot of assumptions necessary to show one way or the other what would have happened.

I asked Moses Abramovitz, God rest his soul, the same question and he said his father died in 1932 and left his older brother with a contract to try and use a German firm's help to manufacture zippers. He said "the workers were paid

40 cents an hour. If they fell to 10 cents an hour would it be equilibrium then?" That was kind of what I was thinking.

Yes well, what lies behind Moses' statement is his assumption, which was very prevalent among people making policy at that time, that the real adjustment, saying prices were flexible, was a code word for saying that wages should be flexible. That's what Moses was talking about, the pressure to cut wages, and that's what Robbins (1934) was talking about in his book written at the time. The intent is not to put all prices and wages down together so as to get more liquidity, but rather to get wages down to change relative prices and put the whole burden on workers. It is morally reprehensible and probably no longer historically possible after the First World War. Barry Eichengreen made the latter point in many publications. It is not just morally bad but politically infeasible after the First World War.

Two of the most powerful paragraphs I've read in all the economic literature on the Depression are what you and Eichengreen wrote regarding this topic in your 1997 paper. I will point out specifically these two paragraphs, but we'll get to that in a moment. Do you think the heavy lifting of explaining the Great Depression has been done?

Well, I think intellectually it has been done, I think the story is pretty clear. There are still lots of details to look up. Charlie Calomiris and Joe Mason (1997, 2003a, 2003b) are publishing papers about bank crises, so there is still a lot to learn about bank crises. I've been working on the German crisis of 1931 and there still are a lot of questions there. I think the main outlines are clear. What is not clear is why this has not been universally convincing. There are a lot of people who are involved in this who only take a US point of view or who take a very classical point of view and so on and have not adopted what to me seems to be obvious. The real business cycle people whom you were talking about have not adopted it. So there is still some heavy lifting to go. The tree falls in the forest and nobody's there, well it fell but it hasn't made a lot of impact. So I think it's our responsibility, Eichengreen and myself and a bunch of other people continue to write about these things in an effort to convince more and more people of this point of view.

You have said that the distinction between actions and regimes is critical in understanding the Great Depression. Is this the point that singling out a particular event like the banking panic of 1930 is not as important as understanding the regime in which actions are taken? Could you please elaborate on this point?

I think this is a critical point. I was actually introduced into this by Tom Sargent. Parts of this come from all over economics and this is the issue of expectations that I keep coming back to. If you do a single action then is this a change in the government's policy or is this not? Let me give you an example from current politics. Condoleezza Rice has just had her confirmation hearings to be Secretary of State and she asserted that she is going to woo the Europeans who have been antagonized in Bush's first administration. So, in our minds, envision a meeting where she goes over and sits down with the French and she says, "Oh we love you. We've had little minor disagreements but our aim is to work together" with the French or the Germans. How are they going to interpret this? This is where the distinction between actions and regimes comes in. If they take this action, that is Condi Rice coming and sitting down and making these statements as the symbol of a new regime, that is to say as a real change in policy, then they will take this very seriously, they will act on it and we will go off in the direction that comes from whatever happens as they respond to this meeting. If on the other hand they take this as an isolated action, but not a change in regime, then they will say, "OK, the Bush administration is going to be nice at this moment for this purpose but the policy regime that they are working with is for the US to go alone" and then they will not take this action very seriously. Maybe they'll be polite. I hope they'll be polite, but they won't do much of anything and the action then will have very little effect. So, here is the distinction, which is that if you take an action contrary to a regime that it is seen as being contrary to the regime it will have minimum impact because it will be seen as an aberration and it won't be seen as a large thing. So while it may have some effect, the individual action will have very little effect. If on the other hand the regime changes, then the actions interpreted as changes in regime will seem to have larger effects. The difference of course is not in the actions, which are the same actions, but in the perceptions of the people who are undergoing these actions and responding to them.

Then it will lead to different expectations on their part?
Well, depending on what has happened to the regime. The point is to change the regime you don't just do the one action, you do more. So in fact what might happen if Condi Rice went over to talk to them and said we really want to work with you and so on, then what the French and Germans might say is "OK that sounds lovely, here is what we would like to do." Then they would wait for stage two to see if Rice or Bush or Rumsfeld or whoever it is would follow through. Then if they followed through they'd say, "Yes the regime is changing, the event is important." But if the US administration did not follow through, then they would say, "This is an isolated action and not a change in the regime." Therefore, it would have very minimum impact.

Thus, you reject the idea that the death of Benjamin Strong was important since this is about regimes and mentalities and not personalities.
Yes, I think that's true. There is a theory of personality that says when in church people act church and I think that the economic analog of that is when

in central bank people act central bank (*laughter*).

That's very nice, thank you. You even showed in Strong's memoirs where he believed in the gold standard.
Absolutely.

Why do think the US didn't follow the United Kingdom in leaving the gold standard in 1931?
I think that the Hoover administration thought that was a terrible thing to do. If you look at the financial press at the time in the fall of 1931 when the Fed raises the interest rate very sharply, that action gets almost universal approval in the American financial press. There is essentially no political constituencies anywhere in the financial community or people in places of responsibility saying we should expand and so on. I'm not saying that there was no one who thought this, but there was no one who was in power that ...

Thought we should expand?
Yes, that the government should be expanding rather than contracting. There was Woytinsky in Germany who was saying this was a crazy policy, and of course he got kicked out. There were people in the US who were saying things like that, but like Woytinsky, they were fringe people. What I'm trying to say is it's not the case that nobody ever thought of expanding. That's not right. It is the case that the people who did think of these things were ridiculed by the orthodoxy, they were shunted out of power and they were not able to influence policy.

Given the gold standard do you think that, as Moses Abramovitz (1977) stated, the endogenous nature of the money supply made increasing the monetary base by whatever was necessary to avert the Depression economically impossible?
Oh yes, well that's the whole point. Because when you're on the gold standard then the central bank preserves the exchange rate. That's what the Fed did in 1931, raise the interest rate in the midst of a very bad recession.

You have said the failure of open market operations purchases in 1932 is evidence that the Fed was severely limited by the gold standard. Is this because of the presumed speculative attack it would generate and subsequent gold losses?
Yes. People are still working on this. It is the idea behind the Hsieh and Romer (2004) paper and also Epstein and Ferguson (1984). It's a fairly complicated thing. The open market purchases were affected by the international impacts in terms of fears for the gold standard and also the domestic impact which was the impact on the banks when interest rates went down. While we know that

both of these things were present, I think these are the kinds of things that still need work. We don't yet have a good handle on how important the international was versus the domestic or vice versa.

Was gold binding for the United States in 1932?
Well the gold *standard* (*Temin emphasizes the word* standard) was binding in the sense that we were adhering to the gold standard and deflationary policy. I don't know mechanically if that's the quantity of gold. Frankly, we had enough gold that we could have done anything more or less that we wanted to do. So, in some technical sense, probably gold was not binding. But historically, the fears of the gold standard and the adherence to the gold standard were binding in terms of policy.

Now I'm a little bit confused.
What are you confused about?

Well, Hsieh and Romer (2004) say gold was not binding, they had all kinds of gold to conduct open market operations and therefore this is a failure of policy. This is a monetary policy mistake and something else should have been done because they have the room to do it. Now, you just told me they had the gold to do it.
Yes, but wait, wait, wait (*Temin says it in a friendly tone*). First of all, the Hsieh and Romer paper had a lot of technical problems to it. So don't take it all quite so seriously. Has that been published?

No sir, it has not as of this moment.
Well, I think probably for good reason (*Temin chuckles*). [P.S. it was published in the March 2006 *Journal of Economic History*.]

Alllright (Parker stretches out the pronunciation indicating he is ready to move on).
But aside from that, the distinction they are making between the gold standard on the one hand and policy on the other hand is not valid. That's the distinction I was making earlier between ahistoric exercises by modern economists going back and historical elements, historical decisions made at the time. The policy at the time was the gold standard policy. Now, there may not have been a one-to-one relationship between people's concern for the gold standard and the amount of gold in Fort Knox or the New York Fed. I think there is a bit of a mystery, not illuminated by that paper (*Temin chuckles*), but there is a mystery as to why Americans were so wedded to the gold standard that they allowed various aspects of the gold standard to influence policy as much as they did even though we were not running out of gold. And the rise in the discount rate

in October of 1931 is a good example of that. You see, one of the problems in the Hsieh and Romer paper is they're talking about the summer of 1932 and they are asking people, in their experiment, in 1932 to think that the Fed was trying to stabilize prices, to expand and so on. This is the same Fed that six months earlier had zapped the economy in no uncertain terms when there was a tiny gold outflow relative to the amount of gold that the US had. So, these people would have had to make a disconnect, that the Fed in 1932 was different than the Fed in 1931. Come back to the point of actions and regimes, that there was a different regime in the Fed in 1932 than there had been at the end of 1931. Well, it was all the same people (*laughing*), it was all the same statements, there is no evidence whatsoever that you are dealing with a totally new Fed at this point. So that's another way to see that it's ahistorical. Part of this is you put a modern person down there to think about it and look at the magnitudes and you say what would they have done? Well, you know, it is fine to kind of look at the model, but it doesn't really tell you about what was going on in the summer of 1932.

Is it hindsight then to label policy as being inept or failed?
No it's not so much hindsight as it is, forgive my saying so, bad history. This is what Friedman and Schwartz gave us 40 years ago. They said the Fed made a mistake, it was inept. Well, why were they so inept? It's because Benjamin Strong died. Well that's their story. But it's basically a silly story. It doesn't help you understand the history. As we look back at George Bush invading Iraq some will say it was a mistake. That could be the end of the analysis, people not trying to figure out why he would want to do this thing. What was it that led the US to get into this position and all the things that followed from it? Are we going to be satisfied to say, "Well, it was a mistake, we shouldn't have done it?" No. The aim of history is to understand what people do. We understand it when we do things well, we try to understand it when we do things badly, we ought to try to understand it when we do things badly but they still turn out well. That's what we're trying to do, to figure out why people did what they did. That's really separate from what is basically a judgmental statement of saying "OK, they were in that and made it bad, they made a mistake."

So with the gold standard mentality when the bank panics happened the Fed let them happen to defend the gold standard.
Yes, that's right. They felt that was not their business.

You state that Germany could have followed the UK off gold in 1931.
Right.

Do you agree with Albrecht Ritschl's (2003) claim that after the experience of the 1920s Germany needed a credible, nominal anchor for the mark and thus stayed on the gold standard long after it should have left?

I think that's a reasonable point of view. I'm not enough of a scholar of Germany to really know whether that's true. And I'm not sure that Ritschl, given that he knows a whole lot more about German history than I do, really knows that either. It's a respectable point of view, but we don't actually know it. What he's saying, the form of it, is that if the Germans had devalued this would have created such expectations of a hyperinflation like the 1923–24 hyperinflation that the German economy would have collapsed. That's the expectations argument and regime change kinds of thing. My gut sense of this, and I may be wrong because Ritschl is a very good economic historian and he might be right, but my take on this is that there would have been a way to do it to contain these expectations. Rather than, say, floating the mark if they had said, "OK we're going to sharply devalue the mark and hold the line," I think that would have been more or less meaningless but economically it might have then reassured people and not set up these expectations. One point Ritschl is clearly right about is that it was harder for the Germans to float their currency than it was for the British or frankly even for the US. The US wasn't eager to do it without having had a hyperinflation so it might be correct that the Germans were even less willing to do it. Of course you have to explain why the British, who had previously been staunch supporters of the gold standard, suddenly said, "The cost has gotten to be too great, we can't do it. We're gone." Of course what's interesting about Germany in 1931 is that they see Britain going off gold and people don't like it, they think it's bad and it's beggar-thy-neighbor and so on and so forth, but the world didn't collapse. The German cabinet meets at that point and says "should we do the same thing?" So it's interesting and it's kind of open. If they were willing and had the guts to do it, maybe it would have been worse. But the problem is that things turned out so badly in Germany that almost anything would have been better (*Temin laughs lightly*). One tends to think that might have led to some real problems, but there was this chance that it might have really not.

I think given the history we know I'd have taken my chances.
That's exactly right.

God help all of us.
Eichengreen and I wrote a similar counterfactual that appears in Balderston (2003).

Ben Bernanke once said to me that counterfactual historical exercises are not worthwhile if you ask a question like "What would have happened during the civil war if Robert E. Lee had an F4 fighter jet?"
You're right.

But if you ask reasonable questions from what's reasonably known from history they're very useful and that's one of the things you and Eichengreen do in that paper. I thought that was a very useful exercise you guys conducted. Yes.

James Hamilton (1988) said that "the gold standard could not have come at a worse time or for poorer reasons." I've always liked that phase. How about if we add, given what you've said from your book Lessons from the Great Depression, *"and adhering to it mandated deflation where it was the worst of all possible policies."*
The gold standard came in the nineteenth century when it was actually quite useful. Perhaps the gold exchange standard or the return to gold in the mid-1920s was at the worst possible time. And yes, deflation was very hard and it was a very bad policy.

Do you think the Fed saw 1929–30 as a repeat of 1920–21 and thus saw no reason for alarm? Let me just go on here if I might. The contrast and the similarity between these two periods to me is interesting and I would like you to expand on it if you would. The recent real business cycle literature is caught up in trying to explain the differences. Why did we have high real interest rates in 1920–21 with no depression but yet we had it here and had a depression? Yet, they don't mention anything about what I thought was your well-thought-out explanation about the differences. There is no mention of that whatsoever. I'm scratching my head and thinking it was a war-time economy in transition and Temin talked about this 16 years ago.
Yes, well I'm scratching my head with you. The exchange rate regime is very important and it was very different. We had the flexibility to adapt in 1921 and we didn't in 1929. How much of this the Fed realized I don't know. I would want to go back, and I've dipped into Meltzer's book *A History of the Federal Reserve, Volume I*, but I haven't read it with this question in mind. And I don't know whether in 1929 the governors were looking back at the 1921 experience and asking whether this was really the same thing or whether they were thinking of this by itself.

Eichengreen speculates there might be something to that as well in Golden Fetters. *It was a changed world in 1929 and it wasn't the same. This isn't my daddy's Edsel any more. It's a changed vehicle.*
That's right.

Milton Friedman admits in my book Reflections on the Great Depression *and in the 2004* Cato Journal *that if he were to re-write Chapter 7 from* A Monetary History of the US *he would make it more international in scope and give France a bigger role in the Depression.*

Yes, I saw his comments.

Do you view this as being along the lines of the research agenda you've been voicing over the last 15 years and is this not progress?
Yes, yes, yes, but only limited progress, of course (*Temin laughs*). But I was certainly very gratified to hear Milton say that.

OK. He's a nice fellow by the way.
He is a nice fellow, absolutely, but not always correct (*Temin smiles*).

Why do you suppose the gold standard was not suspended nor was deposit convertibility in the Great Depression?
You mean before 1933?

Correct.
This is the same thing I've been saying before, which is that this is holding on to the gold standard and the gold standard was the free flow of gold. People just didn't mess with it.

It wasn't credible back then to even talk about abandoning it and you've said this too, but it's almost as if it was an apostasy to even talk against the gold standard.
Yes, well it was. If you go back to Roosevelt's presidential campaign, it was extremely vague regarding what it was he was going to do. He didn't commit himself one way or the other.

What's your assessment of the Japanese experience? They started to have trouble right around the time that Lessons *from the Great Depression was published. Do you have a few salient things you'd like to say about it?*
Not really. I was in Japan a couple of years ago and they were very interested in *Lessons from the Great Depression* and I talked a lot to the Japanese about regime change and the academics I spoke to all loved it. And of course, it had zero impact on anybody. I think the problem of Japan, for people outside Japan, is that various people keep recommending particular things to do. But the problem appears to be that the particular things are all within, here we come back to it, a policy regime that is supported by all kinds of organizations and people within Japan. And until you can change some of those things, it's very hard to make big changes. As to how much has to be changed and how hard this would be to do, you have to ask somebody that knows much more about Japan than I do.

In your 2002 tribute "Moses Abramovitz and open economy macro" you state, "some American economists have adopted the view of the United States' role

in the world economy espoused by Abramovitz while adhering to the model of the Depression from Friedman. This is of course an inconsistent view." Can you expand on that please?
Yes. I felt Moses, in these papers that he never quite followed up, was promoting the kind of open economy macro that Rudy Dornbusch popularized about a decade later.

He wrote those papers, Abramovitz (undated) and Abramovitz (1977), in the mid-to-late 1970s.
So it's about a decade or so, but he was ahead of the curve. The point is that he was thinking about an open economy. So it's very nice to have Friedman say he's thinking about international effects; more now if he wrote it, he would put those in. But it comes back to the same thing. Is he going to put in a paragraph saying "France had a lot of gold too" and that's the only change he's going to make? Or is he going to think about the fact that in an international economy you have all of these effects going on and then you have to think about what the exchange rate regime is or is not? That's why I think it's inconsistent. I think a lot of literature that is purely focused on the US and does not think about these implications is just wrong. We were the 800-pound gorilla with the big economy, but we still were not the whole world. Even now we are still not the whole world.

How do you like the approach of Eichengreen and his conclusions in his "Still fettered after all these years" paper?
I thought that his conclusion was that his book *Golden Fetters* was holding up rather well.

The book is holding up rather well, but yet you can say that for the United States policy mistakes and the bank panics have the preponderance of explanation, and for what happened elsewhere different explanations work for different countries, but it's the gold standard that links them all together. Yet the bank panics and policy mistakes can be some of the things that drive the US explanation.
Yes, I think that in the US the problem with banks, coming largely from our unit banking structure, were much more severe than in other countries. Now that you say it, I remember again what he said. Yes, I agree with that totally, which is that he is saying that it's the gold standard that gives rise to the deflationary force in the early 1930s, but the way this works out in different countries depends on the institutions and policies of the individual countries. There is no reason to think that is going to be the same and it probably was different in the US than in, say, Germany.

But policy mistakes though?

Well I don't use those terms.

OK then, I won't ask you about things that you didn't write (laughter). *Would you not say that leaving the gold standard and the regime change of Roosevelt and the changing expectations it generated was the reason for recovery and why it commenced when it did? Is that the signal the iron grip of the gold standard had been broken?*
Yes.

So this gets back then to the opening questions. What was it that ultimately led to this regime shift especially since, as you and Wigmore (1990) indicate, the first 100 days of Roosevelt's administration were nothing like what could have been anticipated from what he said about economic policy during the campaign and before the inauguration?
Exactly what I said at the beginning, which is the way to get regime change is you have new people coming in. They were learning on the job. I think it's quite clear one of the reasons that they had not talked about it was that they hadn't thought it through and I think Roosevelt was thinking on his feet. He was a bright guy and he didn't always do it perfectly, but I still give him high marks.

So, what ended the Great Depression once and for all?
Well, two things. What ends the downturn is going off gold. Then the economy expands, but the expansion is a bit like the expansions in Europe in the 1980s and the US now where you have GDP growing, but you don't have full employment. So if the issue is how did we get back to full employment then the answer has to be World War II. There are debates as to whether it's from fiscal policy or monetary policy, but I think those are details. The real stimulus is the War.

Now I'd like to specifically point out some things you wrote. One of them was what you said in Balderston (2003), that only by making "the respectable unrespectable, and vice versa" was regime change brought about. That just seems to me some of what it takes for regime change, you really have to be pushed to the brink. Secondly, on page 15 in your 1997 paper with Eichengreen, these two paragraphs: "Calling for lower wages is the discourse of the gold standard because this call follows from the mechanics of the monetary system. Countries on the gold standard cannot devalue their currencies and allow the demand for exports to determine their exchange rate. They cannot expand the money supply to stimulate domestic demand, for doing so would push up prices, provoke gold exports, and weaken the exchange rate. For them, the only way to reduce prices is to reduce costs of production, and the largest of these costs is labor." And, "The unions were reluctant to bear

these costs for a variety or reasons. They did not share the apocalyptic vision of the central bankers. They were not secure enough to trade current sacrifices for purported future gains. They had participated in the war effort and now expected recompense. Their reluctance to agree to wage reductions rendered the restored gold standard of the interwar years fragile and inflexible and transformed it from the guarantor of stability into the transmitter of the Great Depression." Those two paragraphs to me were very powerful paragraphs.
Yes, I think that's right *(Temin laughs)*. I think that's right.

It goes to explain a lot of why assumption number 4 that Kitson talks about, that the burden of adjustment would be borne by prices and not quantities, wasn't going to be the adjustment mechanism now. The same ability to deflate they had before the 1920s wasn't going to be there afterwards, after World War I and labor movement and so on.
That's right. The point here is it's a long period of time, these are the same governments in the late 1920s and early 1930s that had called upon people in 1914 and beyond to defend their country and lay down their lives in a very bloody encounter for their country. Then it was said afterward, "As a result of that we are going to give you a voice and say you are part of the country since you are doing this." And then for them to try to revert back to a system where the people should have no voice ...

They take most of the burden of adjustment as well, correct?
Precisely, they take most of the burden. What's interesting, and this requires a historian of thought much more than a economic historian to figure out, is that in the labor parties of both Germany and the UK, the leadership had gotten co-opted by the traditional gold standard people. It was really the rank and file that objected to this, not the leadership, because the leadership was very orthodox.

Something else that struck me in reading was just how counter thinking outside the gold standard was. You point out (Eichengreen and Temin, 1997) that Hoover thought any deviation from the gold standard was collectivism. If you didn't believe in the gold standard, then you were a socialist or something.
Yes, there was a lot of rhetoric. There was a lot of this extreme sense that if you give up one corner of what you are doing, then the whole thing falls apart.

Were the British still worried about inflation after they left the gold standard and thus they had a reluctant recovery?
Well, they were worried about it for about six months and they wanted to reconstitute gold and they wanted to avoid inflation. You know it seems crazy, but that seems to be what it was and they were convinced by people like James

Meade, and six months later they lowered interest rates. So, I think that fear of inflation affected policy for about six months, but not thereafter.

I should tell you a little anecdote from Abramovitz that never made it into Reflections on the Great Depression *or on the taped interview. When I went to Stanford to interview him, we were walking out of his office and he put it together and he said, "You know something, Jean Baptiste Say had dyslexia." So I thought about it and I said, "We've just been talking about the realization that aggregate demand is really what we should be looking at with the Great Depression. That's it, Say had dyslexia and demand creates its own supply!"(roaring laughter). He said, "I knew it all along. Jean Baptiste Say had dyslexia." I said, "Thanks a lot for that. I'm going to share that some day." What are some of the lessons of the Great Depression that have been learned or need to be relearned? Do you have a ready answer for that?*

Well, there's some in the book and I haven't really gone back over them. A lot has changed in 15 years. The particular thing at the moment that strikes me is that when you set off in a bad policy direction, then the cost of correcting it will be reduced if you don't go all the way down. The longer you hold on to it the harder it is to recover. That's the counterfactual kind of argument that we did in the Great Depression, so I believe that. The other lesson I think that I've learned since writing *Lessons from the Great Depression*, and if I were to write the book today I would emphasize more than I emphasized in the book, is the interaction of economics and politics. There I have economics and ideology and so the ideology was there and as a first approximation I think ideology is fine. But to go down to a second approximation, to get a little closer to it, the ideology is reflected in the politics of different countries and people are intertwined not just in the overall ideology but in bargains, commitments, statements, analogs, all sorts of things that are going on. These various entanglements make it hard to change and I think that comes out very clearly in the German case where the politics gets involved, but I think also in the US case where you have Hoover and the Fed sort of acting together. So I think the story, were I telling it now, would have the politics drawn a little more richly to talk about not just the people in the throes of this ideology, but that they are also structurally in a political situation which had been constructed under the ideology and so to shift the regime you would also have to shift a certain amount of the political bargain, the political structure, the power structure, the kind of sense of responsibility, a whole variety of things. That makes it harder to do. It also makes leadership, when people can do it, all the more surprising and more unusual and more praiseworthy.

What do you think of the Austrian explanations of the Great Depression? The credit boom, overinvestment, the mismatch between capital goods and long-lived goods and short-term consumer goods, the Hayek/Von Mises stuff.

Well I think that these things are a bit like the real business cycle stuff, they're looking for technical things at the time. You get much more mileage out of the approach that I've taken and that Eichengreen has taken. Now the ritual that people are going to is to take this longer view and think, yes technically it might involve imbalances between credit and between long-lived and short-lived goods and all different things. But the reason for these imbalances is the shock to the economy of World War I. The reason these things couldn't work out was the straitjacket of the gold standard and the interaction of those two things that leads to having all these problems. Tracking the effects and understanding the details of this gets you back into some of these things. I tend to think the work of Irving Fisher in fact is really very useful and very important. I don't know if you know one of his essays was recently republished in the *Journal of Money and Credit Banking* (Dimand, 2003) which I think is a very good thing to do and I think also it's a very excellent essay.

Yes sir, I am aware of it. It is worth reading again.
Yes.

In your Federal Reserve of Boston Symposium (1998) paper you come out and say that the Depression was not caused by a single shock but rather by a series of shocks that drove the economy further from equilibrium. In addition, the breakdown of the banking and legal systems crashed it. So, Eichengreen in his recent "Still fettered" paper still calls it "the mysterious first year" and what I'd like to know is, given your explanation, what makes it so mysterious any more?
Yes, I don't think it is so mysterious. But I do think you need to think of the Depression as happening in two stages and that's why the summer of 1931 is very important. Because if you hadn't had the currency crises in 1931, then you would have had a bad recession, but it might come out with people talking about parallels with 1921 saying that yes that's the way it looked and so on. The earlier recession is a bit mysterious, but not really mysterious. It's not due particularly to fiscal policy because the governments were very small at that time. But both in Germany and the US, monetary policy had gotten very deflationary and so that may have been enough to start the downturn. That comes in late 1929. Then in 1930, at least in the United States, consumption collapses and we started talking earlier about various people who have tried to explain this. It's my view this is still not fully explained, so to that extent Eichengreen is correct, this is still a bit mysterious. But in a larger sense, I think we have come to understand this recession was part of the attempts in the late 1920s to bolster the gold standard and it wasn't converging to an equilibrium, but in fact it was oscillating and got to be large enough to cause currency crises in 1931.

Eichengreen (2002) mentions in his paper some secret meeting on Long Island in 1927 between major central bankers of the world where the Fed for a time was trying to coordinate these gold standard policies.
I don't know about that meeting but the Fed was expansionary in 1927 to try and help the British because the British after the general strike were in trouble. No one has ever really put this together yet. I have a draft of a paper that was an idea of how to do it, but I haven't gotten back to it.

Don't be like Abramovitz now, we want to see those papers.
Yes, yes (*laughter*). I've got some other things going on, but there was some reason I stopped it, but I can't remember what it was at the moment. There is a loosening in 1927 which I think is part of the effort, and people said it at the time, to help the British who were in trouble after the strike. That looseness then may have set off the expansion that led to the stock market boom. And so what you got then by that loosening was that the Fed, in a sense, loosened too much for the US and then had in 1929 to tighten up too much for the US. That's what I mean by instead of approaching an equilibrium we're starting to oscillate. That would take the story back to the gold standard and back to the post-war settlement. But, as I say, this is an idea I have, but it hasn't been worked out yet.

We are converging to an equilibrium ending soon, in case you're wondering.
OK, good.

Do you see the Asian crisis of 1997 as being like the Depression currency crises of 1931 except it's Asian now instead of German, American and British?
Yes. Although, I do see a big difference between them because in Germany I don't think this was a banking crisis, I think it was a currency crisis. Remind me to give you a copy of the paper that Ferguson and I (2003) wrote on the subject. It's a twin crisis in the sense that both banks and currencies failed. But twin crisis is a generic term and in the German case, which is terribly important, it's not bad actions by banks but rather political things that lead to the currency crisis in the summer of 1931. So, I think that countries differ and yes, these are similar crises, but no, the analogy is not exact.

This graph here is from Cecchetti (1998, p. 182, Figure 2). Given the resumption of the gold standard is it reasonable to expect the Fed could have discounted as they did in the 1920s?
Yes. The problem for the Fed was that after the stock market crashed they reduced the discount rate just as fast as they could. Friedman, I think, forty years ago said they were probably still behind the market rate of interest. I think that's probably right. They didn't turn around fast enough. They did in

October. The Fed's response when the stock market crashed was very good, but just one month, just a little bit of a thing going on there. It's awful to say "I'm running just as hard as I can." Then other people say, "you're not running fast enough." It's a terrible thing to say. But it is true that conditions really did turn around and the Fed tried very hard to keep up with it and I think they weren't bad, but they weren't out in front. They would have liked to be and in looking back we all would have all liked them to be out in front, but I'm not sure they could have been. This comes back to an old question of Charlie Kindelberger's which I would love to have people work on.

Another good fellow, God rest his soul.
Yes, absolutely. In 1929 one of the reasons that things collapsed so dramatically is because of the agricultural crisis and its dramatic fall. And the reason for this dramatic fall is because all the cartels collapsed. That's got to be part of the story. It's not just the stock market collapse, but also the collapse of these cartels that turned things around. It is hard to fault the Fed in the sense of not saying immediately "oh we have a turn around." But at some point it is legitimate to say they should have seen what was going on, say in 1930, and said, "It's true we've already gotten the interest rate down really low, but maybe we need to try to do something even more." That's what Friedman and Schwartz argue, that there are various opportunities when they could have done that and some make more sense than others. Certainly in the early stage in 1930, I don't know, it's an open question. It's something that would be interesting to think more about.

But after the summer of 1931 ...
After 1931, no, then the Fed has already picked its side.

That's a good way to say it. That's one of the reasons I do this because you can say things in a salient way that reading all the literature you'll never "get it" (Parker snaps his fingers) *like you said it right then.*
Yes. OK, good.

In viewing real business cycle models, can we treat these models much as you wrote about the perfect foresight model in your paper "Notes on the causes of the Great Depression" (1981), "the Depression could not have happened in such a world and we do not need to discuss it further"? (Temin chuckles). *Would you say that the model that implicitly denies depressions is used to explain the Depression?*
Yes, I think that's quite right. It does make it very hard (*Temin chuckles*). I don't follow it and I don't know the literature. But I don't think it's going to be very illuminating.

You don't think this was a labor–leisure tradeoff or due to productivity shocks?
No, and I'm writing something for *The New Palgrave Dictionary of Economics* and right up front I say this is not a labor/leisure choice.

No Great Depression, no World War II?
These counterfactuals are really hard and Niall Ferguson has edited a 1999 book called *Virtual History* trying to get people to think about things. I think if there hadn't been a Great Depression, the probability of a Second World War would have been much reduced. There is this whole question of whether the Nazis would have come in and so on, but I think it is likely that we would not have had the Second World War.

I always ask everyone this last question. Could it happen again? Could we have another one?
Well the answer that I give, again possibly speaking more plainly than I write, is no we will not have another Great Depression that is exactly like the 1930s depression. But we could have an economic collapse and where it comes from is people getting into situations in which their aims are not economic prosperity, but some other set of aims. If you think about the Bush administration, which is accumulating debt and getting to ever greater imbalances in the world economy, one has to think they are pursuing an objective that is different from economic stability at the moment. If they bring it off and we get into this world they're envisaging, whatever it is, then everyone will look back on them as great heros and maybe they are depending of course on whether we like the new world. But there are a lot of dangers and a lot of slips and if the whole thing collapses then we'll say, "Yes, this was like the Great Depression. This was holding on to a theory for too long."

I liked Moses Abramovitz's answer. He said, "... who can forecast how the underlying features of the economy will change over time? It may make us more vulnerable to great disasters we can't envision now."
Right.

Let's leave this like it is. Thanks so much, Professor.

Ben Bernanke

Ben Bernanke was raised in Dillon, SC, entered Harvard College in 1971, and graduated in 1975 summa cum laude. After Harvard, Dr. Bernanke went on to graduate school at MIT, and completed his Ph.D. in 1979. His first job was at the Stanford Graduate School of Business. In 1985 he accepted a tenured professorship in the Woodrow Wilson School at Princeton University. He was Howard Harrison and Gabrielle Snyder Beck Professor of Economics and the Chairman of the department of economics at Princeton University when he was appointed by President Bush to the Federal Reserve Board of Governors in 2002. Thereafter, he was appointed Chairman of the Council of Economics Advisers from June 21, 2005 until January 31, 2006. He assumed the duties of Chairman of the Federal Reserve Board of Governors on February 1, 2006.

I spoke with then Governor Bernanke in his office at the Federal Reserve Board of Governors building in Washington, D.C. on May 9, 2005. Given the enormous workload that Dr. Bernanke has always maintained, I was given one hour of his time and I had no intentions of abusing his kindness. One hour, to the minute, with Chairman Bernanke begins now ...

You once told me that you thought macroeconomists had two sides to their brains. One side was for modern macro and the other side was for the Great Depression. Do you still feel that way?
I think to some extent that's true. But there has been a lot of interest among macroeconomists in looking back at the 1930s. There has been work in the context of modern macro models by people from different parts of the profession, for example, work by Cole and Ohanian (2004a) on the National Recovery Act period which applied modern calibration models. There has been work by Christiano, Motto and Rostagno (2003) that tries to look at the monetary policy implications of the 1930s in a modern dynamic stochastic general equilibrium type model. There has certainly been considerable interest among international economists in looking at the effects of fixed exchange rates and their implications for domestic and financial stability. So, I think there is still some divide, but I think there is an increased interest and ability of people to use both sides of the brain simultaneously.

Have your views on the importance of debt deflation as a transmission

mechanism changed or been modified at all over the last 22 years? Do you give it any more or less weight than you did before?
I have always thought and I still think that it was part of the story. I don't think it is the entire mechanism by any means. But we have seen similar mechanisms taking place in Japan for example. The deflationary period contributed to the stress of the banking system with the implications that had for the real economy. There have been periods also in China where deflation has proved to be a problem for the financial system.

Recently?
Not so recently, but a few years back. So, I think there is some evidence both from the 1930s and the present that debt deflation can be damaging. We had concerns about deflation risk in the United States as well in recent years and clearly one of the concerns was that falling prices would increase pressure in financial markets. So I think debt deflation is an important channel. I have never thought it was the only channel. But it does have a role to play.

Have the literature and the profession finally acknowledged that the financial effects of deflation are not simply redistributive? I have read it in your Federal Reserve Bank of New York Quarterly Review *article (Bernanke, 1993a). You bring it up again in your book* Essays on the Great Depression *that Fisher had a hard time when he came out with his debt deflation hypothesis convincing people in academic circles. Does the profession recognize that it is not simply a redistribution of wealth?*
I have done an extensive amount of work with Mark Gertler and others exploring how shocks to the economy working through the financial system can have amplified effects on real activity, the so-called financial accelerator. One mechanism is price changes but other mechanisms are affected as well. For example, if there are shocks to productivity that in a purely frictionless world might have very modest effects, when the shocks are combined with concerns about financial stability the effects can be magnified. So I think if you construe these financial models to be broader to include real-side effects as well as deflation or inflation effects, there is increasing interest in the idea that financial conditions play a semi-independent role in the transmission of shocks to the economy.

Do you think we can go as far as to say that we have our hands around "the holy grail of macroeconomics"? Eichengreen and Temin (1997) have said "the modern literature can be regarded as having substantially solved the riddle of the Great Depression" and it is the gold standard explanation. Is that so?
I think Barry Eichengreen, Peter Temin, Jeffrey Sachs and others who introduced the gold standard into the analysis made a very important

contribution. I think we will never have the full story. There are many issues associated with why wages, for example, didn't adjust more quickly in the face of large pressures from the monetary system. There are issues about the role of financial crises, banking crises, exchange rate crises and the like, independent of changes in the money stock. But I do think that the only theory that explains the timing and the widespread nature of the Great Depression has to involve, broadly speaking, monetary and financial issues which in turn are intimately connected to the gold standard.

If I may, I'll break the Depression down into several different questions. What started it? Why was it so deep? Why did it last so long? Why did it spread so completely? Why did recovery come when it did? Is there any one of those segregating questions that you think remains a mystery today?
I don't think of any of them as a complete mystery. I think we have ideas about all of them. I think we still may be missing some complete explanations in terms of the quantitative magnitudes. For example, there's a good monetary story that explains why the initial downturn occurred and secondly why the decline in the early 1930s was severe. We are only beginning to get a sense of what we would need to understand and see why these effects were as large as they were quantitatively in an economy that was presumably more flexible than the one we have today. With respect to the recovery, the gold standard had a lot to say about that. We know from Eichengreen and Sachs (1985) that leaving the gold standard was very strongly correlated with the recovery process. But once again, there is quite a bit of variation across countries in the speed of recovery. We need to better understand why, once the monetary contractionary forces were removed, the recovery was not more powerful than it was. In the case of the United States some scholars like Cole and Ohanian (2004a) and others have argued that the National Industrial Recovery Act, which reduced the flexibility of wages and prices, was a significant contributor. That may be true, but the question remains as to whether or not that theory can explain the sluggishness of the recovery, the extent of unemployment during that period and more seriously, can it explain the similar performance in other countries that did not have the same type of program but may have had other interventions in wage–price movements.

Different institutional arrangements as well.
Different institutional arrangements, different political forces and the like.

You have said before that the aggregate supply puzzle remains the biggest unexplained part of the whole story of the Great Depression. How close do you think Cole and Ohanian's (2004a) piece comes to accounting for the post-1934 US experience?
I think it would be hard to deny that on net the NIRA policies promulgated

after 1933 slowed the recovery by reducing the speed with which wages and prices adjusted. Again, I have some concern as to whether or not we can fully explain the slowness of the recovery. Certainly some other types of inertia may have been at work such as a lack of confidence or the slow recovery of the financial system. I think we haven't yet parsed that 1933–37 period into monetary–financial, real, and wage–price components, so I think that remains a challenge. And again I would reiterate that we are at an extremely early stage in understanding why similar slow recoveries were seen in a number of other countries that, at least as far as we know, didn't have the same kinds of interventions. Nevertheless, the work by Cole and Ohanian (2004a), which follows up on earlier narrative analyses by Michael Weinstein (1980, 1981), is a very important element and is certainly worth pursuing further. But we still have some way to go before we completely understand that recovery period.

Perhaps it's related to ask then what's your view regarding consensus in the literature on the Great Depression? Eichengreen's paper "Still fettered after all these years" seems to me to say there that there is a role for both domestic policy mistakes and the gold standard and Romer has for some years admitted that the gold standard plays a prominent role in understanding the spread and nature of the Great Depression. Is there really much debate left?
I think there are debates about details, about the role of individual central banks and other policy makers in initiating and propagating the Depression. But there currently is a pretty broad consensus about the monetary–financial underpinnings. The main resistence to that still comes from some people, but not all, of the Minnesota persuasion like Cole and Ohanian who are arguing that productivity shocks and other real side factors may have contributed to the decline. I don't think that view is plausible for describing the overall decline in the world economy and the close correlation of those declines across countries. But I think it may be of some interest in explaining some of the differences across countries in terms of the timing and severity.

But to go back, I think broadly speaking there is a lot of agreement now on the broad framework in which the Depression is analyzed, with a lot of details yet to be filled in. It doesn't mean the debate is forever closed. I'm sure that new generations will have other issues to raise *(both chuckle lightly)*.

Do you know anything about the Einzig (1937) data that have been used by yourself and also Hsieh and Romer (2004) to try and measure the forward premium on the dollar? This is something about which Eichengreen (2002) has expressed some doubt. If there was more information on how the Einzig data were constructed, maybe that would provide part of the answer.
I don't recall the details of how they were constructed. I think they must have been taken from quotes in financial newspapers that had some kind of prices for forward exchange rates. The problem with those forward quotes is that

except for periods of extraordinary stress they usually tend to follow interest rate differentials and the like. That is, since you have covered interest parity there is not going to be a great deal to explain there. So, I think they are useful in the same way, for example, that Hamilton's (1992) commodity price data are useful. But they are only loosely connected to the phenomenon you are trying to understand.

Something you just brought up, what is your take on the recent flurry of real business cycle papers on the Depression? I observe you were on the discussion panel for the Cole and Ohanian (2000) paper in the NBER *Annual. If we thought we had the Depression explained before, they present a whole new set of questions. Ohanian has indicated the whole line of research basically addresses the question "what is preventing people from working and producing more?" What are we learning?*

There may be a point, as I mentioned earlier, that we don't have the supply side completely nailed down. We've seen how monetary and financial disturbances created massive changes in aggregate demand and prices. The question is how do those changes manifest themselves in terms of real output and employment? A Keynesian view is that wages were sufficiently sticky that they couldn't keep up with the downward movement in prices. So wages adjusted too slowly and you had real wages that were higher than market-clearing levels that created unemployment and reduced output. A response to that which I don't think is entirely compelling but needs to be taken into account is that we don't really have very good data on actual paid wages as opposed to contracted wages or reported wages which may have been somewhat different from actual wages. So that remains a somewhat incomplete story.

The other general approach, which we talked about already, is the possibility that declining prices and panicky capital flows generate financial instability which in turn has real effects via financial markets. Again, I think it is part of the story, but it is not a story that we have modeled in detail. I think there is a lot more to understand about that. So I think that Cole and Ohanian raise some interesting questions that deserve to be looked at, but I don't think that they have presented a viable alternative to explaining why both output and prices fell so sharply in so many countries between 1929 and 1933. For example, productivity shocks would generate movements of output and prices in opposite directions rather than the same direction.

And they would reduce real wages and not raise them.

They would reduce real wages. Also, it might be worth mentioning that Alexander Field published a paper in the *American Economic Review* in 2003 which argues that rather than being a period of technological decline and productivity decline, the 1930s was in fact a very technologically progressive and creative period. Technological progress and inventions were endogenously prevented from being taken into the economy because of the fall in output and employment that was making it unprofitable to start new businesses in that environment. A similar story has been told by Michael Bernstein in his 1987 book. So, it is very difficult to point to productivity shocks that could either explain the severity of the Depression or account for the broad movements of prices and output in the world as a whole. I think it is useful to try and think harder about how markets adjusted to these shocks. But I don't think that the broad monetary–financial perspective is going to be overturned in the near future.

You said in your 1996 paper with Carey that the real business cycle models really do not have an explanation of why these shocks hit everyone around the world at virtually the same time and yet they were more persistent in the gold standard countries. They do not really address this point.
That's right. I think one of the things that I found very stimulating and got me working on the international Depression, as opposed to my earlier work focusing on the US, was precisely this set of facts presented by Eichengreen and Sachs (1985).

And Choudhri and Kochin (1980).
And before that Choudhri and Kochin (1980), exactly. These facts increasingly showed how the cross-sectional pattern of recovery was very closely tied to exchange rate regimes and monetary policy. My own work with Harold James tried to extend those results to a larger number of countries and a larger number of variables and we found exactly the same types of cross-sectional differences that can be accounted for by purely monetary influences. I think that is a very important fact and one that any successful theory of the Depression has to account for.

Isn't that one of the strongest historical macroeconomic relationships we have? The relation between when recovery commenced and when countries left the gold standard?
Well, when you are trying to identify the sources of the Depression it's useful to have some kind of cross-sectional variation in policy so that you can identify differences in response. All the countries in the world essentially declined in about the period 1928–29, which can be explained by the monetary collapse and the contraction of the gold standard. But it is not inconceivable that some other factor could explain the worldwide decline in output. Temin (1976a) in his earlier work, for example, tried to do that. The abandonment of the gold standard though took place in a staggered way which depended very substantially on politics, on previous institutions in history, and on a variety of factors that were not endogenous to the degree of output and price declines. Therefore it provides something similar to the natural experiment talked about

by Friedman and Schwartz (1963). It's a quasi-natural experiment where you have differences in policy choices which arise at least in part from factors outside the current evolution of the economy. Those differences give you some ability to identify the effects of these movements because by looking across different countries you can see the differences in responses in relation to the differences in the policies followed in those countries. In this case you get a very clear relationship not only between the abandonment of the gold standard and economic recovery, but many other variables such as wages, interest rates, exchange rates and prices all moving the way we would have predicted if the abandonment of the gold standard amounted to a monetary expansion and a reflation.

Romer (in Snowdon, 2002) has called the US decision to stay on the gold standard "perhaps the biggest policy error of the Depression" and labels the Depression a result of failed policy. On the other hand, Peter Temin told me after 1931 the Fed had "picked their side" and thus their actions should not be construed as policy failures. Their behavior was not a "shock" or "inept" but was a continuation of the path they had chosen to defend the exchange value of the dollar. What do you have to say about this? Was it a failure of policy or not?

I think the distinction is not a fundamental one from the point of view of explaining the Depression. Romer may be thinking of a policy failure as a point-in-time decision, perhaps within a general framework for policy, whereas Temin in a lot of his work has emphasized the idea of regime choice. The idea that, for example, the devaluation of the dollar in 1933 was a regime change that generated new expectations and a new policy regime in general. I don't see a fundamental contradiction. It's clear that the theories and policy frameworks of the time suggested that sticking to gold and maintaining the gold value of the currency was the only way for long-run stability. The problem was they had reached a new environment where the political calculations were different, for example the power of domestic constituencies vis-a-vis the orthodoxy of currency stabilization had grown more powerful. The institutional structures supporting the gold standard, for example the use of key currencies in place of gold as a reserve, reduced the stability of financial markets compared to the classic period. And as Eichengreen (1992) pointed out, the degree of cooperation among central banks had been reduced by World War I and the "peace" that followed. So, what had been a successful policy regime in the nineteenth century turned into a very dangerous policy regime in the twentieth century. Policy makers didn't understand or know how to respond to that. They went with what they had, which is understandable. I agree with Temin, it was something bigger than a policy choice. It was really an attempt to stay within an existing framework and an existing regime. But nevertheless, some policy makers like Takahashi in Japan, for example, understood that the gold standard was causing trouble and he abandoned the gold standard very quickly. So, I think a better organized, intellectually more cogent approach might have led the US to abandon gold earlier on and therefore would have avoided some of the severities of the Depression.

So why do you suppose the gold standard was not suspended nor was deposit convertibility during this time? Moreover, why didn't the US follow the lead of the UK in 1931 and leave gold? Eichengreen and Temin (1997) have said "that the solution to the Depression might lie in rejecting gold was beyond the pale."

Well again, I don't really disagree with him. I think the kind of errors people made were much more serious than, say, the Fed raising interest rates by 25 basis points when they should have cut interest rates by 25 basis points. They were of the form where we have this framework for policy and we don't have the ability to look beyond it and see the alternatives. When the British went off gold in 1931 the story is that the Chancellor of the Exchequer, while taking a bath, was informed of the abandonment of gold and he said something to the effect "I didn't know we could do that." Of course he could do that. The United States didn't have to do that because the US, like France, had accumulated large gold reserves during the interwar period, and even prior to that in the case of the US. As a result, the pressure on the dollar never reached the stage where essentially there was no choice but to abandon the gold standard. All the countries in the early stages with very few exceptions, like Japan, did their best to stay on gold as long as they could and only when institutional factors like financial crises, banking problems or just the pressure of the external drain became severe enough they found themselves forced to abandon the gold standard. So, I guess I agree with Temin in the sense that it was a problem of paradigm and not a problem of decisions within a paradigm.

Let me just complete it then: do you think Temin is correct that it was the resumption of the gold standard and the status quo ante and the attempt to preserve it that gave us the Depression? After the War the world had changed and trying to put the pieces back together, particularly with the gold standard and its mentalité, led the world economy down the wrong path.

Yes, I agree with that. It is understandable that people like Montagu Norman, Benjamin Strong and Emile Moreau would be attempting, from their perspective, to re-normalize the financial system. For them that meant going back to the gold standard. The British for example had been on the gold standard for several hundred years and had only abandoned it periodically during wars. They always returned but they always returned to the original parity because they felt to return at a different parity was to lose faith with the bond holders and others who counted on price stability. The British were unfortunate in a sense in that it was remotely feasible that they could actually go back on the pre-war parity because it required only perhaps 10 to 20 percent deflation to get back there. So it seemed feasible to do and they did it in 1925. But the effect was deflationary pressure which meant that Britain suffered substantial output and employment losses even prior to the actual 1929 debacle. The French had the good fortune that their inflation during the War had been so great that it was simply impossible for them to consider returning at the pre-war parity. So they chose a parity which turned out in fact to be quite favorable to them relative to the British and allowed them to stay on the gold standard for a longer period. Also the nature of the gold standard changed in the 1920s. There was the issue of trying to provide enough reserves, which led to a pyramiding of reserves using key currencies. And again, I talked about some of the other reasons why the gold standard was inherently less stable in the 1920s and 1930s than it had been in the nineteenth century. Perhaps a wise monetary economist could have predicted those things. Keynes to some extent did. He was very much against the 1925 resumption. But from the perspective of the central bankers, they were not economic theorists, they were not, most of them, economists, although economists didn't generally disagree with them. Their view was that this was part of the necessary reconstruction of the international system. That's why they undertook these actions even though the environment had changed enough that what had been stabilizing in the nineteenth century was potentially destabilizing in the twentieth century.

Do you see the evils of deflation, whether it was anticipated or unanticipated, as the greatest villain in the story of the Depression? And given the ruinous inflation of the 1970s, is not then price instability, either up or down, one of the greatest sources of economic instability in the last century?
That's true and I think that's why both conservative and liberal economists are generally agreed that price stability, certainly in the medium and long term, is the most important objective for modern central banks. In some cases, central banks have codified that objective in terms of an inflation target. In others, like the Federal Reserve, it remains more implicit. But nevertheless, there is a strong commitment to maintaining price stability in both directions. I think it is interesting that the Federal Reserve in its May 2003 statement indicated for the first time the concern that inflation may be too low as well as too high, thereby essentially making clear that the Fed has a range for inflation that's considered consistent with a dual mandate.

Deflation and inflation are destructive perhaps in different ways. For example, deflation has particularly insidious effects on debtors whereas inflation perhaps robs more from creditors. The adjustment of wages maybe different in the two circumstances. The inflation of the 1970s was primarily monetary but it had other factors as well such as the oil price shocks and so on. There are some differences but I think the broad conclusion that the policy for a central bank is to maintain medium-term price stability is widely accepted. In many ways this is a return to the gold standard in the sense that they too valued long-run price stability and put the highest value on long-run price stability and thought the gold standard was the way to get there. What they didn't fully appreciate was the potential for collapse of money supplies in the context of the gold standard that could generate major price instability. Likewise, Milton Friedman in evaluating the Depression came to the conclusion that monetary stability was the key. So he suggested stable money growth as being the primary objective. Both the price of gold and the quantity of money though turn out to have somewhat loose relationships to the ultimate price level. And so where we are today is central banks are stepping away from intermediate targets like the money supply or the price of gold and looking directly at inflation as an objective of monetary policy. Ultimately that's achieving what these other systems were trying to achieve, but more directly.

Looking at Figure 2 in Cecchetti's 1998 paper "Understanding the Great Depression" which shows Fed discounting behavior from 1919 to 1934, does this not show the failure of the Fed to be the lender of last resort? Eichengreen has argued that, since we were on the gold standard, if the Fed had provided liquidity it would have called into question our commitment to gold. But even though they were on the gold standard, the graph shows little was done before Britain left gold, when all agree the Fed had some room to do something, and the first and second banking panics pass with discounting barely even registering a pulse. I saw that graph and was somewhat taken aback by it and I'd like to know what your impression is.

Well, I was aware that the Fed was not very aggressive in rediscounting loans in order to support the banking system. There are two alternative explanations for that and I think both have some validity. One is that at various times they were concerned that increasing the money supply would accentuate the external drain. This goes back to Walter Bagehot who talked about the dilemma of trying to deal simultaneously with an internal and an external drain. Essentially that easy money and lower interest rates could help support the liquidity of the banking system but increase the pressure on the gold standard. I think it was Wigmore (1987) who talked about the final crisis in the 1933 banking crisis, which eventually led to the bank holiday and the abandonment of the gold standard, having been driven very directly by a run on the dollar which not only affected gold stocks but precipitated withdrawals from banks. A lot of other countries like Germany simultaneously experienced exchange rate crises and banking crises as hot money flowed out of the banking system as foreigners tried to escape from the domestic currency. So, at least in principle the Federal Reserve policy makers would have seen the potential contradiction between internal and external drains and it may have been on their mind at certain junctures. But Friedman and Schwartz (1963) suggest that there was more to it than that. To some extent the Fed may have agreed with Andrew Mellon that liquidation was the prelude to a healthy recovery, that you had to get rid of the dead wood and the excesses of the 1920s.

"Purge the rottenness from the system."

Purge the rottenness from the system, especially since small banks were particularly vulnerable to runs. Indeed there was some correlation between financial weakness prior to the Depression and the tendency to fail, as current scholars have found. There clearly was some view that it was good for the system in the long run to allow the weaker banks to fail. Friedman and Schwartz (1963) also commented on the fact that after the Federal Reserve Act was enacted the informal clearing houses within cities that had acted de facto as lenders of last resort during nineteenth century banking crises were essentially prohibited from acting in that role. So when the Fed failed to provide liquidity there really was no other substitute to help provide support for the banking system.

Temin told me that the Fed didn't think that saving banks was their business back then.

Well that's very odd because if you look at the reasons for the Federal Reserve Act in the beginning, one reason was to provide an elastic currency. The main purpose of an elastic currency was to provide extra money as needed during periods of harvest or planting which in turn was intended to keep short-term interest rates more stable. And the evidence suggests, Mankiw, Miron and Weil (1987) for example, that the seasonality in interest rates declined significantly after the founding of the Federal Reserve. So the Federal Reserve was performing that function. Why do we care about seasonality in interest rates? Well, the high short-term interest rates during the fall and the spring created a shortage of liquidity and often provided the backdrop in which banking panics would take place. Classically, October has always been the month for financial problems. Moreover, politically the Federal Reserve Act follows the 1907 crisis where there had been actions taken by clearing houses and I think by J. P. Morgan to try to avert the crisis but Congress was very dissatisfied with the results in terms of the length of time it took to end the crisis. Also there were concerns about whether or not J.P. Morgan and others had turned the situation to their own financial advantage by cornering the money market. So, the rationale for the founding of the Federal Reserve was to provide an elastic currency to avoid these liquidity shortages and to support the banking system. Moreover, classic central banking theory, such as Bagehot's book *Lombard Street*, talked about the responsibility of central banks to accommodate internal drains. So the Federal Reserve should have been cognizant of these responsibilities.

I would be surprised if it was a general disdain for the banking system. It was probably more so the case that they were concerned about what I mentioned before. Either that supporting the banking system was potentially a risk to the maintenance of the gold standard or, probably more importantly, that some purging of the banking system was a necessary prelude to full recovery.

You once said to me that counterfactual historical experiments make no sense if you ask questions like "How would US history be different if Robert E. Lee had an F4 fighter jet?" Do you think it is ahistorical and hindsight to ask how things would be different if the Fed had increased the money supply by what was necessary to keep money growing on its 1920s growth path? I'm thinking here of McCallum (1990), my paper with Fackler (1994) and Bordo, Choudhri and Schwartz (1995). Did the endogenous nature of the money supply under the gold standard and the gold standard mentality of the time make this unfeasible?

What I meant by that earlier comment was that an interesting counterfactual needs to be something which is plausibly within the range of what might have happened. While the Federal Reserve could not have waved into existence a modern financial system or a modern monetary system, it was within their powers to make monetary policy different from what it was, to change their views or theories about what the appropriate approach to monetary policy was, and even to abandon the gold standard in the extremis, as a few countries did. So I think it is meaningful to think about alternative policy paths in that sense. Indeed, in blaming the Federal Reserve for its role in the Depression what you are implicitly saying is that you think a feasible alternative policy path would have had better outcomes.

I said in Reflections on the Great Depression *that it took Hamilton's 1987* Journal of Monetary Economics *piece for the profession at large to acknowledge that money really was tight during the Depression. Is that too harsh a view?*

I think that there is a remarkable amount of prescience in the Friedman and Schwartz (1963) description of the Great Depression. They were focused primarily on the United States and so their emphasis on the international factors was less than what subsequent work placed. But they pinpointed back in 1963 the general point that monetary policy had become tighter in the late 1920s. For example, they emphasized the Fed's attempt to prick the stock market bubble by raising interest rates quite significantly during that period. And they talk in various places about the effects of that on the operation of the gold standard and the money supplies of other countries. Peter Temin in his work talked about the interaction among major industrial countries operating through the gold standard in the late 1920s. I think that some of the contributions that have come from him and others are to note that the United

States was not the only source of contraction. France was an important source of contraction and there were also developments in Germany and the UK as well that contributed to the overall crisis. So I don't think it's quite fair to say that no one was aware of the fact that there was a significant contraction in the late 1920s. But I think what Hamilton (1987) did to some extent was address the quantitative question, which is was the contraction large enough and widespread enough to help to account for the beginning of the great contraction? I think his work added to that understanding. Eichengreen (1992) also contributed to that point by noting that the gold standard promulgated tight money to other countries which then fed back on the United States. So the effect was multiplied via the international monetary system.

Christiano, Motto and Rostagno (2003) again raise the phoenix of a constant real money supply in their paper and claim "to the extent that there was some tightness in monetary policy, it was relatively small, certainly by historical standards of the time." If the nominal money supply and prices both fell by 50 percent, the real money supply would be constant and thus would be evidence that there was no money supply shock. Is it me or is this a new source of confusion?
I don't want to be too hard on Christiano because I know he has done some very interesting work subsequently which actually shows monetary forces to have been fairly important in the 1930s. But with the argument above what I would emphasize is that with nominal debt contracts and nominal wages that are less than perfectly flexible, a decline in prices that is proportional to a decline in money can be very contractionary (a through the debt deflation mechanism and (b by raising real wages above the equilibrium level. So I don't see any inconsistency between the monetary story and the observation that real money stocks didn't fall.

One of the lessons of the Great Depression you have pointed out is that fixed exchange rate regimes can be dangerous and destabilizing (Bernanke, 1993b). You wrote that before the Asian crisis of the late 1990s. You still feel that way, do you not?
Yes I do. I tend to agree with the so-called bi-polar view of exchange rates. Exchange rates should either be flexible or they should be extremely hard pegs, preferably a currency union among countries that share a common currency because they are essentially part of an optimal currency area. I think the experience with pegged rates which are pegged but adjustable shows that they are not able to withstand the pressure of capital flows under crisis situations. They were an important contributor to the disequilibria and the crises that occurred in the 1990s in east Asia and elsewhere.

How might you imagine the Great Depression era unfolding if there had been an inflation targeting regime in place to guide the actions of the Federal Reserve?

Well, now we're getting really counterfactual. I do think, and I think Friedman and Schwartz would agree, that monetary instability exhibited itself primarily through deflation. A price target that avoided deflation would have de facto forced abandonment of the gold standard and would have eliminated a major channel of depression emanating from the monetary system and also would have broken the international links that created this contagion among countries. So I do agree that stabilizing prices is the ultimate lesson of the Great Depression and also of the 1970s. There really is nothing more a central bank can do for domestic economic stability than make sure that inflation remains low and stable over long periods.

Cecchetti and Karras (1994) present an argument describing the decapitalization of the economy, high real rates, portfolio shifts that occur as the nature of money changes, the value of in-place capital falls, deflation and currency holdings place a real, after-tax, riskless floor on expected returns, investment falls and indeed becomes negative, and demand for current output falls. What are your views on this explanation of the forces at work that brought the Great Depression?

Well, the zero bound adds an additional power to the debt deflation argument. If there were no zero bound and if debt contracts were sufficiently short term, then adjustments in nominal interest rates would eliminate significant redistribution between creditors and debtors. So the fact that there is a zero bound, which prohibits full adjustment of nominal interest rates, exacerbates the problem through two mechanisms. One is that, from an ex ante perspective, to the extent that deflation is expected, it puts a floor on the real interest rate which is the negative of the expected deflation rate. Second, from a debt deflation perspective, whether deflation is expected or unexpected, because nominal interest rates can't adjust fully, if debt contracts are of any length, then there is no mechanism to prevent deflation from redistributing huge amounts of wealth from debtors to creditors. So I agree the zero bound is very important. In recent history Japan had trouble with deflation and the United States was concerned about deflation in 2003. The concern about deflation, which after all in the case of Japan was relatively mild in terms of percentage rate per year, was the problem with the zero bound which in the presence of deflation would have prevented the central bank from creating a negative real interest rate as a means of stimulating the economy. The interaction of a zero lower bound on interest rates and deflation, even moderate deflation, can be a very negative force to the economy. So I think that the Cecchetti and Karras argument is quite compatible with debt deflation and financial crisis views and I agree that the zero lower bound is a critical element in explaining why deflation is perhaps an even more serious problem than inflation.

Are there any lessons from the Great Depression that need to be relearned?
As I said before, the two main lessons which I think have been learned to a large extent, but always can be re-emphasized, are first that a central bank's primary responsibility is the maintenance of price stability, to provide low and stable inflation in the medium term, to avoid sharp inflations or deflations and particularly to avoid the instability of expectations associated with an unanchored price level. The second lesson is that the financial industry is a special industry in terms of its role in macroeconomic stability. Major upheavals in the financial system can be extremely disruptive to the economy as a whole and therefore the central bank and other government institutions have a particular obligation to make sure that financial stability is preserved, that banks and other financial institutions are well capitalized and well managed and that there exists a mechanism for responding in the event of crisis, such as the discount window or a deposit insurance system or whatever you need to make sure that the financial system will remain whole even under a great deal of stress.

I always ask everyone at the end two questions. What ended the Great Depression?
We could turn it around and ask why didn't the Depression end quicker than it did? Once the gold standard was removed, and the banking system was stabilized by the banking holiday and the subsequent actions that Roosevelt took, the two main impediments to recovery were removed and there was evidently some natural tendency of the economy to begin to right itself. Indeed, 1933 and 1934 were years of rapid gains in the stock market and even reasonably good economic growth. So the question is perhaps not what ended the Depression but what thwarted the recovery in the mid and late 1930s? Again I think that the wage and price controls of the NIRA and other interventions that tried artificially to reflate through fiat rather than through monetary forces were a major factor. There may have been some elements of hysteresis in that once the unemployment rate had gotten to such a high level, people had lost skills or firms were slow to recover and re-employ workers. But, again, broadly speaking, putting the puzzle the other way, why didn't the economy recover more quickly? Particularly in the early stages after Roosevelt became president it appeared as if things were turning around pretty quickly.

Could it happen again?
Probably not in the same way. But there certainly are risks to international financial markets that could produce very serious instabilities. One scenario that is occasionally described by some economists is a hard landing scenario for the dollar associated with the US current account deficit. I don't particularly find that persuasive, which means it probably willhappen by the time this book is published. So there are stories that one can tell where the

financial system comes under an enormous amount of stress due to some sort of shock be it monetary, financial or real, and the financial system is so complex and so inter-related that one can't rule out the kinds of contagion that were seen in the 1930s. I do hope that central banks have learned enough in the ensuing years to understand the importance of maintaining price stability and of reacting quickly and effectively to shorten the effects of financial instability. I optimistically think that while we could still have financial crises and bad outcomes in the world economy, policy makers know enough now to short circuit the impact before it becomes anything like the severity of the 1930s. Certainly that's the hope anyway.

My 60 minutes are up. Thank you so much.

James Hamilton

Professor Hamilton received his Ph.D. from the University of California, Berkeley in 1983 and he is currently Professor of Economics at the University of California, San Diego. His 1994 book *Time Series Analysis* sets the standard for the profession. Professor Hamilton is also the leading expert on the macroeconomic effects of oil shocks. At the end of the interview I could not resist asking some questions on these topics. His research agenda has concentrated on macroeconomics and econometrics, but the three publications that resulted when he turned his attention to the economics of the Great Depression have been very influential. Moreover, as this interview reveals, the depth at which he understands the issues and the clarity in the way he expresses this knowledge for all of us to understand is without equal. I spoke with James Hamilton in his office at the University of California, San Diego, on March 4, 2005.

Could you give us some background on how you became involved in the literature on the Great Depression?
The Great Depression is the single most dramatic macroeconomic development of the last century. In some ways it might be thought of as the defining event of what macroeconomics studies in terms of just what can go wrong in the economy. If you have a theory of what goes wrong with the economy in a downturn, well that's a great place to explore the theory. If you can't see evidence of your ideas there it's probably not operating anywhere. Something went seriously wrong there and it's pretty important to know what it is.

So you took a look at the Depression and said "There are still behaviors of prices and quantities that need to be explained and I have something to say."
Well, I started more from the point of view of a consumer just looking at what people said and trying to sort out my views seeing whether the concepts I had were consistent with the events of that time.

Was the 1987 Journal of Monetary Economics *paper your first paper on the Depression?*
Yes it was.

You certainly started out with a bang there, I have to say. What is your view on the causes of the Great Depression in the so-called mysterious first year? Barry Eichengreen (2002) has recently said that he seems to think that this is where much of the debate still lies. Do you not think monetary policy can be given the preponderance of the responsibility?

Well, I would say it's pretty clear that the initial downturn was caused, at least in part, by monetary contraction. I don't think there is a lot of room for arguing with that claim. I think that maybe there were other factors contributing as well, but certainly there was a classic tightening of money, raising of interest rates and that surely contributed to the initial downturn.

You say in your 1987 JME *paper that it could not have been the only reason for the downturn, which you just stated is correct. What are some of the other explanations you give weight to?*

The stock market decline is an event you don't want to ignore. It was such a dramatic drop in stock prices. It certainly seems quite possible that that would in itself have effects on consumption spending and investment spending. Now, that then raises the question why did stock prices go down? Was it a rational anticipation of something about to happen? If so what and how were people recognizing it? Why, after all these years, do we still not know exactly what it was they were anticipating? Or was it that there was some kind of excess in the market valuations in 1929? I don't think you can rule out that possibility altogether.

What about the Austrian school ideas of the overinvestment/boom type of explanations that were offered at the time? Do you place any weight in those at all?

Yes, I don't dismiss them out of hand because it's a pattern you do see in other situations. We saw it in Southeast Asia and Mexico in the 1990s for example. You have a similar kind of thing, that everything looks just incredibly rosy and then all of a sudden there was almost a financial panic. People were getting out of their investments, realizing ex post that they made some mistakes, realizing ex post that there was some shady accounting going on, seeing that the boom was flimsier than it had seemed at the time. So, I don't rule those accounts out altogether.

Do you agree with Michael Kitson (2003) that the causes of the Great Depression are one thing, but the extent of the Great Depression is due to the operation of the gold standard?

Yes, I think that is a very good characterization. I divide the Depression into three phases: the initial downturn from 1929 to 1931, turning into a real severe event which really was the Great Depression from 1931 to 1933, and then a very gradual recovery from 1933 to 1939. I think there are three separate questions. What caused the initial downturn? What made it become so bad?

And lastly, why was the recovery so slow? I'm sympathetic to the view that there might be three different answers to those three different questions. I put it that way because, as Friedman and Schwartz (1963) observed, if the economy had recovered in late 1930, we wouldn't be talking about this right now. It really would have looked quite a bit like most of the other downturns, a little more dramatic movement in stock prices, but not that far out in terms of how far stock prices had fallen by 1930, not that far out of line with other experience. It really would have just been another recession. So I don't think we need anything that special to understand 1929 and 1930. Some combination of monetary tightening and what we were talking about, possible overinvestment, maybe some mismanagement and fraud contributing to that, the sort of things that contribute to any downturn I think work satisfactorily for 1929 to 1930.

Any ordinary NBER downturn.
Yes, I don't think it would have really been distinguishable from the others if the economy had started to recover by the end of 1930. So, there is something different that happened from 1931 to 1933 and I think the gold standard is very much front and center of what that was.

Yes, I try to make that segregation as well. We have a perfectly ordinary recession from 1929 to 1930, but then it turns into a train wreck.
Right.

You can't separate that train wreck, it seems to me, from the gold standard worldwide.
I think that's a pretty compelling connection.

Are Kitson's assumptions pertaining to the gold standard also correct? He goes through four different things about what is needed for the gold standard to function. First of all, the gold standard assumes the law of one price. Second, it assumes that the demand for money is stable. "Third, it assumes that the monetary authorities do not intervene to prevent increased gold reserves adding to the money supply. Fourth, it assumes that the burden of adjustment would be borne by prices and not by quantities. This is the pre-Keynesian assumption that the economy tends toward full employment – an assumption that is so obviously inappropriate to the interwar period." Are these really limiting assumptions of how the gold standard functions?
Well, let me say I think he's leaving out what I regard as one of the key issues of this time, and that is a gold standard means that the price of gold, in terms of dollars, is fixed. Therefore, if the price of gold in terms of potatoes goes up, the price of potatoes in terms of dollars must go down. An increase in the relative price of gold must mean deflation in the overall price level. That's just

an accounting identity and it says as long as you're on the gold standard, if you have explained why the relative price of gold went up, you have explained why the overall price level fell. Now, a lot of people talk about deflation in the Depression just in its own right, just looking at the overall price level and implicitly they are assuming that what goes on with gold is some kind of residual, that there is no demand and supply for this commodity and the relative price could be any old thing. I don't think that's the right way to view it economically, I think there is a demand and supply of gold. Now, it's fundamentally coming in part from the monetary system, the international payments mechanism, and a lot of that demand is in fact from central banks wanting to hold gold for purposes of reserves. So, I would, I guess, amplify Kitson's remarks to say I think why that mattered was that there was an increase in the demand for gold coming from the financial instability, that there was an increase in the relative price of gold. I take that as a fundamental.

This is from your 1988 Contemporary Policy Issues *paper when you talk about hoarding on the part of the public.*
Yes. So I would add to these assumptions that there's an implicit view that the relative price of gold isn't going to move very much, that it is basically limited by the supply of mining and so the relative price doesn't change. If the relative price of gold is kind of volatile and wild, it's a terrible system to use because then you're imposing all of this same volatility and wildness on the aggregate price level and we pretty clearly don't want that. So I would say that's an important thing he's left out. All the other aspects he discusses, the maldistribution of gold and problems with cooperation, all of that I would translate into the factors that were causing the relative price of gold to go up and therefore any country that was sticking to the gold standard to experience a severe deflation.

(Parker shakes his head at the crispness and importance of what Hamilton just said) *See, you don't hear much about that. You look in the literature and they don't say it just the way that you have right there.*
Well, that's why I wanted to bring it out when you got here *(laughter).*

Excellent. Milton Friedman recently said that if he had to write the chapter "The Great Contraction" all over again he would give more responsibility to France in propagating the Great Depression. I would think that you would agree with that from what you said in your 1987 paper, would you not?
Well, certainly I would. I do want to point out that *A Monetary History* by Friedman and Schwartz was such a monumental work and the thing that made it monumental was that they had an overriding theme that they were interpreting the whole sweep of economic history in the US. By its nature, when you do that, you are going to leave some things out and you need to

emphasize what is similar across all of the downturns. So I don't know if for purposes of that book it's wrong, but for purposes of understanding the Depression it is different from other downturns, as we were saying, in terms of the magnitude of what happened I think there were some other forces going on. It certainly is the case that *A Monetary History* does not emphasize, to the degree that I think is appropriate, what was going on with the gold standard at the time.

Do you agree with Michael Kitson that the gold standard was "simply structurally flawed" and could not have survived even with cooperation and coordination. Given the maldistribution of gold, the gold standard asymmetry and the speculative volatility that you document in your 1988 Contemporary Policy Issues *paper and the claim, correctly, that it was exacerbated by the interwar gold standard, the gold standard was doomed, no?*
Yes, I agree with that and I'd be sure to emphasize some of the financial turmoil of the 1920s, the hyperinflations and the fiscal challenges many of the governments were facing. I think that compounded these issues.

I think probably two of the greatest paragraphs in the literature on the Great Depression came from your pen when you wrote in 1988 the return to the gold standard "couldn't have been done at a worse time or for poorer reasons," but we'll get back to that. You point out in your 1988 paper that central banks would not have converted their foreign reserves during the Depression if everyone believed the exchange rates between currencies and gold were unalterable. Thus this reserve component made the system even more unstable.
Yes, that's exactly right. It's a fractional reserve kind of system and when everybody gets worried about wanting more reserves it's got to translate into an increase in the relative price of gold.

Would one way to look at this, as in Temin (1989), be that the world had changed? Eichengreen (1992) talks about how capital flows became a much more important part of international transactions during the interwar era whereas at the turn of the century the price-specie-flow mechanism worked well because you basically had the current account. But once capital markets began to open up, then you had also the capital account and the balance payments, the price-specie flow mechanism didn't work quite as well as it did. In addition, with all of the other things we talked about, the hyperinflations of the 1920s, the fiscal imbalances and so on, we had an old apparatus that could not function any more in the different world after World War I. Would that be a correct way to view it?
Yes. I think that there is quite a bit of accuracy to that.

Quoting you now from your 1988 paper "[t]he death blow to the international gold standard, and the knockout punch to the US economy as well, was the speculative attacks on the currencies of these two world finance centers (the UK and America) during summer and fall 1931." So please, do go on. Do you see that as the knockout punch?

Well, I think that's the point at which you would definitely say we are not talking about a regular downturn anymore. We're not talking about a regular recession once you get past those events. The economy really seems to be going into free fall, with the Fed raising interest rates sharply at a time when the economy was very weak, which they did in an effort to respond to the attack on the dollar. So yes, you would have to say we entered a new phase once those events start developing.

Both your 1987 and 1988 papers show the data and you talk about just how dramatically the macroeconomic aggregates began to free fall then. That's pretty convincing. Temin has stated that he sees this behavior by the Fed as a consequence of defending the exchange value of the dollar and not as failed or inept monetary policy. From your 1988 paper it would seem that Temin (1998) is correct that the shock in 1931 was foreign/monetary in nature and given the behaviors of open market operations, as you point out they increase, discounting went up even though the discount rate increased, and the fact that the monetary base increased between June and December 1931 by $433 million dollars, it is hard to fault Fed behavior for the collapse of M1. On the other hand, in your 1987 paper you refer to the counterfactual experiment of what would have happened if the Fed had kept the nominal money supply from falling. It also states that since the Fed was established in part to advert bank panics, then the Depression, in this sense, represents an unambiguous failure of monetary policy. It seems to me that where we're at right now in the literature is to ask was it a failure of policy or was it not? So let me ask, did the Fed's behavior represent a failure of policy or was the gold standard the reason for their behavior?

Let me go back first to a point on which Professor Temin and I disagree, which is what happened prior to 1929. There clearly was a discretionary component of policy that I would say was misguided. This effort to stomp out the stock market boom, in retrospect, surely everyone would agree was misguided. In Temin's research, for some reason, he only started the story in 1929 and what happened after that. After we're already in a recession, OK, we can discuss what the Fed could have done at that point. But I think we should emphasize there were some important mistakes in policy before we got to that point.

You pointed out January 1928.

That's right, they really started tightening back then. They were in fact continuing to tighten even after business had started to turn down, we now recognize in retrospect, in the summer of 1929. Now, once you get to 1931, I guess I'm agreeing with Professor Temin in that, as I was saying before, I take the increase in the relative price of gold as a fundamental fact of the time and if you are going to maintain the dollar price of gold you have to have the deflation. It was the deflation, and the collapse of the monetary aggregates that go with that, that was a big part of the problem. So I agree with him, I guess, to the extent that I think what we really needed in order to have a better monetary policy was to abandon the fixed exchange rate between dollars and gold.

Professor Temin put it very succinctly. He said after September 1931 the Fed demonstrated that they "picked their side."
That's right.

Do you have sympathy for that point of view?
I do. I think that was the whole point of raising rates in the fall of 1931. It was to prove the US was going to stick with this no matter what. It was a sad mistake with serious consequences, but they did persuade the markets that that's where the US is going to go. They did eliminate that potential run on the dollar ... but at what a cost.

This is one point of debate right now with Romer and Eichengreen, among others. Was the Fed fettered in 1932 or not? Did they meet these binding gold points? Do you have a view on that?
Well, are you bringing up at this point the Hsieh and Romer (2004) evidence?

Yes.
What they do is they say in 1932, from what happened, there is evidence that the Fed did have the ability to increase the base without having effects on the price level of gold and I agree with that. But, I think what we're talking about is the fall of 1931. There was a substantial, significant outflow of gold in those weeks that we're talking about. It came right after Britain had been forced off fixed exchange rates and so I think these counterfactuals are kind of missing that key part of the story. I think very much in 1931, just as we were saying, the Fed picked a side and the side they picked was unambiguously "we're sticking with gold."

Romer and Hsieh have to try to explain why a speculative attack wouldn't have occurred or how if they had tried this they would have had that latitude. It could have been very nonlinear and gotten out of hand very rapidly.
Absolutely. That's how these things go.

Do you have any other comments about the gold standard literature in general? That's just an open-ended question.

Well, I think we've covered it. I do think it has emerged as something of a consensus that, as you were pointing out, it was sort of underplayed from the Friedman and Schwartz summary. Now I think most scholars are agreeing that it's a pretty important part of what went on in causing the Great Depression in the sense of what happened to make it an extreme event.

Are you as impressed with the solid relation between leaving gold and the recovery and when it commenced as I am? It seems to be one of the most robust empirical macroeconomic relationships that one can find throughout economic history.
Yes I am, because remember these big movements are not measurement errors. It's not an accident. There were huge downturns in these countries and a very dramatic recovery, so the timing of that is not something you want to dismiss casually and the fact that it does correspond so strikingly with when countries abandoned the gold standard is also to me very persuasive.

Why do you think the US did not follow the United Kingdom in leaving the gold standard in 1931?
You know that's a good question. As we were saying, they wanted to convince markets that this is where they were going to go. Of course there were international traditions, that this shouldn't happen and the market should be able to right itself and if we just made sure money was sound that would perhaps happen. I think there was confusion about exactly what was wrong and exactly what would clear it up. Dan Nelson (1991) had some interesting work where he shows some creditors were actually mistakenly thinking that this was in their interest to avoid the kind of inflation that would happen if we went off gold.

God rest his soul.
I don't myself know. I think there's a fog of war in these kind of things in designing policy. I think it's easy to go wrong. I'm not sure how to answer your question.

Eichengreen and Temin (1997) say it was the mentalité of the gold standard – if we just stick to this everything will be fine – and that may have a lot of value. Why do you suppose the gold standard was not suspended nor was deposit convertibility? It had been done before in times of crisis, it was done during the panic of 1907 and yet it wasn't contemplated. It seemed to have fled from their minds.
It's just as we were saying, they picked a side. Of course, if you are going to defend the gold standard the most important thing is to be very resolute about it and very dogmatic and everybody knows here is what we're doing and no we're not going to entertain arguments about it. As soon as the word gets out

that maybe we're not sure, maybe we will go off, of course you magnify all of the speculative pressure. It is true that in that kind of environment you do have to pick a side and you have to be firm about it and they picked the wrong side (*both laugh gently*).

You also mentioned in your 1988 paper the worldwide hoarding of gold by private parties. There was a risk of holding any currency in the world at that time and all that changed the world money multiplier.
That's right. It changes the world money multiplier when we look at it or changes the world relative to the price of gold, which is what I keep coming back to, in terms of requiring a deflation of any countries pegging the dollar price or pegging their currency to gold.

What a rotten system, I have to say. Looking back of course, what a rotten system.
Yes.

Do you think arguing that the Fed could have conducted the counterfactual experiment of keeping the nominal money supply constant is an ahistorical approach to explaining the Depression?
As we were saying, if you start to move the price level around and don't have a story for what you're doing to the relative price of gold, you're implicitly supposing that gold is just a residual that just does whatever it needs to do to accommodate your theory. I frankly don't understand that way of thinking about things. I don't think you can talk about manipulating various nominal magnitudes without doing something to gold at the same time.

But then changing the money supply would be one way to change the relative price of gold and should the Fed have been thinking in those terms?
No, I was agreeing with Temin, that you can't do that. In 1931 your best policy option is to abandon gold. If you're going to stick with gold you have to do what the Fed did, which is to say "we're tough and we're going to do it."

That's what Temin has claimed. The kind of magnitude it would have taken to change the money supply in order to get to the desired results was just beyond contemplation at that time.
You mean with the collapse of the M1 multiplier the magnitude of the base expansion.

Correct. So, why do we talk about things that could never have been in the first place? I suppose that's correct, but yet at the same time Sweden was on a price level stabilization program. There was the Goldsborough bill in May of 1932 that ordered immediately raising the price level back to pre-

Depression levels. There were over 50 bills in Congress ordering the Fed to increase the money supply, and also what was said by the New York Federal Reserve. So it's not as if people were not talking about it and it's not as if the man from Mars came down and started talking about it. But yet they picked their side. We keep coming back to that.
Yes.

If you'll permit me to read the following from your 1988 paper: "[t]he most important element in the success of any national gold standard is the public's confidence that the government's fiscal soundness and political imperatives will enable it to pursue indefinitely a monetary policy consistent with long-term price stability and continuous convertibility. By this criterion, returning to the international gold standard during the mid-1920s could not have come at a worse time or for poorer reasons. Clearly, the gold standard was reinstated precisely because the fiscal and political chaos since 1914 had made it impossible for many governments to reform their monetary policies in the absence of a gold standard." You also have a paragraph that says "[i]t sometimes is asserted that a gold standard introduces 'discipline' into the conduct of monetary and fiscal policy when none existed before. Indeed this was the primary reason that the world returned to an international gold standard during the 1920s. I cannot think of a more naive and more dangerous notion. A government lacking discipline in monetary and fiscal policy in the absence of a gold standard likely also lacks the discipline and credibility necessary for successfully adhering to a gold standard. Substantial uncertainty about the future inevitably will result as speculators anticipate changes in the terms of gold convertibility. This institutionalizes a system susceptible to large and sudden inflows or outflows of capital and to destabilizing monetary policy if authorities must resort to great extremes to reestablish credibility." So I would just like to give you your "props," as they say nowadays in today's language. Those are two of the most powerful paragraphs I think I've read anywhere in the literature on the Great Depression and you're to be congratulated for just how simply and effectively I think you communicate the point.
Thank you very much. The gold standard does not operate by itself and just because you say you're going to do something, markets have a healthy degree of skepticism about that. They are looking at what your real incentives are, not what you say you're going to do or even what your law says you're going to do now because laws can change and what you do can change. If you've got a fundamentally non-credible commitment to fiscal stability, then putting some kind of window dressing out there isn't going to fool the market. It's going to create more uncertainty by the market as to when you're going to give up the game and that uncertainty is itself a very destabilizing force. So I think that's what definitely happened in the 1920s.

And that's what made that whole system so volatile.
It made the system so volatile and it caused countries to try to hoard gold so that they could withstand this kind of speculation. The whole premise that you can kind of create credibility by fiat is flawed. You create credibility by being credible. And if you can be credible, if you have your fiscal house in order and your monetary house in order and everybody knows it, you don't need gold then to persuade them. You're doing what you need to do and you'll have the stability for that.

You have a demonstrated record.
Yes. A long demonstrated record or at least the kind of reform where you have solved the problems that got you into the mess in the first place. To me that's much more important from the point of view of policy than having some kind of rule that we think is going to force us to have discipline or persuade the markets we're really serious this time.

Every time I reread your Contemporary Policy Issues *paper I learn more. There is stuff here that no one has talked about since your 1988 paper in just the same way. These things are not talked about enough so let us please just mention and discuss them. You talk about the behavior of the Treasury bill rate and how it can be solely attributed to the increased probability of devaluation in 1931. You talk about the change in the spread between Treasury bills and foreign private discount rates during 1931 and how this reflects the impact of the gold standard and the uncertainty of remaining on it. Again that doesn't show up very much in the literature at all. Also, "[t]he events of the fall of 1931 clearly were far more serious in their consequences for domestic credit than were the domestic banking panics preceding them." Note the behavior of the Treasury bill rate to corroborate this idea. Only minor perturbations from the downward trend were evident from the first two banking crises but the T-bill rate climbed 200 basis points during the last half of 1931. Moreover, the same can be said for the behavior of M1, output and prices. They nosedived more after September 1931 than they did after the banking panics by a good margin. Kindleberger (1986) has said that Friedman and Schwartz didn't go far enough after 1931 in saying that the British action didn't have any impact on US Federal Reserve policy and you would agree with that, would you not?*
The British action, I think, precipitated the run on the dollar and then that precipitated the hikes in interest rates in late 1931 that we were just talking about.

The British leaving gold and the run on the dollar also had consequences for those behaviors of the money supply, output and prices that you point out. That's one of the reasons why they took such a large nosedive.

Sure. It's a classic contraction and it's a classic response to a run on your currency. You raise the interest rate sufficiently high to persuade those people to hold dollars after all, despite their jitteriness about it. In doing that, however, you make the cost of borrowing that much higher for an economy where nobody could afford it to begin with, investment was in the tank anyway. It's a terrible thing to have to do from the point of view of what the economy is going through at that time. It's the only tool you have though to restore that demand for dollars.

You also talk about how the decision not to go off gold in 1931 created an environment for unanticipated deflation and greater price uncertainty. Other than the obvious work that you did there on commodity prices that led to your 1992 American Economic Review *paper, this uncertainty of regime change is probably one of the first references I've seen to "unanticipated deflation." Because if they thought they might go off and then they didn't, we're talking about well, "when are they?" or "are they going to?" and that creates price uncertainty there.*

Surely it was and as you were just saying nobody knew for sure what was going to happen and that was one of the fundamental problems with the gold standard. You don't know whether they're going to go off and that just adds to all the other problems.

Yes, and credibility is out the window once you start asking that question.

Right.

I assert in my first book that it took your 1987 JME *piece for the profession at large to acknowledge tight money. Do you think that's too harsh?*

Well, as we were saying, I think Temin (1976a) did divert the discussion a little bit away from what happened before the downturn. So perhaps I did play a role in calling people's attention to that question again, which I think is a very important and a very interesting one. It had been a little bit obscured in the debate over some of these other issues of what was happening in 1930 and 1931.

It seems to me that even as late as 1981, in Brunner's book The Great Depression Revisited, *some people were still basically denying that money had much of a role at all. The way I view it is that your 1987 piece was trying to put that to rest.*

It wasn't my intention when I started to write that to put anything to rest. It was my intention to try to sort out the facts in a way that I could make sense of them. I guess I ended up persuading myself that there were some very important developments in 1928 and 1929 that were really where the story got started. My paper just put together the case as I saw it.

You lay out the case for tight money where you say it's not the fall of the real money supply that indicates tightness but rather a slowing in the rate of growth that's the appropriate measure, whereas, some of the profession seem confused on this point, even today I might add.

Again I think that's one diversion that Temin's (1976a) book may have led some people down. In every hyperinflation in history we see the real money supply fall as there is a flight from money. The converse happens, not quite as dramatically, in a deflation. The real money supply is going to go up and it's only when you're ignoring rates of growth of the price level that you're lulled into this notion that, "Well, I can just look at the levels of the real money supply to decide whether money is tight or not." It's just not the right way to think about things.

What are your views regarding dynamic stochastic general equilibrium (DSGE) models applied to this particular literature and what we have learned? They seem to do great in helping us understand the recovery.

That's right and I think people have worried about that for some time, that there was a whole lot of the New Deal legislation which did not sound like a prescription for making the economy run better, encouraging labor unions and encouraging monopolistic restrictions on output. That can't be good for the economy and it seems pretty reasonable to me to suggest that it is part of the answer to that third question of why was the recovery so slow. I agree with you. I think that is interesting research and they are the kind of models that are well suited for thinking about that. But, the other basic ingredient of these dynamic stochastic general equilibrium models is the notion that productivity shocks are a big, driving force behind economic fluctuations. Well, if you think about it, suppose you ran a retail store and you've got the same store this month as last month. You've got the same number of people working this month as last month, but fewer customers came in your door this month, so your sales fall. Now, if you think of that in a production function sense, your inputs are the same, your output has gone down and you are going to measure that as a productivity shock. The way this literature has traditionally done things, it's a negative Solow residual. Whereas, in terms of the economics, it's not a supply shock, it's not a productivity shock, it's purely a demand shock and it's being called a productivity shock because this is the framework we're using to think about things. We don't really have a model that's consistent with fundamental market failure. The model insists that the market works and therefore we just can't have as productive a store in this environment. Now, Christiano, Motto and Rostagno (2003) have a little bit more sophisticated measure of productivity shocks than I'm discussing because they do try to take into account some capacity utilization, which is a step in the right direction. But the overriding point is still there. These things that are thought of as productivity shocks are, in my view, to a large degree demand shocks. And furthermore nobody has ever explained to my satisfaction what these negative productivity shocks are. I understand positive productivity advances. I understand very clearly that the rate of new technological discovery and implementation might be random and we might have faster growth one year than another because of that. That makes perfectly good sense to me. What I don't understand is why we are less productive this year than we were last year. What exactly is it about technology that is producing that? I don't think that the DSGE modelers have ever answered that question in a very satisfactory way. Their answer in part seems to be "well look, we've calculated this Solow residual and that thing is negative so there must have been one." But to that my answer is, well you've measured this thing alright, but to me it's a demand shock that you've measured. On one hand I applaud the effort because making sense of the Depression, as I was saying, is sort of the number one task of macro economists and that's good if we have the courage to take the facts seriously and try to fit our model to them. But, I really am troubled by that whole literature in terms of postulating the existence of this thing, a negative productivity shock, without ever explaining to me just what it means.

Just stepping back one step here, maybe this should be viewed as these models are just beginning now and they're ultimately going to become more and more elaborate as time and research effort go on so that even though the framework may seem somewhat clunky right now, it will get better over time and we can learn more?

Well they are getting more elaborate. I mentioned capacity utilization and there are all these things in the efforts we've been discussing that are more complicated than the first efforts along these lines. My reaction to Kydland and Prescott's (1982) original paper was "Oh, that's great, that's a neat idea. Now the second paper in this literature ought to tell us what these productivity shocks are." Well, that was 23 years ago right? I'm still waiting for that second paper (*laughter*). It seems it is almost a social phenomenon. They have all agreed that they don't have to answer that question for us. They don't have to tell us "here is what that productivity shock is." I guess it's because they don't know the answer and so they'll tell us something they do know. But I don't see that that has been the research imperative for this approach even though it's now coming to be kind of dominant in the profession. I do not see a research imperative by the practitioners of that approach to identify "here's what the productivity shocks are, here's how we can corroborate them independently, and here's how I think they are operating." From Kydland and Prescott (1982) on it has always been this black box and that to me is an unsatisfactory scientific approach.

I'm probably mistaken, but I can not find where Bernanke (1983a) or Fisher (1933) make explicit mention of the transmission mechanism requiring a distinction between anticipated and unanticipated deflation. I believe you are one of the first, if not the first one, to connect these dots in your 1987 JME *paper. How did you come about doing this? Do you agree with me that you're the first one to use that?*

I didn't notice particularly that I was and I didn't think that was going to be my big insight, although when you ask that I can't point to you and say, OK here's who else was talking about that specific issue. Again, as I told you, I was just kind of taking the basic facts and trying to put them together and it seemed pretty obvious to me that this was one of the key questions that was sort of implicit in what was going on and perhaps my pointing that out was relevant for some of that discussion that followed.

That is the first time that I could find it. Calomiris (1993) has said that "[a]nticipated deflation still could have had a depressive effect on the economy, as argued by Temin (1989); but it would not have produced financial distress, since agents anticipating deflation would reduce interest costs to offset the capital loss from debt deflation." I assume this means that people would shift out of different maturities and refinance at lower interest rates as deflation happened. Does this not depend on the duration and mean reversion characteristics of the price level and thus is not quite so cut and dried as Calomiris suggests?

Well, it's not cut and dried because for one thing you've got a floor on the nominal interest rate of money which is zero. Furthermore, if money is giving a real yield of some significant positive amount, all other interest rates have to be adjusted upward from that. So no, I don't agree with that, that just because deflation is perfectly anticipated it is going to have no consequences. I don't agree with that statement.

Cecchetti (1998) has pointed out that the postal savings rate had a minimum floor of 2 percent so that's the binding floor that should properly be viewed for the United States. So, if it goes from 0 percent to 2 percent that makes it even more stark.

Yes it does. There are stories you can tell of why it might have had big effects if it was anticipated. But I have trouble interpreting the evidence as saying that it was anticipated. To me the evidence points to deflation being largely unanticipated.

Even at the short-run horizons as Cecchetti (1992) argued?

Yes. I think people were not anticipating events even as they were unfolding. That's my view.

In your 1992 AER *paper you conclude "[t]hat decreases in particular relative prices, rather than in overall consumer prices, are key to understanding this year," that is 1930. Could you please elaborate on that point? Is this related to Kindleberger's (1986) commodity price story?*

Well first, it's just the observation that there were huge drops in commodity prices relative to the overall price level. The overall price level did not decline that much in 1930, but you find a number of specific agricultural products where there is a huge effect. We often talk of debt deflation in an aggregate macro sense, where we are sure it's the aggregate price level that goes in there that we are talking about. But if you're a farmer and your revenue is coming in from selling your wheat and your wheat revenue in nominal terms has just completely plummeted, it's the wheat price rather than the overall price level that matters for your ability to fulfill your debts. If you can't and the agricultural banks fail, then you have the whole story. So my point was just that there were big movements in relative prices at this time. I'm persuaded that they were unanticipated, they were big enough to have very profound implications for these particular markets. Sometimes perhaps we are lulled in macroeconomics into just thinking of the representative firm or the representative household and we are missing these kinds of points which may have been quite important at the time.

Especially for the beginning.
Right.

Cecchetti (1998) has said that he thinks that the whole notion of a liquidity trap is a nominal/real confusion.
Well, I do feel that the talk of a liquidity trap is something I have never had too much sympathy for. For example, in Japan it has come up again with all kinds of papers arguing that is what is going on there. One of the reasons I have such a problem with it is I don't see why the central bank has to buy only the shortest term government security. There are all kinds of other assets out there, there are all kinds of other open market operations that would increase the monetary base. And you can't tell me the prices of all of those assets are totally unresponsive to what you do with the money supply. That's crazy, that Japan could have bought up the stock exchanges of all the world and nothing would have happened to the value of the yen.

That's what Ben Bernanke said to me one time, "if the Bank of Japan could increase the money supply and not cause inflation they could buy up all the assets of the world."
Yes, exactly (*laughter*). So I have never been a fan of the whole liquidity trap idea. It's something that got into textbooks early, people thought it was sort of a cute idea, but I have never believed that it was an important part of the picture in the US in the 1930s or Japan in the 1990s or any episode that I am aware of.

It's like Bill Murray in the movie Groundhog Day – *he kept coming back in the same dream – oh no the liquidity trap is back again.*
Yes, yes.

Just to finish up on the literature, even the work that Dan Nelson (1991) did, for example, argued that people were perhaps anticipating deflation to some extent. So, you still don't see that any of it was anticipated so that high ex ante real interest rates played a part in the story?
Well in some ways I would like to because, as we were saying, I think you could get some pretty concrete explanations going for how that might have happened. But I just found that evidence unpersuasive. You can read the newspapers all you like and pretend you know what investors were thinking. I can't read today's *Wall Street Journal* though and tell you what investors think right now from that. Economists always want to look at markets, where are people actually putting their money, rather than read the opinions of the pundits. And, if you look at futures markets, boy, they sure were not anticipating any of what happened to wheat or corn or any of that.

What ended the Great Depression?
Well, getting off the gold standard got us out of that second phase and into the third phase. Getting out of that finally, I would say it was the fiscal and monetary stimulus of World War II that got rid of the demon altogether.

What are the important questions remaining that need to be answered about the Great Depression in general?
I think we still have not come to grips with exactly what is the nature of the transaction frictions or coordination frictions that are at the core of what can go so spectacularly wrong. We are thinking in our conventional models that it is something about how prices do not adjust, but that has always struck me as simplistic. When you look at the Depression and prices were falling as dramatically as they were, something else is going on.

I have felt that way too about the sticky wage explanation. It's not satisfactory to me. If only wages had fallen 70 percent instead of 50 percent we would have gone back to a Walrasian equilibrium. It doesn't seem right to me.
Yes, I don't think it is. I think the alternative of what really is the nature of the coordination problem, the nature of the friction problem, we still frankly do not understand.

Could it happen again?
In my opinion, in the United States, no. Because the Fed certainly has the power to prevent this. The intellectual and academic tradition in the Fed is such that I can't conceive of them ever again allowing this magnitude of deflation,

this magnitude of a drop in the monetary aggregates, and while all that is going on the economy crashes. It is inconceivable in my lifetime that would happen in the US. Now, I look at Japan and I am just baffled at why the Japanese have put up with this inept monetary policy there for so many years. They have done the same kind of things. They deflated the heck out of an economy that was already down and bleeding. Why did they do that? They apparently perceive some kind of institutional constraint preventing them from the kind of monetary expansion that they need. I don't understand enough about Japanese culture and Japanese intuitions to understand why those constraints are as powerful as they are. But I can say from my perception of the US that I can't conceive of that kind of problem. And I have to tell you that there was some discussion in the popular press a few years back, not so much now, that deflation may be coming back. I never put a bit of credibility in that. One thing the Federal Reserve can do for sure is it can prevent deflation. You can argue about the limits of monetary policy in all kinds of other ways and you'd be right. But the one thing the Fed can do for sure is prevent big deflations. It's not hard and the historical experience suggests that deflation can be a very unpleasant thing. I think it is inconceivable that we would go through that same thing again.

Do you think the Fed should be the arbiter of security prices? Do you think they should have a role in trying to stop bubbles from happening if they think one is happening?
Not at all, because the whole story of a bubble is that nobody can figure out what is going on. People are betting their money that it's not a bubble and how does the Fed have the added wisdom to be able to perceive this? I think they called things pretty wrong in 1929. It is a degree of understanding that human beings and the government wouldn't have and nobody can have, it's the ability to say "here is what the price of stocks ought to be." If you have an opinion, go ahead and put your money there and more power to you if you get rich from it. But to say that the government is going to decide that for all of us is hubris that is potentially dangerous.

OK, a couple of off-the-cuff questions now. What is the long-run equilibrium price of oil?
You know that is a tough question. What's happened in the last year is there has been this big surge in global demand, particularly coming from China. People are wondering can global production keep up with that? If you look far enough into the future, the answer has to be no. The Chinese are increasing their use 6 percent a year, you can not project that rate, it just does not work out. So, sooner or later, the demand for oil has to stop growing. Sooner or later oil production has to peak and what that means is the price has to go up. Now, it is possible to me that we are seeing part of that process now. I think there is

a change in the world that people are not tuned into enough. It's a world market, it's not the US any more. It is what's going on in Asia that is where the future of the world really is. They have been buying a lot of it and that's been driving up the price. Another thing I think is that it used to be that oil was priced in dollars and I am not sure that is true anymore. The dollar has depreciated very significantly over the last year and if you look at the price of oil in euros, it's not that big a deal. Again, I think because the US is a less important player in the total world consumption now than it used to be, our whole idea that we always want to think of oil as being priced in dollars might be mistaken. I'm sure what we are seeing in part is just a reflection of the depreciation of the dollar. So those are some issues relevant to answering your question, but whether the answer is $45 dollars a barrel or what, I don't know.

I am not a conspiracy theorist or anything of the kind and I never have been. But can we see the next couple of decades developing into a competition between the US and the Chinese securing oil supplies?
Well, I think we are natural competitors in a lot of ways. I worry more about the geopolitical kinds of issues. So far the Chinese are not trying to flex their muscles and influence other places, but they could. So if you were just looking at it from a positive kind of theory, you might say this is a potential source of friction that is going to develop. Now, on the other hand I think China's growth has come because they have de facto abandoned part of the whole communist ideology and I think the people there are very much persuaded of the benefits of economic freedom. In that sense, I think the allies of the US have always been the countries that want freedom. That is where we stand and our real enemies are the countries that are opposed to that. I see China's future as one of freedom because I think it's economic freedom that is fueling their economic success, and everyone there has to want that. I would say that is a positive development with room for potential. So I think it is something we want to be very careful with in terms of our policy with China. We ought to be very aware of these issues, but I don't think inevitably it has to go one way or another. As for specifically competing over oil, since we are both oil consumers our interests often coincide. We both want to see the Middle East stable. Sometimes our geopolitical interests are going to be different from theirs, as we saw in 1973, we had some differences with some of the oil consuming countries in terms of our other foreign policy goals. So maybe that's the kind of friction you could see developing. I think it is something to be aware of, but it's not something that I am in dread of.

My complaint is that when it comes to things like North Korea, the Chinese a lot of the time act like they don't have a dog in this fight. That troubles me a great deal. Well, Wal-Mart alone takes 1 percent of Chinese GDP.
Right.

If something happens in North Korea, I don't know what they think is going to happen to our trade with China. We take 40 percent of their exports, they have a dog in this fight and I wish they would start acting a little more like it.
Well you're right, but I guess I see a basis for optimism there though. These things take time. You know, it is kind of a crazy situation, but I don't think it has to end badly.

There is recent talk in journalistic circles about a Manhattan project for fuel efficiency. Thomas Friedman has talked about this, like him or not, and Fareed Zakaria in Newsweek *has recently mentioned it. Do you pay any attention to that at all?*
Well, you know there is a tremendous incentive for private markets to do this, there are huge profit opportunities. I think Toyota and Honda are going to be reaping them, for example, with these hybrid engines. I don't think that is a fad or just a trendy thing. I think that is definitely going to become very important, and the reason it is going to become very important is basic economic pressure. I have more confidence in Toyota's and Honda's ability to develop that than I do in the Department of Energy or somebody else if you put them in charge of it. You might argue there are some kind of coordination or networking issues with the way we use internal combustion engines and there is some truth to that. But I would have skepticism about a Manhattan project kind of label for the problem we have. If the price of oil does keep going up you are going to see all kinds of technologies develop.

I always go wobbly when the government starts picking winners and losers.
Yes.

That's it. Thanks so much, Professor.

Robert Lucas

Robert Lucas won the 1995 Nobel Prize in Economics, in the words of the Royal Swedish Academy of Sciences, "for having developed and applied the hypothesis of rational expectations, and thereby having transformed macroeconomic analysis and deepened our understanding of economic policy." I thought it vital to the theme of this book to ask for Professor Lucas' assessment of the economic literature on the Great Depression for three reasons. One, his stature in macroeconomics is obvious. Asking him about the issues surrounding the greatest macroeconomic event in history could not possibly be more appropriate and fitting. Two, he published a paper with Leonard Rapping on the Great Depression and has done some creative thinking on the interwar era. And three, he continues to have a great deal of influence on Lee Ohanian, Harold Cole and others who are currently pursuing a research agenda focused on topics related to the Great Depression. I spoke with Robert Lucas in his office at the University of Chicago on October 13, 2005.

In your interview with Arjo Klamer (1984) you said you see the Friedman and Schwartz story together with your and Rapping's (1972) story as very good explanations for 1929–33. For after 1933 you said "[I] really don't know. There are many aspects of what happened after that I can't figure at all. But I do not think that unemployment is the center of the story." Could you please expand on what you meant by unemployment not being the center of the story.
I don't know what I meant back then. But a lot of economists, and I would include myself, think it is more interesting to look at an employment rate, take the total number of adults of working age population and look at the fraction of those people that are working. The distinction of what the people who are not working are doing with their time, whether they are sitting around at home, whether they are taking care of their kids, whether they are looking for a job, is less important than how many people are working and what those people are producing. So I don't think we need to look at unemployment as "the" defining characteristic of a depression. I think of it as a fall-off in production. Those things are so closely related, obviously periods of high unemployment are periods where production is falling well short of where it ought to be.

Any thoughts on why it took so long for the Friedman and Schwartz story to catch on and gain credibility?

(*Lucas laughs*) I'm the wrong person to ask. I was a student at the University of Chicago in the 1960s and a student of Friedman. So I bought the story hook, line and sinker from day one. I think the rest of the profession was much more focused on what you do to get out of the Depression as opposed to what got us into the Depression in the first place. So the Keynesian idea was that countries are going to bounce in and out of recessions for God knows what reasons, we do not really care what the reasons are. What we need is some way to get ourselves out when it happens.

How about not going there in the first place, that's important too, isn't it?
Well, from the Keynesian point of view that was not so central. But it kind of begs the question, why on earth did a society which had been using its resources pretty fully for a while just start leaving resources of all kinds idle and plunge into a depression?

When there were people who want to consume more food, clothing and housing and people who want to make things and you can not get them together.
Right. I think that is a central question and I think that Freidman and Schwartz faced up to that from the beginning. That's why I think their book has lasted so well. It focused on the right questions and took a serious crack at answering them.

In your paper with Rapping you mention the employment decisions of the household involve, among other things, deciding whether a shock to employment is permanent or temporary and the choices households will make depend on this perception. Would you not say then the implications of the model are that the inability to discern the Depression, at least in the beginning, as a temporary or permanent shock is responsible for much of the behavior of employment perhaps from 1929 to 1931?
That's the way I looked at it. People were out of work in 1930 looking for a new job, expecting the kind of wages that they were earning back in 1928–29 and it took them a long time to realize that those jobs weren't here any more. Prices and wages had fallen and people had to revise their hopes and aspirations for pay downward. As the thing goes on and on more and more people get wise and people take jobs in 1932 that they wouldn't have even looked at in 1930.

Would you kindly elaborate on the features of the model and why you feel it fits this period so well.
Well, Friedman and Schwartz are concerned with the nature of the shock that kicks us into the Depression. They focus on declines in the money stock, which are clearly linked to declines in spending, and what they show is that the 1929 Crash did not really initiate anything. So we can't think of the whole

Depression as unfolding from October 1929. The 1929–33 period involved a succession of contractions to the money supply, one after the other, each one of them huge. It's like having three hurricane Katrinas hit New Orleans a month apart. Just when you think you are digging out of the first one, "whamo," and then the same way the third time around. Friedman and Schwartz document that quite clearly in their book. So Rapping and I tried to construct a theory about how temporary shocks to wages and prices could reduce employment or increase unemployment. Our theory didn't really tell you why that unemployment should last very long. So we need new shocks to keep people off balance, and Friedman and Schwartz described those shocks. One, two, three, all the way down to 1934. You don't need a theory that has a lot of persistence in the responses to account for those movements in employment and output. OK, by 1934 those shocks are over, and there is not another serious monetary shock for three to five years, something like that. So according to Rapping's and my model the system should have snapped back to something like full employment by, say, 1936. But it wasn't anywhere close to full employment by that date. So when I was talking to Klamer, I had in mind that distinction. We have a half-way decent story to get us down from 1929 to the 1933 trough. From there on it's hard going.

Ah, but not lately, because I'm going to follow this up.
OK.

Since that interview with Klamer in 1982 there has been a lot of stuff written about the economics of the Great Depression. I'm sure you're impressed by the work of Cole and Ohanian, especially their 2004 JPE piece, in trying to unravel the mystery that is post-1933.
Right.

I know you and Lee Ohanian have discussed this extensively. You have said before, after 1933 "I can't figure at all." So let me ask you, can you not now begin to "figure" what went on post-1933?
Well Friedman and Schwartz talk about the NRA, the National Recovery Administration, as a harmful thing. They do not have any ability to quantify its effects. Rapping and I echoed that but we made no progress in quantifying it. So what Lee Ohanian and Hal Cole have done is to start to take a much harder look at the quantitative nature of those New Deal actions, not just the NRA, in a model that lets them start to quantify the effects of those policies on the real economy. And, you know, they're getting big effects. So they're basically saying "Let's not look to monetary policy for any help in explaining what went on from 1933 after. Whether you give it a lot of credit or not for the 1929–33 period, let's look at fiscal policy, regulation, the whole New Deal package for the explanation of why the recovery was so damn slow."

The cartelization of industries, price fixing and on and on.
Yes, price fixing, the support of industrial unionization and the wage fixing that went along with that, and just the general chilling of the investment climate. Someone undertaking an investment project in the middle 1930s had really no idea what kind of tax environment or regulatory environment he was going to be living in over the life of the plant he was trying to build. That is not the way we encourage investments.

One of the things that floored me about that paper is they reported that Harold Ickes "received identical bids from steel firms on 257 different occasions between June 1935 and May 1936."
Well that was encouraged by the New Deal: producers were asked to get together to pull the economy up and all they did was to pull themselves up (*laughter*).

Certainly I think monetary and financial theories play a major part in the explanation of the Depression. You said to Klamer that units are not supposed to matter, but yet we have the Great Depression. So units do matter and they matter a great deal, otherwise Friedman and Schwartz never would have had any material for the book and the Depression would not have happened. Anticipated deflation caused high ex ante real rates, deflation caused debt deflation, deflation caused high tariff rates, deflation and asymmetry in the gold standard caused the US and France to drain the world of gold and deflation caused much of the rise in real wages. So deflation is the key to understanding the Great Depression, without deflation these things do not happen. And deflation happened because of the behavior of the money stock. Thus the Depression can correctly be viewed as a monetary phenomenon. Do you not agree with that?
It's pretty close. The debt deflation mechanism is not one of my favorites. I think the tariff policies in the late 1920s, although they were terrible policies, I don't think they played much of a role in causing the Depression. The connections you are drawing between money and deflation, deflation and economic activity I think are right on. Cole and Ohanian wouldn't agree with you, but I would.

In a recent paper they do say money accounts for 33 percent of the Depression, but we will talk about that shortly.
OK.

Additionally, given the ruinous inflation of the 1970s, is not then price instability, either up or down, one of the greatest sources of economic instability in the last century and would you say that maintaining price stability is one of the key lessons for central bankers to learn from the Great Depression and the Great Inflation?

Yes (*Lucas says emphatically*). Price stability is important for its own sake if people make plans on the basis of the prices they think are going to prevail when they retire or when they harvest their returns from an investment project. If people are totally in the dark about those matters, it just raises hell with their decisions. The biggest change that I think has gone on since the 1960s and 1970s is this. No one ever said that inflation was a good thing to do, that we should ignore it. But the idea was that there was this tradeoff and you had to focus on inflation *or* focus on full employment and high output, you had this choice to make. So when their policies led to inflation, they would say, "Well that's too bad, but it's just a by-product of all this prosperity we are getting." I think that choice is nonsense. We now understand that there is no tradeoff and periods of price stability are not periods of high unemployment or low growth. There is no systematic connection between those two variables. So when it comes down to the central bank, central bankers can and should be and mostly are focusing exclusively on the control of inflation. That is their job. That is their only job. Once you understand what your mission is, you can do it a lot better than when you don't have any idea (*laughter*).

I like it. Is there any embellishing of your story on the Depression that you would like to do? Is there anything other than Friedman and Schwartz and Lucas and Rapping that you find compelling in explaining the Depression?
Well, you have already talked about Cole and Ohanian. I think they are going in exactly the right direction and have made real strides.

If I could just read one more quote here to try to put that in perspective, you said in your book Studies in Business-Cycle Theory *that "[i]t is, at least for me, the working out of these highly abstract but explicit models that is the* source *of ideas for constructing new econometric models, criticizing old ones, or reading the classics from a fresh viewpoint" (emphasis in the original). So Cole and Ohanian with these abstract models, if nothing else, are giving us a fresh viewpoint on an old problem.*
Yes, I agree completely.

"The only aggregative economic policy implications we see for events like the Great Depression are the standard ones: if possible avoid aggregate-demand shifts which cause them; failing this, pursue corrective demand policies to make them as brief as possible." That is what you and Rapping said in your comment to Rees (1970). Any further enlightenment to this very straightforward prescription?
That's a little more Keynesian than I would be now. We thought Rees was way out of line, so we tried to leave him out in left field.

Friedman said if he had to rewrite the chapter on the Great Contraction, he would give more weight to the actions of France. Do you want to discuss what role you give to the gold standard in explaining 1929–33 and the worldwide nature of the Depression?

So many other people on your list have thought more about this than I have. I remember during the Kennedy years, when we were still on the gold standard although it was of no importance to us, the Kennedy administration thought it was important. If you ask Alan Greenspan "Why are you so worried about inflation?" he'd say something sensible about what inflation would do to the domestic economy and to people's ability to plan for the future and so on. Well, what Kennedy would say is if we have too much inflation we are going to depreciate the dollar relative to gold. So the gold standard was used as kind of a litmus test for seeing how you were doing in your anti-inflation policies. If people were trying to transfer your currency into gold, that was a sign you were too inflationary. At best it's a symptom. It didn't make a damn bit of difference to the US economy in the 1960s whether you were on or off gold. That shouldn't have been the constraint on Kennedy. But on the other hand, if you took that constraint away, and that was the only constraint we had, then we could sail off into an inflation. It's a symbolic thing but sometimes symbols are important.

You said in Klamer (1984), "In the 1929 to 1932 period they went back to World War I and looked at how the economy was run then. They didn't have a good inventory of ideas. It was too quick. They couldn't cook up fundamental new ways of dealing with things on such short notice, so they grabbed something that was handy. And that's what societies always do in difficult situations." Peter Temin has said that it was trying to re-establish the world as it was before World War I and the intransigent adherence to the gold standard that drove the world economy into the ground. The resumption of the gold standard and the status quo ante and the attempt to preserve it is what gave us the Depression. After the War, the world had changed and trying to put the pieces back together, particularly with the gold standard and its mentalité, led the world economy down the wrong path. Sounds like maybe you and he are saying the same thing here.

No, no (*Lucas says emphatically*). We are not saying the same thing at all. Here's what I am saying. Hugh Johnson, who ran the NRA, his background was in the corporatist management that Woodrow Wilson adopted. I'm not talking about the pre-World War I world, but the way in which the US government ran World War I. What did we do? We got union leaders, corporations, all the big shots in the economy together and they agreed on what we wanted to produce and how we wanted to produce it. Union leaders and businesses that didn't go along were thrown in jail or something like that. It was kind of a centralized "let's get together and run the economy from Washington D.C." thing. Well, we won the War and a lot of people came away with warm memories of that period. Not Eugene Debs who spent the War in jail, but Bernard Baruch who made his name as a manager during those days.

So when Roosevelt was elected he called on Baruch and asked "what do we do?" Baruch, who knew no economics and was proud of that fact, thought back to World War I and said "let's get the team back together, the big shots and the corporations together and let's plan the economy from Washington. We'll just plan our way out of the Depression like we planned our way out of the War." That was the model that Hugh Johnson had in mind for the NRA. It's not exactly a proletarian or fascist model, but it's a central planning take on how you get things done in the economy. And Herbert Hoover too, by some accounts, had that view on how to operate during the Depression. It led to a lot of incredibly stupid policies. So I wasn't thinking of nostalgia for the pre-World War I days. That would have been a good thing to have in my opinion (*Lucas chuckles*). But a wartime economy is not a model for how you run a society.

But as far as re-establishing the gold standard is concerned, people thought that before the War the gold standard made the economy very stable. They tried to reinstitute the gold standard and the world had changed. The gold standard was dysfunctional for the world after the War. They grabbed for dysfunctional things and tried to reapply them to a world that had changed after World War I.
The British had a hell of a time recovering from World War I. People attribute that to the fact that they stubbornly tried to restore the value of the pound to its pre-war parity with gold and it kept the economy down through the 1920s. That was not the problem in the US. We had a great decade in the 1920s. We grew like hell and it was just a great time for a capitalist democracy. Well, until 1929.

You have also said "Nominal wages and prices came down by half between 1929 and 1933. Why would anyone look at a period like that and say that the difficult problem would be to explain rigid wages? I don't understand it. But I can see how someone trying to explain 1934 to 1939 could be puzzled about rigid wages. I have been puzzled by that too." I have felt the way you felt for some time. Do you still feel that way?
Yes.

Moreover, have not Cole and Ohanian (2004a) helped to solve that puzzle from 1934 to 1939?
Yes, I think they have. There was a jump in nominal wages by something like 10 percent in 1934, right in the middle of 24 percent unemployment. I think that was upward pressure from New Deal policies. That's the line that Cole and Ohanian are spelling out and they are working that out.

Do you think the heavy lifting of explaining the Great Depression has been done?

No, as I say, I think there are trouble spots. I think Cole and Ohanian are the only game in town for the latter part of the Depression, and they are a *serious* game (*Lucas emphasizes the word* serious). But there are some problems with the theory. Any theory of price fixing is such that if you try and raise prices artificially in one sector, spending is going to shift off into the other sector and people are going to shift their spending from the high-price sector to the low-price sector. If too much of that happens then you are not going to decrease output. You are just going to change the composition of output. So getting a depression by the fixing of prices one way or the other has to deal with that issue somehow and I don't think Cole and Ohanian have it figured out yet.

Lee Ohanian indicated to me that Prescott said to him the Depression "is a fascinating episode, it is a pathological episode and it defies explanation by standard economics. We need new theories to understand the Great Depression." I'm sure you feel this way, do you not?
Yes.

So the route they are going down is the route we need to go?
Well, there are lots of routes for new theories but they are right to keep looking at it. In economics we like to think we know everything. So it takes a real effort of will to admit that you don't know what the hell is going on in some areas. So Cole and Ohanian had the guts to just look at this period and say "None of these theories I can take off the shelf makes any damn sense here. Let's start over" (*laughter*).

If we thought we had the Depression explained before, Cole and Ohanian and others present a whole new set of questions and analysis using real business cycle models. Ohanian has indicated the whole line of research basically addresses the simple question "what is preventing people from working and producing more? What is stopping people from making trades that would make people better off?" Cole and Ohanian (2000) attempt to undo much of what we thought we knew of monetary and financial theories of the Depression. Moreover, Cole and Ohanian's 2004 working paper "Deflation and the international Great Depression: a productivity puzzle" presents results that attribute two-thirds of the Depression to productivity shocks and one-third to monetary shocks and they do so in an international investigation. They set up an econometric horse race and money does not dominate like one would suspect if extant theories were truly dominant. So let me ask you broadly, and you can take this anywhere you want to go with it and your answer can take any shape you wish to give it, what are we learning?
I'm not a fan of that 2004 working paper. Econometrically I think there are better ways to use that cross-sectional data than what they did. But it is awkward. If you look at Canada and the US during the Depression period, if you take Friedman and Schwartz and the monetary collapse as explaining our

downturn, the Canadians had a similar downturn during the same period but they didn't have a monetary collapse.

Or a banking collapse.
Right. So they had a spending collapse, maybe you do not want to get too fancy about where the spending collapse came from. You know we had our spending collapse because the money supply contracted. And I suppose they got theirs because Americans stopped buying Canadian goods. Iowa had a Depression too but I don't know if the money supply in Iowa fell during that period. But I guess I'd have to have better reasons than that for giving up on the monetary explanation. The timing and the magnitudes are just right, totally convincing, if you go back and read the Friedman and Schwartz chapter on the Great Depression. But how did it work? We should be able to write down an economic model that kind of explains the workings. How did it happen that bank failures and monetary declines translated into huge movements in employment and production? We just don't have a decent theoretical model. Maybe Rapping and I thought we had, but I don't think we did and I don't think anyone else does now either. I think that has been the problem right along. Is there some other explanation for the 1930s? I don't know. I told Prescott I'd hate to have to rewrite the Friedman and Schwartz book where the role Friedman and Schwartz assigned to monetary collapses is assigned instead to productivity shocks. Where is the productivity shock that cuts output in half in that period? Is it a flood or a hurricane? If it really happened, shouldn't we be able to see it in the data?

And we can't put our finger on it, can we?
We can't put our finger on it.

You have said that research during the 1970s forced you toward a general equilibrium point of view that was essentially the same in substance as the view taken by many pre-Keynesian theorists. Why do you think that most economists at the time were so clueless regarding the Depression and why was it such a disaster for the profession?
The Keynesian view was that a capitalist economy was a pretty shaky piece of machinery, it is pretty prone to instabilities. It can break down for all kinds of reasons. So what we want from economics is to be like a mechanic. You come in with your car and something is wrong, your mechanic can diagnose what is wrong and fix it up. How did it go wrong in the first place? He doesn't know and he doesn't care. All he knows is this tire is flat, it hit a nail. I don't know what happened to it, but I know how to fix tires and I will fix it for you. That was the kind of Keynesian attitude, not so much telling us how we got into trouble, but telling us how to get out. Government projects, tax stimulus, interest rate reductions, these are all ways to get things going again. That was kind of the Keynesian attitude, a kind of a can-do attitude. It is a healthy

attitude in a way, a kind of attractive attitude you know, we are ready for anything. But remember if it ain't broke don't fix it. You have to have a limitation on that attitude or you are going to over-manage the system (*laughter*).

What about the people who were still sticking to Say's law? There were a lot of people back then who advanced Say's law as the main prescription of what was going on. It seems in hindsight they were pretty clueless.
Prescott and I argue, and you can find this in the paper "Methods and problems in business cycle theory" in my *Studies in Business-Cycle Theory* book, that the general equilibrium theory that Arrow and Debreu and other mathematical economists developed in the 1940s and 1950s is a hugely flexible piece of machinery and it is a lot more useful really than Arrow and Debreu imagined it was. You can twist that model around and you can deal with uncertainty, you can deal with dynamics, you can deal with a whole lot of stuff. It's a great piece of equipment for thinking about applied economics. I think in terms of macro, Prescott and I were the first people to catch on to what a powerful piece of equipment it was. But the old fashion Say's law, Patinkin's book, and Hayek, all these guys who were smart as hell, thinking about great problems, their view of general equilibrium theory became archaic or outmoded after Arrow and Debreu redid it. So when I talk about general equilibrium now, Say's law doesn't come up.

Thank God! (Parker says with loud laughter).
It's not that there is anything wrong with it exactly, it's a kind of nineteenth century thing which, given the available equipment they had, was useful. But we can do better now.

The tradition in macro has been to segregate the twentieth century into the pre-World War I, interwar and post-World War II eras. Do you consider the Depression to be a different kind of economic fluctuation than what has been known in both kind and magnitude or is it an example of another business cycle fluctuation that has been "in essentially unchanging form for at least two centuries?"
That's a real good question, that's a real good question. I would have been solidly on the fact that the Great Depression was another instance of a familiar event that had happened many times, although perhaps not on as large a scale. That is the view Friedman and Schwartz took. Prescott and the real business cycles guys have pushed me way over to thinking that a lot of the more modest recessions can be accounted for in real terms. You don't need to appeal to a monetary collapse. I have estimated that the fraction of US instability in the post-war period that you can contribute to monetary policies is 20 percent at most. Eighty percent of the fluctuations have been real in origin. The fluctuations have been tiny. So from that point of view, the Great Depression

stands out as kind of a singular economic event. The point of view that Cole and Ohanian take, that the New Deal policies did it, is specific to the 1930s kind of theory. Do you know what I mean?

Yes I do.
There is only one New Deal, so if we were going to talk about the panic of 1893 or something like that, Cole and Ohanian would have to get another story for that one. Friedman and Schwartz's hope was to have a single story that kind of works for all these events. They were trying to show in their book that they had one and I don't know. I don't know. I was raised on that view and have maybe moved quite a bit away from it under the influence of Prescott.

Ben Bernanke has said that business cycle models should explain both the post-war and interwar eras and we should not have two sets of models to explain both. What do you think about that?
Certainly that's what every economist would want. Like any scientist we like unified theories and you respect a theory that accounts for a lot of events much more than you respect a theory constructed to account for one event only. But you sort of take what you can get, right? (*Lucas chuckles*).

Did the Great Depression set up the 1960s and 1970s and the use of fine tuning macroeconomic stabilization policies?
Yes. Absolutely. I was there (*Lucas laughs*). We were raised on the 1930s and came out of the 1930s saying we would never let that happen again.

What are some of the lessons from the Great Depression that seem to have been forgotten today or have to be continually relearned?
There are so many lessons. I feel we over-reacted to downturns in our country and other countries. So you have a decade of rather slow growth, people think it's over for us, it's over for Japan. You know Japan is a highly wealthy, sophisticated, developed country. They have their good years and bad years, but they are never going to fall much behind. The Depression was such a collapse, we haven't had anything like it in the post-war period in any country, any one of the advanced countries.

So it is Chicken Little thinking, that "The sky is falling!"
Yes, that's what I think. Maybe it is a hold-over from the 1930s. Or maybe it's what David Brooks thinks, unless you're a pessimist you're not viewed as a deep thinker (*laughter*).

What ended the Great Depression?
Well the War was what ended the Great Depression. When Pearl Harbor happened the unemployment rate was still well above 10 percent. That whole long period from the early 1930s was a period when the unemployment rate

never got below 10 percent. I said I wasn't supposed to talk about the unemployment rate (*laughter*).

I don't believe in censorship anyway, so you talk about whatever you want to talk about.
OK. Output or whatever you want to look at, the economy is never really running full steam ahead until the War.

I asked all the economists of the interwar generation this because it is a question I am deeply interested in and now I want to ask you. Can poverty and the distribution of income be correctly viewed as separate?
Well if you mean by poverty an absolute, the living standard has just grown enormously in the United States. Certainly in the post-war period it has been a rather smooth 2 percent per year growth in average living standards. So when people say that poverty isn't changing, to say that you have got to keep raising the standard of what you mean to be out of poverty over time. Certainly if you define poverty as anyone would have, say, in 1948, there are damn few people left in that situation now in 2005. We care about it but I think the focus on distribution tends to distort the analysis of economic policy. It leads us to think the only way you make me better is by making you worse off, that there's some kind of a zero-sum aspect to it. *All* (*Lucas raises his voice and stretches out the word* all) the lessons of economics since the industrial revolution have run against this idea of a zero-sum game. People are worried about China and India growing now. We've gained enormously during the periods where we have been most open, with immigrants coming from abroad and we are buying from abroad. We have always tried somehow to get low-income people around the world, let them get rich selling to us. Whether they come over here and work in plants like the Poles, the Italians and the Jews did 100 years ago or we go abroad and buy from people. It doesn't make a hell of a lot of difference. The thing is Americans gained too, we all gained enormously during those periods. The fastest periods of growth for the United States have been periods of rapid immigration and openness to trade.

Imagine that.
So I think if you worry, as a country gets rich and starts to develop, some people get really rich and some people don't get rich at all. So you say, "My God, inequality is growing" and that's what we are seeing in Russia now. Certain people in the United States are orders and orders of magnitude richer than I'm ever going to be. I just don't take that as an injury to me.

And good for them.
It is not making me worse off, it is probably helping me.

If I'm better off and richer and you are no worse off, the distribution of income

is going to be more skewed toward the rich, but it doesn't violate the Pareto principle. Why is that a bad thing?
Why do we take that as a bad thing? You know the basis for it. When some disaster hits like in New Orleans it just seems awful to us that a subset of people got shafted and nothing happened to the rest of us. So it is natural to want to give and support these guys. Giving to people in need is certainly a decent impulse that none of us disapproves of.

Certainly not.
I don't think that the government should be the only agency that does that, but if it does some of it that's fine with me. I am not an enemy of the welfare state. But that's a different issue from resenting or preventing people from getting super-wealthy, wealthier than I am. The US system is kind of loaded against capital accumulation. Moving to something like a flat tax wouldn't be a gift to the wealthy, I don't care if they get rich or not. It doesn't hurt me if the rich get richer just as long as the country grows faster. I'll take a piece of that.

Paul Samuelson has said he thinks that it is unfair and hindsight to say that the Fed should have increased the monetary base by whatever was necessary to avert the Depression. What do you think about that?
Friedman and Schwartz's chapter on the Great Depression has a lot of description of debates that went on among Federal Reserve people and others during those early years. There were plenty of people at that time who advocated policies to maintain the stock of money that would have worked. There were people who knew that, it is just that the people running the Federal Reserve didn't do that. And they have some amazingly ignorant and stupid quotes from Federal Reserve people in that book. So you know, they chose that course of action. Somebody knew enough to prevent that course of action.

I once found a Brookings Institution paper about the NRA, where they explained it exactly. The report said we had a big fall in prices and the NRA was trying to push prices up. It sounds like the NRA is trying to get us back to where we were in 1929. But they are pushing up the supply curve and we have got a downward sloping demand curve. They are going to push us even worse into the Depression with this. So the people who wrote the report said what they want to do is push out the demand curve and increase spending and that's the way to reflate and get us back to 1929. Whoever wrote that report understood exactly why the NRA was misguided and what kind of policies would get us to the right place. So I don't know. I think we could have done better based on what we knew. A lot of people were giving much better advice than the actions that were actually taken.

There were actually several pieces of legislation about wanting to target the price level here in the United States. As an example, the Goldsborough bill and several other bills like it made it explicit that it was the Fed's job to keep the

wholesale price index at the average level of the 1920s. This and similar legislation was defeated many times because people were addicted to the gold standard and the real bills doctrine.
So it's sort of what we call inflation targeting now.

Yes sir or even price level targeting.
That is interesting.

OK then, the last question. Could it happen again?
That's why Friedman is disturbed by the Japanese experience. He said he would like to think that the answer to that is no, because we have learned so much about how to conduct monetary policy. When you see a sophisticated economic system like Japan stumble on for a decade of slow growth for what appeared to be, at least in part, monetary reasons, it makes you stop and think.

Thanks so much, Professor.

Lee Ohanian

Lee Ohanian received his Ph.D. from the University of Rochester in 1993 and he is currently Professor of Economics at the University of California, Los Angeles. He previously held positions at the University of Minnesota and the University of Pennsylvania and he currently is a consulting economist at the Federal Reserve Bank of Minneapolis and a research associate at the NBER. Together with his colleague Harold Cole at UCLA, Lee Ohanian has taken the lead pursuing a research agenda that has committed itself to taking a fresh look at both the old and new questions regarding what we know (or thought we knew) and do not know about the economics of the Great Depression. If you thought the heavy lifting in explaining the Great Depression has been done, you have not met Lee Ohanian. He had a lot to say and I was ready to listen to an iconoclast in action. If it does not come through in this interview, then let me assure you the enthusiasm with which Professor Ohanian speaks about his research agenda is immediately evident and refreshing. I spoke with Lee Ohanian in his office on the campus of UCLA on March 7, 2005.

Would you please provide some background on how you got involved in the literature on the Great Depression.
I can go into this in as much detail as you want.

I want you to say what you think you need to say, as long as it takes, it does not matter. I have nowhere to go and all day to get there (laughter).
OK. As a kid, I was always fascinated by the Depression. My father, my mother or my grandparents would often talk about how terrible it was. Even forty years after the Depression, they would talk about it and you could look in their faces and see how much pain they still felt. It was hard for me to reconcile the Depression with the US economy that I observed. I would think "What caused the Depression? What made things so bad?" And that's one reason why I went into economics. I was always interested in macroeconomics, and a lot of my interest in macroeconomics came from the Great Depression and, more broadly, macroeconomic history. I went to do a Ph.D. at the University of Rochester, given their great reputation in macroeconomics. I wanted to write a dissertation about the Great Depression. When I arrived, I talked with the macroeconomists there, Bob King, Alan Stockman, Tom

Cooley, Charles Plosser, Mark Bils, and Jim Kahn, and asked them "What caused the Great Depression, what made it so bad, and what made it last so long?" They smiled in an avuncular way, and said that is probably not the best thing for a graduate student to write a dissertation on, too risky a topic. I ended up writing a dissertation that intersected economic history with macroeconomics about how US wars were financed.

After three years at the University of Pennsylvania, I went to the University of Minnesota. The macroeconomists at Minnesota spend time at the Federal Reserve Bank of Minneapolis and I did that as well. I spent hours talking with Ed Prescott. One day I asked, "Ed, what do you know about the Great Depression? I have always been fascinated by it but I have never seen anyone write down formal models to try to sort it out." Ed's response was "It's a fascinating episode, it's a pathological episode, and it defies explanation by standard economics. We need a new theory to understand the Great Depression." And I said "OK ..." (*laughter*). Ed is brilliant, but sometimes he speaks cryptically, and you have to think a while about what he says to really understand him. Shortly after that Hal Cole and I were eating lunch at the Minneapolis Fed cafeteria, we started chatting about it, and we decided to learn more about it together. And if you are on staff at the Minneapolis Fed, they ask you to write one article for their *Quarterly Review* per year ...

So the result was Cole and Ohanian (1999).
Yes. Hal and I were influenced by Ed's view that standard theory couldn't account for the Depression. Obviously, the growth model with constant long-run technological change is not going to give us the right answer about the Depression, but we thought that we could turn the model on its head, and use the model's failures to point us in a useful direction for understanding the episode. The neoclassical model can take almost any shock as an input; Friedman and Schwartz talked about monetary shocks, Meltzer talked about trade shocks. We can then use the framework to quantify the relative contributions of these shocks. Our analysis identified two main questions: "What caused the Depression?" and "Why didn't the economy recover after 1933?"

The second one was certainly illuminated by Cole and Ohanian (2004a). I am going to talk about it later on, but that is one of the best papers on the recovery that there is out there.
Thank you. It is nice of you to say that. With our 1999 paper, we analyzed the basic macroeconomic data: output, consumption, investment, labor supply, etc., and then looked at shocks that are commonly studied in the business cycle literature to determine if those shocks could have plausibly led to the Depression. The first shock we considered was a productivity shock which at the time seemed strange because it is a 40 percent downturn, and it is natural

to wonder how productivity could have generated such a large decline. Our goal was to objectively examine productivity shocks as well as other shocks, including monetary shocks, banking shocks, trade shocks, and fiscal shocks, to see how far we could go in quantitatively accounting for the Depression.

Many shocks were negative between 1929 and 1933. There was deflation, there were declines in broad monetary aggregates, there was a large decline in productivity, which I will talk about a little bit later, and there were banking panics. There are several candidate shocks between 1929 and 1933 that could have contributed to the Depression. But the most striking finding – from the perspective of theory – is the post-1933 economy. Post-1933 shocks indicate that the economy should have experienced a fantastic recovery, as productivity dramatically increases. Field (2003) argues that the best decade for productivity growth was the 1930s, but all of this growth came between 1933 and 1939. Productivity fell substantially between 1929 and 1933.

But you also say that productivity returns to trend by 1936.
Exactly, productivity returns to trend by 1936 and remains on trend or is above trend after that. In addition, the money supply grows rapidly, and deflation is halted almost immediately by 1933. Roosevelt institutes banking reforms, and banking panics stopped after 1933. These positive forces should have fostered a strong recovery. But there was very little recovery. Employment is 27 percent below normal in 1933 and remains 21 percent below normal in 1939. A large, negative shock must have derailed what should have been a dramatic employment recovery.

Let me stop you right there, because I want to interject a second question to kind of wrap this together. You correctly point out that theories of the Depression have to hold water in a general equilibrium model since direct effects may be offset by indirect effects and it is important to account for these. I like the simple elegance and crispness of the way you phrase your discussion of the Japanese economy in the Economic Dynamics *interview in 2000, when you say "[w]hat is preventing people from working and producing more?" Is this the essence of your line of inquiry for the Great Depression?*
Absolutely, you hit the nail on the head. Some factor must have been restricting the free trade of labor services. That is the key to understanding the 1930s. We can quantify the size of this factor using the first-order condition that equates the marginal rate of substitution between consumption and leisure to the real wage. This first-order condition holds in many classes of models. In the 2004 *JPE* paper, Hal and I documented that this equation was off by about 120 percent during the New Deal period. (*Ohanian writes the following equation on a note pad:* $MU_l = MU_c * W$.) The right-hand side of this equation is the marginal benefit from work: I can work a bit more at the market real wage rate, and obtain more consumption which I value at the marginal utility of

consumption. My opportunity cost of working is the marginal value of forgone leisure. In depressions, hours worked are low, so the marginal utility of leisure is low. Consumption is low, so the marginal utility of consumption is high. Even more puzzling, the real wage in certain sectors was 25 percent above its normal level. You put these numbers into this equation and you get a bizarre result: the left side of the equation is declining, while the right side is rising substantially. Why weren't people working more, given the high wage and low consumption? There must have been a major factor that prevented labor markets from functioning as they normally do. That little marginal rate of substitution equation really drove home the very weird nature of the recovery. And that took us into the paper that came out in the *JPE*. In our 1999 paper we hinted at Roosevelt's policies ...

(Laughing) *You have a good way of doing that. You always ask the next question on what you are working on at the end of your last paper. I wish I was smart enough to do it myself. It's like we really need to know what happens here, and then son-of-a-gun, 12 months later there is a paper by Cole and Ohanian answering that very same question. So I have to hand it to you* (laughter).

I wish to point out that we certainly are not the first people to ever suggest that Roosevelt's policies were a possible impediment to recovery. There are lots of intellectual antecedents for what we did. One of the first challenges we faced was trying to convince people the policies really did have a major effect.

When you say people, are you saying historians, economists, or economic historians in particular?
A number of economists, economic historians and historians. I exchanged correspondence with Robert Barro and his view was the recovery was proceeding normally, and then the Fed derailed it with reserve requirement increases. And it is not just Barro, a number of people have this view. Many historians argue that New Deal policies did not contribute to the weak recovery. For example, one of the best-known books in this area is *New Deals*, by Colin Gordon, which argues the NIRA had little effect. It is a fascinating book of almost 400 pages, yet there is not a single table or figure with data that supports this thesis. In contrast, Hal and I tried to assemble a convincing case about the impact of the New Deal. In Cole and Ohanian (2004a), we obtained monthly data on prices and wages, and we show that relative prices and real wages across many industries jumped when the policies were adopted. That evidence really convinced me. You observe an industry wage and its relative price jumping 30 percent after a code of fair competition is adopted, and you ask, "What else could have caused this?" And those high prices and wages remained high through the 1930s.

You also point out the ones that did not write a "code of fair competition."
That is about as close to a controlled experiment as you are going to get.
Yes, we found this striking case in which bituminous coal mining negotiated
a code of fair competition, and wage and prices jumped. But anthracite coal
mining never formed a code, and there is about a 40 percent difference
between bituminous coal wages and anthracite coal wages. When I found that
data I thought "this is fantastic!" I ran upstairs to find Hal and yelled, "You
have to see this!"

You also picked up on the fact that even though the Supreme Court ruled it
unconstitutional, de jure, that ruling was never enforced. On and on and on
in 1938, 1939, 1940, people basically just ignored the ruling.
Yes, this fact was also a key point in establishing the impact of the policies. A
common view was "the NRA was over formally in mid-1935, and it didn't
have any impact before that." In fact we had a rough draft of the Minneapolis
Fed paper in 1999, and Hal gave it at the Money and Banking Workshop in
Chicago. Ed Prescott was on the faculty at Chicago that year and was very
supportive of the work, and was telling Bob Lucas, Jim Heckman, and Lars
Hansen about it. I went with Hal to Chicago to see how people reacted to the
paper. Hal gave a really wonderful presentation. You know how Chicago
seminars are, they can be very raucous. But Hal had the audience virtually
entranced, well, at least for the first half hour! It was a lot of fun, there was a
lot of interesting discussion, and Ed, Hal, and I stayed out until two or three in
the morning, talking about the paper, and the Depression, and I remember that
Ed was really excited about how well the paper was received. Anyway,
regarding the impact of the policies, I think it was Jim Heckman who said
during the seminar "everybody knows these policies were over in 1935." We
did face a lot of resistance along the line of "how could these policies continue
to have any impact?" The *JPE* paper documents the institutional history and
in that paper we showed how Roosevelt was able to continue his policies after
the NRA was declared unconstitutional. We made the case by showing changes
in prices and wages, and by showing that the antitrust laws weren't enforced
after the Supreme Court's decision. In fact another question came up at the
Chicago seminar, I think it was from Gary Becker who said, "The economy
rose at the beginning of World War II. How could that be with these policies?"

There you go again. You asked that question at the end of Cole and Ohanian
(2004a). My guess is you have got a working paper coming out pretty soon.
It's fascinating. Roosevelt does a complete "about face" in WWII regarding
these policies, and we have this beautiful statistic regarding the wage relative
to productivity. Economic models tell you which data are central for
understanding the impact of a policy. The model in our *JPE* paper tells us that
the impact of Roosevelt's cartel policies can be observed in the wage rate

relative to productivity – the higher this ratio, the greater the depressing impact of the policies. The ratio of the wage relative to productivity is 30 percent higher in 1939 compared to 1929, but it falls during the war, and is almost back to its normal level by the end of WWII. We see that when the New Deal policies are adopted, the economy remains depressed, and when those policies are removed, the economy booms. Another issue was developing the theoretical model. This was a challenge because dynamic stochastic general equilibrium (DSGE) models are not always easy to use.

I wouldn't think so.
They are being adopted by a lot of people in macroeconomics now, but they can be difficult to solve. We needed a model that was really tailored for the period, a model that really captured the essence of the NRA.

Yes, like that insider–outsider model you put in there with the labor dispute negotiations. Bernanke called for those types of models a decade or more ago.
Yes, that is the essence of the NRA. Roosevelt had this mistaken idea that too much competition was responsible for the Great Depression. He thought if nominal prices and wages rose, then the economy would return to normal. So he said, "Ford and GM, you guys collude. But we won't let you have the goodies of collusion unless you give some of the rents to labor. If you reach a labor agreement, then we'll let you sign a 'Code of Fair Competition' that allows minimum prices and quotas on new investment." We developed a dynamic bargaining model in which the government permitted collusion, assuming a wage agreement was reached with labor. These repeated games are more complicated than competitive equilibrium models. With this in mind, we developed the simplest possible model. Still there is an imperfect competition bargaining structure within a dynamic general equilibrium model. It took a while to hammer that out. The issue then becomes quantifying the impact of the policy, because at the end of the day, the $64 dollar question is "are these policies responsible for 90 percent of the slow recovery or only 5 percent?" Parameterized models let us make these kinds of quantitative assessments. We found that about 60 percent of the weak recovery was due to these policies, 40 percent to other factors.

OK, let's move on. In Cole's and your paper "Re-examining the contributions of money and banking shocks to the US Great Depression," you stack the Great Depression up against other major deflations and require theories to explain those as well, using this as a consistency criterion. You are not the first to ask why, although the deflation was about the same, the output response in 1920–22 was milder than in 1929–33. I don't know that we have a satisfactory answer yet. Using current theories requires saying some things were present during 1929–33 that were not present in 1920–22 in order for

extant theories to explain the Depression. You then go on to "level" practically all the theories that there are regarding the Depression and what we thought we knew about money, high real interest rates, debt deflation and bank failures. So I call this "the terminator paper" (Ohanian laughs). *So I have to hand it to you, it has been fun working up this interview and watching an iconoclast at work, which I think is a compliment.*
(*Ohanian chuckles*) OK.

Moreover, your efforts, regardless of how they are received, should be lauded for trying to shed new light on our biggest macroeconomic problem. Eichengreen and Temin both feel that the heavy lifting in explaining the Great Depression has been done. I bet you don't feel that way.
Let me think for a second before I answer this. The short answer to your question is no. The Depression is one of the most fascinating macroeconomic questions. There are big differences between the answers from economic historians and the answers from macroeconomists. A lot can be learned by intersecting the two approaches and that's how I'm trying to pursue this. The reason macroeconomic questions are so hard to answer is because there are many endogenous variables, like output, employment, prices, wages, returns on capital ...

Bank deposits.
Yes, they are all endogenous variables. It is important to use the machinery of modern macroeconomics to sort out cause and effect during the Depression, and this machinery can help improve communication between economic historians and macroeconomists. I am hoping that economic historians start using this methodology. About 10 years ago, I gave the paper I wrote with Cooley on post-war British growth at the University of Iowa. Deirdre (then Don) McCloskey was on the Iowa faculty then. She was very positive, and predicted that these methods would become the future of economic history, much as cliometrics changed how quantitative economic history was performed much earlier. And some economic historians, such as Mike Bordo, have picked up on these tools. The big breakthrough for Kydland and Prescott in their 1982 *Econometrica* paper "Time to build" is that it made general equilibrium models quantifiable in a sufficiently rich way as to use them to seriously study macroeconomic time series. Broadly speaking, economists agree that addressing the Depression – or other macroeconomic episodes – means to define a set of shocks, feed them into a model, and quantify how those shocks affect macroeconomic variables. The challenge for understanding the Depression is that output is about 40 percent below trend in 1933. This suggests that a very big shock is needed to account for this magnitude of decline. We are now able to construct different types of models, put in various shocks and evaluate the impact of those shocks. Because the enterprise of

studying depressions with DSGE models is still in its infancy, I disagree that all of the heavy lifting has been done. It is exciting that Kydland and Prescott, V.V. Chari, Ellen McGrattan, Tim and Pat Kehoe, Fabrizio Perri, Fumio Hayashi, and others are picking up on these ideas, studying other depressions using similar methods, as well as extending the procedures that Hal and I have been using. There is much more to be done and I am excited about that.

You have taken the literature off in a different direction, so whatever comes out of it, let's see.
Economics is exciting. You and I both know it is a calling. People have disagreements about what the answers are and people address those questions in different ways. Only good things can come from that.

Alright, let me ask you some more specific questions about "the terminator paper" as I call it. Do you think people were expecting prices to return to the antebellum level after WWI and yet were not expecting such behavior after 1929 as prices were stable for some time? Thus the nature of the two deflations was different. Couldn't these two deflations be viewed differently because of that?
Most modern monetary theories stress unanticipated deflation reducing employment and output. It is striking that the deflations were roughly comparable, in fact the 1920–21 deflation was even faster than the 1929–33 deflation, but there was a small recession in 1920–21, versus the Great Depression in the 1930s. So understanding the Great Depression versus the 1920–21 recession would require that the 1920s deflation was anticipated, but the 1930s deflation was unanticipated.

But then wouldn't that have made ex ante real interest rates more the story than in 1920–21?
Yes, we address that in the paper. As you correctly point out, if this was the key difference, then we should see very low nominal interest rates in 1920–21 and high nominal interest rates in 1929–33. But the pattern is the reverse. Nominal interest rates and ex post real interest rates were much higher in 1920–21 than during the Depression. In 1920–21 nominal rates were 4 percent to 5 percent, but close to zero in the Depression. This suggests that capital markets were more accurately anticipating the deflation of the 1930s than that of the 1920s.

A purely deflation–monetary theory of the Great Depression faces the major challenge that the monetary contraction that precedes the Depression is small, both in absolute and relative terms. The New York Fed discount rate rises about 150 basis points between 1927 and late 1929. (There was no Fed Funds market at this time). This is smaller than a typical post-war monetary contraction. Feeding this sequence of higher rates into the Christiano,

Eichenbaum and Evans (CEE) (2005) model, which is tailored to generate a significant impact of higher interest rates on output, generates a small recession. In 1920–21, the New York Fed discount rate rises about 250 basis points, and the CEE model comes close to generating the small downturn of 1920–21. Consequently, that model – or any plausibly parameterized monetary model – will tell you that the 1920–21 downturn should have been more severe than 1929–33.

Temin (1989) has talked about how price behavior was a transition from WWI. I have always found that to be a pretty persuasive argument. Additionally, a big deflation happened after a big run-up in the price level right after the war. A big fall after a big run-up can maybe cancel out the debt deflation component in 1920–21. And most importantly, the gold standard was not there in 1920–21 and was there in 1929–33. That is one thing that explains perhaps why we get that difference in behavior in those two episodes. I guess I wanted to ask why do you basically not talk about the gold standard at all in your "Re-examining the contributions of money and banking shocks to the US Great Depression" paper?
That is a very good question.

One of the premises of your paper is that you have to find something that was there in the later period that was not there in the earlier period to explain the difference in behavior and that is one of the things that fulfils that requirement.
I don't find the gold standard story convincing, because the gold standard is simply a vehicle for transmitting deflationary policy from one country to another – it is nothing more than that. The gold standard constrains the types of monetary policies any individual central bank can pursue. In Eichengreen's view, deflationary policies in the US are exported to the rest of the world through the gold standard. So the gold standard view of the Depression is nothing more than a deflationary explanation. Cutting to the chase, deflation/monetary contraction is the key shock in the gold standard literature. As we have discussed, the pure deflation story of the Depression faces significant challenges.

You had another point which was about coming out of WWI. I agree with you that the US typically deflated following wartime inflations. That is why Hal and I examined nominal interest rates before the 1920–21 recession. The fact that nominal rates were quite high in 1920–21 indicates capital markets were not anticipating the deflation at that time.

In your "Re-examining the contributions of money and banking shocks to the US Great Depression" paper, bank suspensions were important across both

the 1920–21 and 1929–33 episodes. Did deflation and monetary policy have
any role in bringing about bank suspensions?
Bernanke (1983a) has argued that bank failures and suspensions were *the*
major reason why the Depression was so deep and lasted so long. In the paper
we contrasted banking variables between 1920 and 1921 to those same
variables between 1929 and 1933. The fraction of deposits in banks that
suspended operations was larger in 1929–33 than in 1920–21. Of course, the
key is quantitatively how important is that difference for understanding the
severity of 1929–33. Ben's regressions didn't shed light on that question, nor
did the regressions provide a theoretical framework for measuring the size of
the banking shock or for quantifying the impact of that shock. We pursued that
in a variety of ways, and found the contribution of banking shocks to be small.
Like Bernanke, we assumed that there is "relationship capital" between
borrowers and lenders that is match-specific. For example, if I always borrow
from you, but you close your bank doors, I need to borrow from the bank down
the street, but they do not lend to me because they don't know me.

We developed models that stressed "relationship capital" in borrowing
arrangements. The models featured both internal and external finance, with
banking services as an intermediate input in a constant returns to scale
technology, and used those models to address two sets of issues. The first
quantified the size of the banking shock and the impact of that shock on output.
The second used the models to determine if changes in other variables are
consistent with banking problems having a large exogenous impact on
employment and output. Our model indicates that the size of the shock is equal
to the fraction of deposits in failed/suspended banks. This was very small,
around 1.5 percent of deposits each year in the Depression. And production
theory implies that to a first-order approximation, the impact of the banking
shock is banking's share of value added, which is about 1 percent. So the
impact of the banking shock on output in this model is 1 percent multiplied by
1.5 percent, which is virtually zero. Even if we use the value added share of the
entire financial sector (12 percent), the impact is still close to zero. Moreover,
the share of valued added doesn't change much over the Depression, which
indicates that this first-order approximation is accurate.

Now, it is reasonable to conjecture that there may be other models which
deliver a bigger bang from that banking shock. We therefore used the theory
to consider the question "If bank failures did have a major effect, how would
other variables change?" The theory predicts that if banking did have a major
impact, then firms should have substituted towards internal finance from
intermediate finance. But the opposite occurs. Corporate profits fall
substantially and firms are paying out cash like nobody's business. Their
internal cash was being depleted during a period in which the banking theory
predicts the opposite should happen. If business was in trouble because loans
were scarce, then why are they paying out all this cash? Banking theory also

predicts that the states that had the most severe banking panics should have had the worst depressions. We tested this and found there is no correlation whatsoever between state income and the severity of the banking panic. And if banking was the major factor, then we should see historically enormous spreads between the interest rates on the highest quality paper and the interest rates on marginal paper. We don't – the increase in the spread on Baa paper that we observe in the Depression is smaller than the increase we saw in the 1980–81 recession. In fact the increase in the Baa/government spread in the Great Depression is about the same as you'd see during an average post-WWII business cycle. Given the previous literature, it would have been a lot easier for us to say "We got the banking story to work in a DSGE model, and it worked just like you guys thought it would." But it didn't.

Your "Re-examining the contributions of money and banking shocks to the US Great Depression" paper casts doubt on the inflexible wage hypothesis as the timing of real wage changes does not coincide with movements in output other than in 1931. Moreover, the movements of the real wage are too small and affect too little of the economy to be of much importance. Also the indirect, general equilibrium effects of other industries having falling wages offset this effect. This result was robust to a number of alterations in the model parameter values. What is the short answer on why this result differs from Bordo, Erceg and Evans (2000b) who find that 70 percent of the downturn is from sticky wages?

OK, the short answer is Bordo et al. assume the entire economy was subject to this wage stickiness, and they use an increase in the real wage that is much bigger than what we measured for the distorted sector. Regarding their measurement of the real wage, they don't take into account any kind of trend growth in the quality of labor. I am not sure why. They ignore any kind of productivity change, such as the standard approach of defining trend productivity change to be 2 percent. Moreover, there were changes in the composition of labor during the Depression. Typically, the average level of human capital rises during downturns, as job loss tends to be concentrated among lower productivity workers, and any measurement of the wage needs to correct for compositional change. Hal and I performed these types of corrections, and found that the economy-wide wage was not high. Regardless of that issue, it is clear that the entire economy was not subject to high wages. The farm sector, which comprised about 25 percent of employment at that time, was clearly not distorted by high wages. And their model counterfactually predicts a huge increase in labor productivity. But perhaps most important, any wage-based explanation must explain why wages did not fall. It is implausible that nominal wages were "exogenously sticky." To see this, suppose I am working for you during the Depression. Unemployment is 25 percent, profits are negative, the economy is going to hell, there is no question you are going to tell me "Lee, I am losing money hand over fist. You know that nominal wage that hasn't changed in the last 2 years? If you want to still work here, you are going to have to take a cut." And there is no doubt that I – or anyone else – would take a wage cut in those circumstances. Given these reservations, there are two ways to go. One is to try to address these issues in the Keynesian framework. Bordo, Erceg, and Evans are talented, and I hope they pursue that. The other approach is one I am taking. In current work, I am re-visiting the initiating causes of the Depression. The labor market changed enormously beginning in November, 1929, including the relationship between employment and wages. Wages in the industrial sector among the largest firms were unchanged for quite some time. My new work pursues this in a model in which labor policies changed substantially. But it is very different from the Keynesian sticky-wage view.

OK. Why can't the negative productivity shock that you documented in your "Re-examining the contributions of money and banking shocks to the US Great Depression" paper be consistent with Cecchetti's decapitalization story and thus have an explanation as to the sources and reasons for the change in total factor productivity? Decapitalization should manifest itself in very large and highly persistent productivity decreases. Why can't the productivity shock story be consistent with that decapitalization story?

They are two separate issues, though together they could have a significant effect on the economy. To see they are different, suppose the government puts interest rate controls on the economy so that the real borrowing rate is at least 10 percent. Certainly investment is going to go into the tank. But we measure productivity shocks using the traditional Solow method, which defines productivity change as output change less the weighted sum of changes in labor and capital input. So the low investment you refer to will be accounted for in the measurement of the productivity shock. Now, variable capacity utilization is a different animal. Variable capacity suggests that the standard Solow method will yield mis-measured productivity change because the capital input is mis-measured. I tried to address this issue, and other issues about measuring productivity in the Depression, in a 2001 paper.

You did, in your May, American Economic Association piece.

Yes, I measured productivity by adjusting the capital input for plant-closings, and assumed that the plants that remained open operated on a normal schedule. This particular pattern of utilization was observed in the auto industry. I received a letter from Robert Solow about that paper. He said he found this work interesting, but wondered how the results would change if I adjusted for reduced utilization of factories that remained open. I then did some other calculations where I made assumptions about utilization changes in operating capital. Even after these adjustments, there is still a large productivity decline.

Of course, you know what this means: people say "Holy Toledo, Lee, what are you talking about? Productivity fell 12 percent in the Depression, isn't that implausible?"(*Ohanian chuckles*). I think about these issues seriously, and I take into account potential caveats. I tried to do that in that 2001 paper and you still measure a large productivity decline.

In your 2001 AEA paper you mention organizational capital as one potential source of lower productivity after discounting five other sources from capacity utilization to increasing returns. You only briefly mentioned this in your conclusions to Cole and Ohanian (2004b). Is this a theme you are going to pick up again?
I would like to pursue that. I am not sure if you would like to hear about future ideas I have or not.

This book is about the literature on the Great Depression ...
OK. After 1932, the government intervenes in the economy in a really unprecedented fashion. There was labor market intervention that really increased unions' bargaining power and at the same time significantly restricted what firms could do during strikes. Before 1933 if workers in Flint, Michigan gave GM a hard time, the National Guard was called in and a few unionists would get shot. After 1933 GM auto workers take over the Fisher body plant. No car bodies can be produced so no cars can be produced. So naturally, Alfred Sloan is mad as hell and he calls the governor of Michigan and says, "We need to knock some heads together." The governor tells him, "This is a private matter, I hope you can sort it out." There is evidence suggesting that firms saw these changes coming down the road. Unions in Europe had become powerful before the 1930s. The 1920s were a period where capitalists' share of income was at an all-time high and workers were not getting as big of a piece of the pie. So when I think about organizational capital, I am thinking about industries that are earning high profits, paying their workers low wages, but understand that these good times won't last forever. This would lead to changes in the organization about how the business was run from top to bottom.

My thinking has evolved since that 2001 paper. In addition to productivity, I am thinking about alternatives along the lines of economic inequality. I might be pursuing a theory based on inequality because in the United States the peak of income and wealth inequality is around the late 1920s. In the 1920s, a period of remarkable productivity growth, labor productivity is about 25–30 percent higher in 1929 than in 1919, real wages are almost the same in 1929 versus 1919. Some economic historians have estimated that as much as 95 percent of the workforce received no real wage gains whatsoever in the 1920s. Hopefully, in a couple of years I will have more to say about this.

That's a historian line of research that I thought had withered and died.
It is. I have been reading a lot about the 1920s and it is such a different and remarkable decade. And when you think about the Depression, you also notice that it is also such an interesting and singular event. I may be pursuing connections between the 1920s and the Depression including this idea of anticipations of substantial government intervention in the economy.

Let me get to my one of my major questions and everyone wants to know. If you have these productivity shocks, what were their sources, what explains them and where do they come from? Please tell me.
Yeah ...

Remember, I asked please.
Yeah, that is the question I ask myself and that's the question Prescott asks himself. Sorry about getting long winded, but you are asking very good questions that do not have easy answers.

My initial reaction was that the productivity shocks were the consequence of unmeasured changes in utilization and/or changes in the composition of output and workers. I made plausible adjustments for those factors in that *AEA* paper, and found that there are still large productivity declines after those corrections. I hope that more people will pursue this issue. I wish I had a real good answer to give you. It would make my life a lot easier (*laughter*). My view is the theory with the greatest potential is based on organizational capital. Corporations had enormous power in the 1920s: an awful lot of GDP was controlled by about the top 100 corporations in the country, non-union labor had absolutely no bargaining power. Worker productivity rises by about 30 percent in the 1920s, non-union wages are flat, and there are enormous gains in profits. According to Paul Douglas, that was an important reason the stock market was so high in the late 1920s. I think the most fruitful avenue is firms understanding that the good times are ending, and modifying their organizations in anticipation of a much different labor market. There is some evidence suggesting this was the case. I will be pursuing this in future research. So the short answer is "Randy, I wish I knew" (*laughter*). I think I will have more to say in a couple of years.

That's fair enough. Gertler (2000) also criticized you, as does Bernanke (2000), for not using cross sectional data in your "Re-examining the contributions of money and banking shocks to the US Great Depression" paper. So I guess your response is the 2004b paper, "Deflation and the international Great Depression: a productivity puzzle", is it not?
Yes, that's the response. In the discussion of our *Macro Annual* paper, Ben stated that the monetary/deflation story is clearly supported by the international cross section. Bernanke, Temin, Eichengreen et al. tell a particularly simple

story about deflation, sticky wages and depression. So Hal and I developed a model of that story, in which monetary contraction generates deflation, which in turn raises real wages. We also included productivity shocks into the model, and decided to run a "horse race" between the two shocks, in which we calculated the fraction of output change caused by each shock, and the fraction of price change caused by each shock. We worked on this paper for a long time. We had to develop some new techniques to construct the bounds on the contribution of the shocks.

That's a nice twist there.
Usually one constructs variance bounds for mean zero random variables. But our shocks are not mean zero because it's a depression, so the money shock on average is going to be negative and the productivity shock on average also turned out to be negative. We constructed bounds on the importance of the shocks. Productivity accounts for between 55 percent to as much as 85 percent of output change. Money accounts for between 15 percent and 45 percent of output change. The most we could give to money was less than half. And we were shocked by this, given the presumption in the literature.

No pun intended, huh?
(*Ohanian chuckles*) Bernanke's comment at the NBER on our 2000 paper was that the international evidence screams out "it is money". But it doesn't. And there's a very simple reason why it doesn't: monetary theories predict that the countries with the biggest deflations should have the biggest depressions – but that is factually wrong. We fit a number of regressions of output change on deflation, and find that deflation accounts for very little of the international Depression.

Yes, and that is Figure 1, relating deflation and output growth, in your 2004b "Deflation and the international Great Depression" paper.
It's just not in the data.

This paper is worthy of anybody's attention if for nothing else than just to eyeball Figures 1 and 2. It does not lie on that nice 45-degree line in the third quadrant of the Cartesian plane. And it should. And it doesn't.
Exactly. I can't tell you how many times Hal and I have checked that computer program and the data, because there is no systematic relationship between output and deflation. But in contrast, when we back productivity shocks out of the model, and compare them to actual productivity from the data, lo and behold the model productivity shocks line up almost exactly, right around the 45-degree line with actual productivity. We kept thinking there must be a mistake here, this can't be right. We had three graduate students check the work, and it kept coming out the same way – productivity is the dominant

factor. In fact, we couldn't find a specification in which deflation explained very much of the output change. The R-square is about .23 in a plain vanilla panel regression of output on deflation We maximized the potential contribution of deflation in a regression by allowing for separate coefficients on deflation for every country, and we also added fixed effects. Deflation is insignificant in that regression! Our model results, along with the lack of any statistically significant relationship between deflation and depression, show that the deflation story is just not the right one for 1929–33. One could say "OK, I'm going to dismiss everything Cole and Ohanian have to say. I still believe in my heart deflation caused the Depression." But if you want to go beyond a gut feel, then it is incumbent to develop a deflation-based DSGE model in which (a) deflation accounts for the international Depression, (b) the model generates no systematic relationship whatsoever between output and deflation and (c) deflation works as if it is a productivity shock in a growth model. Hopefully others will pursue this, but let me just say it is going to be very, very difficult to plausibly accomplish. I would bet a lot of money against it.

The abstract of Cole and Ohanian (2004b) comes right to the point and claims productivity shocks are more important than money deflation shocks by an accounting of two-thirds to one-third. The main reason is that the empirical data between deflation and output is much different than the money shocks generated in the model. Could you please explain that a little bit?
Sure. If monetary/deflation shocks were accounting for most of the Depression, then there should be a correlation of 1 between output change and price change. But in contrast, the correlation between these variables is negative or close to zero for most of this period. This large difference is the reason why the model assigns such a small faction of output change to monetary shocks and it's the same reason why in those regressions deflation accounts for so little of the change in output.

But it basically goes to almost 1 after 1933 doesn't it?
The correlation between output and price rises a bit, the correlation between real wages and output rises more after 1933, but it is not close to 1.

There is a change in the correlation in 1933 that, it seems to me, makes your model and the work that has been done using it much better at explaining 1933–39 than 1929–33.
The wage–output change suggests that the monetary story has a better chance after the Depression than during the Depression.

OK, what made that correlation change then?
We will need to do more work to sort that out.

It seemed to me that the change in the correlation here from negative to zero to positive is a lot of what is driving what is going on with the results for these models between those two different periods.

That is a possibility. But I suspect that the change in the correlation is associated with differences in the types of labor policies that were adopted across countries. For example, the US had a slow recovery with high real wages, but due to Roosevelt's cartelization policies, not monetary factors. France also adopted distorting labor policies, and had a slow recovery and high wages. Germany had a fast recovery with declining real wages, which coincided with a substantial weakening of union power. So assessing the contribution of monetary factors to the recovery requires taking into account these other important policies. Hal and I plan on doing that in a new paper.

I think my thinking is correct regarding these monetary versus productivity shocks. The productivity shocks you are talking about are all orthogonal to the financial and monetary shocks the way that they are constructed.

The fact that the productivity shocks are orthogonal to deflation suggests that if productivity is endogenous then it is being driven by something other than deflation. To test this, we calculated the correlation between the productivity shocks and a number of variables, including deflation, money, the real and nominal exchange rates, the Bernanke–James banking distress variable, the trade share, and the real value of the stock market. The real value of the stock market is highly correlated with productivity, as is the lagged real value of the stock market. This suggests the possibility of a non-deflation related financial factor, but much more work is needed in this area. It would be great if I had some obvious factor that could explain productivity. So far, it remains a mystery, but at least we have narrowed down the possible suspects. Deflation isn't one of them (*laughter*).

OK, let me ask you this question straight out.

That is fine, you are asking great questions! I've gotten a lot of heat on this stuff over the last five years, so I am used to it!

You mentioned in Cole and Ohanian (2000) that the total deposit-to-output ratio increased 35 percent from 1929 to 1932. Thus intermediated finance and loanable funds were abundant. Is it useful to examine two endogenous variables and then make causal statements thereafter?

I am very sympathetic to your question. The challenge in macroeconomics is that most variables are endogenous, and therefore one requires a formal model. The model in Cole and Ohanian (2000) tells us that the deposit-to-output ratio is a good indicator of the available capacity of the banking system, and thus our model guided us in interpreting those variables. The basic reason is that the scarcest factors of production will fall more than final output. But banking capacity falls less than final output. This interpretation will tend to come out of any model in which banking is an input in a neoclassical technology for producing output. The fact that banking capacity fell considerably less than output makes you stop and think about the importance of banking as a cause of the Depression.

In regard to abandoning the gold standard, if you look at the Choudhri and Kochin (1980) results for example, it seems to me that one of the greatest, strongest, most robust macroeconomic empirical relations we have is the timing of recovery and abandoning the gold standard.
I look forward to more research that addresses this in detail. I agree that the timing of changes in the gold standard and recovery do seem to be important. With that in mind, however, there are a bunch of questions that no one has really evaluated that force one to think more deeply about the Choudhri and Kochin evidence. Specifically, the standard gold standard interpretation implies that countries that left gold expanded their money supplies, and thereby reflated their economy. But this is factually wrong. You can see this in Bernanke's (1995) broader examination of countries that leave gold. Nominal income rises more in the off-gold countries, but it is *not* because they expanded their money supplies more than did the on-gold countries. The rate of monetary increase between on-gold and off-gold countries is the same! Instead, the rise in nominal income in the off-gold countries is due to higher velocity. And that increase does not seem to be due to higher expectations of inflation in the off-gold countries. The challenge facing the gold standard story is that it must explain why velocity rose, and why the standard gold standard explanation – higher monetary expansion in the off-gold countries – is factually wrong. I will probably be pursuing this down the road.

(Parker says the following as if to say he would have to see it to believe it) *I look forward to seeing that. Christina Romer has said that "perhaps the key divide in macro involves how we answer the question 'do nominal shocks matter? – does money matter?'" How do you answer that question?*
I could go on and on about this but I'm going to try to keep this answer short. But this is a really important question and I have a very different answer than Christy.

I didn't come 3000 miles to get the short answer.
Right, I hear you. Here comes the long answer. The key divide in macroeconomics used to be a methodological divide. Twenty years ago a small number of economists used dynamic general equilibrium models to address applied questions. Those *modeling efforts* are often confused with the type of *shocks* that are studied. So I want to draw a distinction between the nature of

shocks, and the methodology of inferring the impact of those shocks on macroeconomic variables. For example, one can study the impact of monetary shocks in *IS–LM* frameworks, or in DSGE frameworks. Twenty years ago macroeconomists at Harvard/MIT/Yale/Princeton were still using *IS–LM*, while macroeconomists at Chicago/Minnesota/Rochester/Carnegie were using DSGE models. But today this methodological difference doesn't exist. The macro faculties at Harvard, MIT, Princeton, and Columbia are largely working with DSGE models. There are debates about the importance of monetary shocks, but not nearly as much as 30 years ago. And the debates are a lot about details. Today there is broad consensus that money is neutral in the longrun. The debate about money is what happens in the short run, and what defines the short run. Regarding my views, I don't see any direct evidence that monetary shocks have either substantial or long-lasting effects on employment or output. For many years, policy makers at the Board of Governors believed that there is a systematic relationship between inflation and the "output gap", basically Phillips curve type reasoning. Andy Atkeson and I wrote a simple paper a few years ago that showed neither the unemployment rate nor other measures of "output gaps" could forecast inflation. The paper seemed to cause a stir within the Fed system. A lot of Fed economists have tried to come up with alternative models to use Phillips curve type models to forecast inflation, but without any real success. I am still a consultant to the Minneapolis Fed, and the President, Gary Stern, and the Research Director, Art Rolnick, tell me that Board discussions of money and the real economy have changed a lot over the last decade. The reason macroeconomists are reaching a broader consensus is because we now have a common methodological component to how we are addressing questions. I see much more consensus in macroeconomics than in other fields, such as labor economics. Unlike macroeconomics, labor has no common methodological meeting ground. There are natural experiment researchers such as David Card and Alan Kreuger, and there are structural econometric estimators like Ken Wolpin and Mike Keane. And there isn't much communication between those two camps. In macro, a lot of the walls between groups have come down since I went to graduate school in the late 1980s. Unfortunately, this has made hiring macroeconomists much more difficult for departments such as UCLA, Rochester, Penn, and Minnesota, because now Harvard, Yale, MIT, and Princeton want to hire the same people we want to hire. A couple of years ago we hired one of the young stars, Aleh Tsyvinski out of Minnesota, but this last year he went to Harvard.

OK, you and Cole pick up the United Kingdom in your 2002 paper in the Review of Economic Dynamics. *You say, "these output and expenditure share data suggest that a negative, permanent shock drove the UK economy onto a low steady state growth path in the 1920s." Temin has identified WWI and all the sequence of changes it wrought as the shock that brought about the*

Depression. Could WWI have something to do with this negative, permanent shock you refer to?
The shock we identify in Britain is a shock that affected the incentive to work, as employment fell substantially, though productivity growth was in line with its historical average. There is a long-standing debate about the importance of Britain's post-WWI unemployment system for the UK economy.

The answers you provide regarding UK unemployment during the interwar years make one sit up and pay attention.
My view of the impact of WWI on Britain is different than Temin's. Britain became very uncompetitive after WWI. For example they lost many of their foreign markets in the steel, iron and textile industries. Their lack of competitiveness, in conjunction with government policies, was an important reason why Britain remained mired in depression from 1920 through WWII.

Here we have the same theme again, what is preventing people from working and producing more? Here is that question again and the UK paper with Cole suggests that government policies that made unemployment lucrative explain much of the behavior of unemployment. There were benefits at 50 percent to 60 percent of compensation even for job loss after one day's employment, housing and rent subsidies, and an indefinite period of payment. People respond to incentives. This is simple economics. If you make it pay to be unemployed what do you get? Unemployment. So here is my question. Can't the same thinking be applied to modern-day Europe and is this not a danger for the US economy, the danger of more and more layers of regulation, laws and taxation that ultimately create disincentives that prevent people from working and producing more?
Hallelujah, absolutely! In my view, and you will see this in the views of Prescott and Ljungqvist and Sargent, government policies account for why hours worked in Europe are so much lower than in the US. At one time, I believe it was in the Netherlands, one could claim disability for a variety of reasons, including factors that are hard to assess, such as back pain and headaches. At one point roughly 40 percent of the workforce was claiming disability, as disability payments were very high. Once the disability insurance system was reformed, the number of people on disability declined substantially. I completely agree with you. Europe has higher taxes and many more labor market regulations than the United States has, and this is an important reason why there is so much less work in Europe.

In your review essay on the book The Defining Moment *you say "Understanding why bad policies are sometimes adopted, and how to prevent them, is clearly an important question ..." I would like to know if you think we have moved any closer to answering that question.*

It is an enormous puzzle because during good times policy makers can take some additional risk – output and employment are high, so government can experiment a bit, and if things go wrong, the loss will be relatively small. During a severe depression, experimenting with bad policies leads to much larger losses. We have moved closer to answering your question in the sense that Roosevelt perceived he was following the best economic advice at the time. His economic advisors thought that the road to prosperity was raising prices and wages. So at some level, bad policies were adopted during the Great Depression because Roosevelt's advisors just didn't know enough. But this isn't a complete answer, because Latin American countries – take, for example, Venezuela and Hugo Chavez – routinely adopt protectionist measures, distort labor markets, and nationalize industries, despite the benefit of recent – and not so recent – advances in economics that tell us those policies are dead wrong. And Latin America represents economic policy failure on a grand scale. Argentina once was wealthier than the US, now they have less than 25 percent of US per capita income. The question of why such obviously bad policies are adopted today is very challenging, and I hope this will engage researchers in political economy.

Your JPE *paper with Cooley "Postwar British economic growth and the legacy of Keynes" seems to be a natural laboratory for structuring the importance of the above question regarding understanding why bad policies are adopted. The damage that was done by the policies of capital taxation seem to be a clear lesson from economic history that people, especially politicians, have to continually relearn. Why is it so difficult for people to acknowledge or remember that what you tax, how you tax it and how much you tax it matter a great deal for the allocation of resources and economic growth? Ed Prescott has been saying this in the* Wall Street Journal *and elsewhere, but is anybody listening?*

One of the reasons economists are in such great demand is because we have to keep teaching simple economics over and over again – basic issues about incentives and markets. The city of Santa Monica, California wanted to adopt a living wage ordinance that would have paid individuals a minimum of over 12 dollars per hour. It doesn't take much economic intuition to understand that if you are not worth 12 dollars an hour and the minimum wage is 12 dollars an hour, you will not work in Santa Monica. It is remarkable how often and how hard we have to teach the simplest economic principles. One reason is redistribution, but that is not the only reason because the types of redistributive policies typically advanced are very inefficient ones. If the goal is to raise the incomes of the poor, you don't do it by raising the minimum wage. My own proposal for prospective policy makers is if you are going to hold public office, you better take some courses from a decent economics program and understand how incentives and markets work.

What ended the Great Depression?

What ended the Great Depression? The reversal of Roosevelt's labor and industrial policies. In 1938 Roosevelt made a speech in which he argued that a hidden cartel system in the US economy was retarding recovery, and he chalked up the 1936–37 recession to labor demands for higher wages. Roosevelt was able to see that his policies were impeding recovery. Immediately after that, he completely restructured the Department of Justice (DOJ), hiring Thurman Arnold as head of the antitrust division, who then tripled the number of attorneys working on antitrust issues. The DOJ pursued ALCOA and a number of rubber companies for antitrust violations. Roosevelt completely undermined labor unions in WWII. Roosevelt received a "no strike" pledge from unions, with the understanding that unions could continue to engage in collective bargaining during the War. Roosevelt then put in place the National War Labor Board (NWLB), who failed to approve a very high wage increase that the steel workers' union negotiated with Bethlehem Steel, known as the "little steel decision." The steel workers' union was naturally mad as hell, but Roosevelt replied that the NWLB was an independent agency and that their decisions were out of his hands. In our 2004 *JPE* model, the distorting effect of labor bargaining power shows up in the ratio of the cartelized wage relative to productivity. In 1939 that ratio was 30 percent higher than it was in 1929. By the end of WWII that ratio is almost back to its normal 1929 level. One of the reasons why employment rose so much during WWII is because Roosevelt unwound those policies. After WWII, the Taft–Hartley Act restructured the Wagner Act substantially and considerably weakened union bargaining power. Even today, nearly 60 years after Taft–Hartley, its repeal remains one of the main union rallying cries. Bill Clinton secured union support in 1992 by telling unions that he would re-visit Taft–Hartley, and he almost lost union support in 1996 because he had not done this during his first term. Perhaps not surprisingly, I will be pursuing the end of New Deal policies and the WWII expansion in another paper.

Yes, in the 2004 JPE *piece you asked what the contribution was of the policy shift abandoning these policies toward the WWII economic boom. I would bet that is exactly what you are working on.*
Yes, that is one of the things (*laughter*).

Alright, the last question. Could it happen again?
Not in the US, because we have learned enough to avoid really bad policies, such as the NIRA. In other counties like Argentina or Venezuela, bad policy making is just a finance minister away (*roaring laughter*).

Christina Romer

Christina Romer received her Ph.D. from MIT in 1985 and she is currently Class of 1957 – Garff B. Wilson Professor of Economics at the University of California, Berkeley. Her main fields of research are economic history and macroeconomics. She has researched the business cycles of the late nineteenth and early twentieth centuries, the causes of the Great Depression, the effects of monetary policy, and the reliability of historical macroeconomic data. In joint work with her husband David on post-World War II monetary theory and policy, Professor Romer has followed in the path of Friedman and Schwartz. I spoke with Christina Romer in her office at the University of California on March 9, 2005.

Could you please provide some background on how you became involved with the literature on the Great Depression.
I would say I have always been interested in macro history, but I started by thinking about business cycles in general. In truth, in my thesis research, I deliberately left out the Great Depression as somehow being too different and so unlike other business cycles. I did not get drawn into research on the Great Depression until the crash of 1987. I was on leave at the NBER and when the stock market crashed it got me thinking that maybe this was going to give us insight into what happened in 1929 and vice versa. So, I wrote a paper (Romer, 1988) on the effect of large stock price movements on consumer spending and investment. And then, as happens with lots of research projects, once you start looking at something more questions come up.

You have said earlier, I think in your "The end of economic history?" paper, that you took Bernanke's (1983b) irreversibility idea and said, "Why can't we apply it to the Great Crash and Great Depression?" So you saw this modern literature and asked, "Why can't we view history through the lens of modern theory?"
I think it was actually a two-step process. I was looking at 1929 through the lens of modern experience. Then, in thinking about both the historical and modern experiences, it seemed to me that Bernanke's theory about uncertainty and investment was both insightful and relevant to consumers.

Cole and Ohanian (2004a) have a nice summary of different wage and price codes and codes of competition you talk about in your 1999 Journal of Economic History *paper. I think that their summary of the National Industrial Recovery Act (NIRA) codes together with your growth rate effect that you talk about provide a pretty complete explanation of price behavior in the latter half of the 1930s, which I really think seals the deal pretty well.*

I think we have come around to an understanding of the NIRA. My vision of Roosevelt is he was just trying anything he could think of and some of the programs were useful and some definitely were not. The NIRA strikes me as one of those classic situations where policy makers saw the correlation that when prices went up the economy was doing better, and they mistakenly inferred that it was a causal link.

I was taken aback with the persistence of the NIRA codes. Even though they were ruled to be unconstitutional, people ignored that for years and years afterwards. The codes were not de jure any more but de facto they continued to have a life of their own. And they persisted as you pointed out in your 1999 Journal of Economic History *piece.*

I think that makes a lot of sense. Once you get businesses used to colluding, then it is hard to say "no, regime over."

Do you see instability in the price level, both up and down, as one of the greatest sources of economic instability in the last century and would you be willing to say that maintaining price stability is one of the key lessons for central bankers to learn from the Great Depression and the Great Inflation of the 1970s?

Oh, (*Romer ponders a moment*) no. I think that price movements are typically a result of output instability, not the cause. In the Great Depression, the huge deflation was not the forcing variable; it was the consequence of an aggregate demand contraction that caused output to be about 40 percent below trend. Likewise, in the late 1960s and the 1970s, the inflation was largely the result of expansionary policy pushing output above trend. So the lesson I take from the last century is that policy should be aiming to keep output at trend. I think, aside from relatively infrequent supply shocks, if you keep output on trend, the swings in prices will take care of themselves.

So are the inflation targeting regimes of the world focusing on the wrong variable?

I think, as a practical issue, it doesn't really matter whether countries target inflation or output. We now have a widespread consensus in favor of low inflation, and I believe in low inflation as much as everyone else. It's just a question of what you need to do to get that. I think if you run sensible, moderate policies that aim to keep output at potential and unemployment at the non-accelerating inflation rate of unemployment (NAIRU), you're going to do fine. Whether, as a practical matter, you get low inflation by looking at the inflation rate or by looking at real output, it does not matter. The only time the indicators give conflicting reports is when there is a supply shock. Then, my own view is you take the hit a little bit in both. When you have an inflationary supply shock you take some of it as output lower than you would like and some of it as inflation higher than you would like and gradually work your way back.

You have done work on the Great Crash, as we all know, and its effect on consumption and income uncertainty. What's the reason for the change between the working paper version (1988b) and the final version in the QJE *(1990)? The neat little model was gone from the working paper.*
Ah, the editor told me it was unnecessary (*Romer chuckles*).

OK, it was not too long, it was unnecessary.
Right. I think it was good for my thinking and the editor, who I think was Olivier Blanchard, said, "I think you could summarize this quickly and go on."

Do you not think Olney's 1999 QJE *paper is a nice complement to your Great Crash paper in explaining why consumption behaved as it did in 1929–30 and that, together with Temin (1976a) talking about the wealth effect and Mishkin (1978) talking about liquidity, autonomous consumption behavior in the early part of the Depression has been explained?*
Yes, I think that all of the papers have chipped away at the issue that Temin (1976a) identified as the thing that was strange in 1929-30: consumption fell much more strongly than usual for the start of a recession. I think they all come together to say there were these many different factors that mattered.

Eichengreen (2002) still sees "the mysterious first year" as a place where much of the debate still lies. You coined that phrase in your 1988 NBER working paper on the Crash. Is the first year of the Depression still so much of a mystery?
No, I don't think it is.

It was a normal NBER recession it seems to me.
There are two things here. I think it was certainly a normal NBER recession, say, between July 1929 and October 1929. I think what is true is that its character changed rapidly at the end of 1929 and in 1930. It just very quickly went from a routine, fairly mild downturn to something that was pretty nasty. You were asking before about all of the different studies. I think part of the reason why I still like my story emphasizing the effect of the Great Crash is that it explains the timing best. The character of the recession changes so dramatically in November and December of 1929. I think that tells you the

layman's view, that somehow the Crash and the Great Depression were related, has something to it. But again, as you pointed out, there were other factors depressing consumption as well in this period. The first year of the Depression isn't a mystery any more.

Given the experience with the Crash and your knowledge of central bank behavior, do you think the Fed has any role in trying to be the arbiter of securities prices?
That's a good question. I think it's not a smart thing for a central bank to try to target securities prices, mainly because it's just not possible. The Fed's influence on stock prices is highly uncertain and variable. And, it is so hard for anyone to predict where stock prices should be, to know if they're overvalued and such things. I think the Fed has to care about inflation and it has to care about output. In general I say, "You run smart policy, you see if we are at trend with low inflation." If we are, looking at the stock market is not going to help you do better. Your job is going to be mopping up if something goes wrong. But if you are running moderate, sensible policies that are not leading to inflation, that are not leading to excessively low unemployment, I think that is going to be the best you can do.

You said in Snowdon (2002) "Perhaps the biggest policy error was the decision in 1931 to stay on the gold standard rather than leave." Why do you suppose the United States did not follow the United Kingdom off the gold standard in 1931? You have said it was a major policy decision and a major policy mistake. What in your thinking was involved in this decision?
Monetary contraction was the fundamental cause of the Great Depression. The Federal Reserve chose to do nothing in response to widespread financial panics. Then in 1931, when Britain went off the gold standard, we decided to raise interest rates to defend the dollar and stay on it. So unquestionably, monetary tightness was a key culprit.

Then the question is where did the monetary tightness come from? Could the Fed have done better, even conditional on staying on the gold standard? And, there is your question of why the heck didn't we get off the gold standard? The paper I have done most recently on the Depression (with Hsieh) argues that even within the constraints of the gold standard, the Fed could have done so much better. I think that's a really important point. I do not like the idea of saying the Great Depression was all ultimately due to the gold standard. I think, even conditional on being on the gold standard, there was so much the Federal Reserve could have done that they didn't do. Then going beyond that and talking about why we stuck to the gold standard, I am not sure I have any insight. You're right that there were countries around the world going off it and we didn't have the sense to follow them. Perhaps part of it was the fact that devaluation was not a decision the Federal Reserve could make. We had a separation of powers, if you want. The Fed was charged with maintaining the money supply and all of that. And yet the one thing they didn't have control over was the constraint put on them by the fixed exchange rate, which was something decided by Congress.

So that was a legislative and executive decision.
Right, so that made things inherently more difficult. The people most aware of what was happening to the money supply and the effect of gold flows were not the people who could decide to abandon the gold standard. That was Congress's decision. And I think Temin and Eichengreen are correct in talking about the gold standard mentalité. There was a sense that the gold standard was a good way to do things and so you can certainly see why people were not quick to throw away what was thought to have been the source of a lot of the prosperity over the previous 30 or 40 years.

"I believe that US monetary policy had a lot of room to maneuver and didn't take it." Those are your words in Snowdon (2002). I would like to hear from you why not. Why wasn't deposit convertibility suspended? They did it in 1907, there was precedent for it, and yet ...
One reason that the Federal Reserve didn't act was that they had a misguided model of how the economy operated. Hsieh and I find that in 1932 they ended their moderate expansion prematurely because they were convinced the policy had already worked and that it wouldn't be useful to expand further if people were going to be unwilling to use the funds.

Or if one Fed bank is fighting against another.
Yes. The structure of the Fed certainly made action difficult. Again, in 1932, one reason for suspending monetary action was that it was difficult to maintain consensus for expansion among the different banks.

Your point about institutions brings up a general idea about the Great Depression. I have often thought about how one reconciles my earlier work that business cycles on either side of the Depression were quite similar with the fact that the economy collapsed in the 1930s. I think the answer is that a variety of institutions can result in a similarly stable economy. Before World War I, we had an economy with little government intervention and it worked fairly well. After World War II, we had an economy with active aggregate demand management, and that has been reasonably stable too. But, the 1920s and 1930s were a transition period. We had lost the market institutions – the clearing houses, suspension of payments – that had arisen to deal with instability outside the government. But, we did not yet have a Federal Reserve that knew what to do. The result was disaster. But, it was part of a learning process.

An expensive learning process.
It was a very expensive learning process and I feel pretty strongly other people could have learned faster (*laughter*).

When it comes to saying that policy could have been different, is it as simple as you said in your comment on Peter Temin's Federal Reserve of Boston paper (1998) that policy must be given part of the blame if other policies were available and understood and/or other conscious choices were involved and they could have done something differently?
I think the fact that other alternatives were known, were available, yes it does mean they could have done something different.

There were over fifty bills during the interwar era in Congress encouraging the Fed to increase the supply of money. There was the Goldsborough bill of May 1932, yet they did not do anything.
I think what Hsieh and I would say is the gold standard dealt the Federal Reserve a bad hand to start with, but then monetary policy makers took it beyond that. They didn't have to do what they did, even conditional on being on the gold standard.

Do you agree with Michael Kitson (2003) who said the causes of the Great Depression are one thing, but the extent of the Great Depression is due to the gold standard?
No question.

Then why is everybody saying there is this big debate about this? I have never understood that.
I think that you are absolutely correct that there is actually a great deal of consensus about the cause of the Great Depression. Eichengreen, Temin, Romer, Bernanke, Bordo, Friedman, and Schwartz all agree that the downturn of the 1930s was caused by a decline in aggregate demand, stemming largely from monetary contraction. In this regard, the mainstream research on the Great Depression is fundamentally at odds with authors such as Cole and Ohanian who stress productivity shocks.

I think there is also widespread agreement that the gold standard played a role in transmitting a contractionary shock in the US to the rest of the world. Where the key debate remains is on the gold standard's role in limiting US policy choices and hence in causing the American decline. Was the Federal Reserve's inaction just the passive working out of the gold standard and just following the rules of the game, as Eichengreen and Temin suggest? Or, were there mistakes beyond that? Friedman and Schwartz say there were alternative policies; the Federal Reserve did not have to do what it did. My own view is that Friedman and Schwartz are correct.

Do you think that the gold standard was doomed to failure and no amount of coordination and cooperation could have saved it given the maldistribution of gold, the gold standard asymmetry, and the fact that the burden of adjustment fell on debtor counties mostly? Was the gold standard doomed to failure?

"I don't know" is probably the right answer. But it seems likely that anything that is contingent on some country playing a managerial role is going to be hard to sustain. A system of flexible exchange rates, on the otherhand, tends to work on its own and no one has to figure out what to do, so it is less fragile. That's why economists like the market system in general. Something that has to be managed and coordinated is going to have pressures and eventually will fail to work.

You said in your Boston Fed paper (1998) that "(w)hile the gold standard no doubt constrained the Fed's behavior at some point in the Depression" gold reserves were sufficient in 1930 and 1931 for the Fed to have responded to the bank panics. You then discuss how they were not constrained through most of 1932, as you show with Hsieh. So then if the Fed was constrained by gold, when were they constrained?

The Federal Reserve undertook a moderate expansion in the spring of 1932. What Hsieh and I show is that the moderate expansion did not set off fears of devaluation. This suggests that they had room to maneuver. What we don't have is the experiment in 1932 where they actually take a big enough and sustained enough monetary expansion to actually get us back to trend. Our strong suspicion is that by 1932 things had gotten so horrible that had the Federal Reserve expanded enough to get the money supply back to normal, this would have caused a speculative attack. So in that way, by 1932 the Federal Reserve was constrained. We view our case study as showing that moderate expansion was possible under the gold standard. And, until at least the summer of 1931, moderate expansion might have been very useful. We weren't yet 25 or more percent below trend.

And more importantly, you also say the British had not left gold yet either.

Right. The way we view the 1932 move is as showing that a billion dollars in open market operations was possible, even in 1932 when things were about as bad as they could get. That wasn't enough to actually fix things in 1932, but it probably would have been enough to fix things in 1930 and 1931. So I would say that in 1930 and 1931 the Fed had enough room to maneuver to probably have counteracted the declines in the money supply. By 1932 they had room to maneuver, but not enough to actually deal with the problem that had become so enormous.

You're taking numbers of what they actually did do. These were actual observed behaviors, then asking what would have happened in 1930 and 1931. In the same era and the same institutions.

But there is one thing about the Glass–Steagall Act of 1932. Could they have done that in 1930 and 1931 without Glass–Steagall? That is one of the things I question.
The Glass–Steagall Act allowed the Federal Reserve to count government securities as collateral for Federal Reserve notes. This prevented the Federal Reserve from having to hold gold above the 40 percent mandated level to back notes. There is certainly much debate about whether the Federal Reserve had enough free gold in 1930 and 1931 to increase the money supply without this change in collateral requirements. Our view is that this is probably a non-issue.

I think that had the Fed wanted to expand in 1930 and 1931 and actually found themselves constrained by the gold cover, Congress would have been happy to give them the Glass–Steagall Act earlier. Part of the reason we think this is that it was passed very quickly in 1932 – within a month I think, and with just three hours of debate. It comes back to what you said about the 50 plus bills in Congress to get monetary expansion. People were chomping at the bit for the Fed to do something and the idea that they would have said "no we are going to prevent you from doing this" does not strike me as plausible. The only counter to this that I can think of is perhaps we needed to suffer for three years for people to get to that point, but I don't think that's true. There was enough consensus for expansion, even substantially earlier, that either the Federal Reserve wouldn't have actually been constrained or the Glass–Steagall Act would have just happened earlier.

How did you come about writing that paper with Hsieh?
Chang was a student in a graduate seminar I taught on, among other things, the Great Depression. I think we both felt that the Eichengreen–Temin hypothesis was such a pretty story that people just jumped on the bandwagon before there was hard evidence. It sounds so plausible, it's nice, and it just struck us as missing something. Both Hsieh and I had been thinking that the 1932 experience ought to be able to show us something. I discussed a nice paper by Bordo, Choudhri and Schwartz (1999) at an NBER conference, where they had a giant model of things and asked what would have actually happened to the gold constraint. I remember Eichengreen's response to that paper was it was missing the whole issue. It was not a question of did we have enough gold following these usual channels, it was the specter of speculative attacks.

He claims in his "Still fettered" paper that Bordo, Choudhri and Schwartz (1999) ruled it out a priori because of a linearized model that precluded a speculative attack ahead of time.
I remember in my comments saying "you really ought to look at the 1932

experiment. It seems to me that is going to be your ticket to answering Eichengreen." When they didn't do it, we did (*both chuckle*). Chang had the idea of looking for devaluation expectations using forward exchange rates.

Eichengreen (2002) has indicated that to be convinced by the results of your paper, he would need more evidence on the volume of activity in the forward market and how forward quotations are constructed. Is there any further evidence regarding these issues?
We have done a number of things. One of the things we have looked at is the classic source of data on these forward rates, a study by Einzig (1937). If you look at where Einzig's data come from they look pretty obscure – some particular bank's little circular. So a big part of the work Hsieh and I have done recently is to go back to more primary sources like *The Commercial and Financial Chronicle* and *The Economist*, getting more estimates on forward rates.

That's a difference in the first draft compared to the second draft of this paper then. You used the Einzig data to start with. Now the 2004 draft uses other data sources too.
We use several. We actually stick with the Einzig data but we check it against several other sources to make sure it is a good source. So that's in some sense a more useful thing.

Not that you know anything about checking original sources ... (Parker says jokingly and rolls his eyes)
(*Romer laughs*) Another change that we have made is to look at interest rate differentials. Expectations of devaluation of the dollar should show up as a rise in the US interest rate relative to that in countries firmly attached to gold. And, since bond markets were unquestionably quite thick, this provides an answer to Eichengreen's concern. We find no rise in US interest rates relative to foreign rates during the 1932 open market purchase program.

Another thing that we do is to see if some episodes identified by Eichengreen as times when expectations of devaluation rose show up in our measures. They absolutely do. This, again, gives us more faith in our measures. We also did a lot of work on 1933 because that is one episode where Eichengreen said we should have seen expectations of devaluation and they do not show up strongly in our measures. So we went back to *The Commercial and Financial Chronicle* and other sources and found that it actually was not until pretty close to when we devalued that people realized devaluation was going to happen.

We think it's *very* (*Romer stresses the word* very) helpful to have a stern critic – it makes you really test whether you think you're right. So Barry has been invaluable on the paper because he pushed us. We have convinced ourselves, now we want to convince him. And, of course, even if we are right about the United States and the Fed having a lot of room to maneuver, it does not take away Eichengreen's more fundamental contribution of showing that the gold standard was important in the worldwide diffusion of the Depression.

Do you not think that Eichengreen's (2002) paper, published since your chat with Snowdon (2002, interview conducted in November 1999), is really in the spirit of what you have believed, and I am sure still believe, that different shocks can matter in different countries and yet the gold standard ties them all together as a transmitter of deflation? This seems to fit well with your statements in Snowdon (2002) and also with the opening of your 2005 Encyclopedia Britannica *entry on the Depression. So bank failures and money can be most important for the US and the gold standard has a minor impact while the opposite is true in the United Kingdom. Why can't this be so?*
I think it absolutely can be so. Part of what I find frustrating is the number of people who are outside the literature on the Great Depression who say, "we still don't understand it." I think it is because everyone is saying there must be an easy, two-sentence explanation of the 1930s. Why, for the most severe, extensive, horrible decline in history, would you expect the explanation to be simple? And I think precisely what all of the research, especially in modern times, has concluded is that it is an incredibly complicated phenomenon with different explanations for different countries. That's the way the world is – things are complicated.

You know, one of the reasons why I got into this literature in the first place is because I looked at the literature pre-Bernanke (1983a) and it was all focused on mono-causal explanations; "I'm right and you're wrong and if you don't believe me then you're an idiot." I thought there has to be something more than this (both laugh lightly). *What's your view of the Cecchetti and Karras (1994) real interest rate/decapitalization story? The nominal rate goes to zero, the real rate spikes up, portfolio shifts occur, the value of in-place capital falls, the nature of money changes, deflation and currency holdings place a real, after-tax, riskless floor on expected returns, investment falls and indeed becomes negative. Basically, you can view the early part of the Depression as a decapitalization story of the American economy.*
That real rates spiked up in the early 1930s is certainly true. But, it is important to remember that the deflation that led to this spike was not some exogenous event, but a consequence of plummeting aggregate demand and output. The deflation may then have had additional effects through the financial market imperfections emphasized by Bernanke or mechanisms such as Cecchetti and Karras discuss.

In your 1992 Journal of Economic History *piece "What ended the Great*

Depression?", one of the things that paper says is recovery was brought about by the Cecchetti/Karras story in reverse and the classic monetary transmission mechanism. One of the standard questions is what ended the Great Depression? Now I would like to ask you, what ended the Great Depression?
I think it was monetary expansion, I think you are exactly right.

Could you teach my wife to say that? (laughter).
I think that people may have missed the crucial role of monetary expansion because the nominal interest rate was already near zero before the start of the recovery. In this situation, it looks as though further monetary expansion could not have done anything. But, expansionary monetary policy can cause expectations of inflation. And the evidence we have suggests that this happened. As a result, real interest rates fell dramatically after 1933.

You also said it was investment led.
The recovery was led by interest-sensitive spending – both investment and consumer durables. Indeed, if you look at what it is that rose in that first year of recovery, consumption of services continued to go down, but consumption of durables went up. That, again, exactly fits with a real interest rate story. It's funny, when everyone was worried about Japan and deflation and could they do anything, I kept saying, for goodness sake, we took an economy in the 1930s that was almost 40 percent below trend and monetary expansion worked then. Nominal rates were zero and all of that, and it worked.

Something that has not been emphasized enough that you have spoken about in the past, and I think needs more attention, is that it was the executive branch of government that was the source of this monetary stimulus. Of course, the 1940 book The Golden Avalanche *by Graham and Whittlesey was the first to talk about the influx of gold from Europe. But you are one of the few sources that speaks of the Treasury's role. You discuss it in your 1992* Journal of Economic History *paper, "What ended the Great Depression?" but you lay out the mechanics more in your 1993* Journal of Economic Perspectives *paper. I want to emphasize that everyone said the money supply went up, the gold came running in, but you are one of the few to emphasize that it was the Treasury doing it. I think that needs to be highlighted and whenever we talk about monetary expansion during the recovery the Treasury's name needs to be mentioned.*
I agree completely. I think the only thing I would say is the Fed could have messed up. I give them some credit for standing idly by while the Treasury was monetizing this gold inflow. In the early 1930s, they certainly showed themselves well able to do stupid things, but this time they didn't. I think that does deserve some credit.

You have said the profession understands the Great Depression very well. Yet the work of Cole and Ohanian (2000) and also Prescott (1999) indicates that they consider the Great Depression to still be a large puzzle. What is your assessment of the research findings they have recently been publishing?
I think it is wonderful when anyone works on the Great Depression. But, honestly, I think some of this research is a giant step backwards. The models that it uses to analyze the 1930s are absurdly unrealistic and limited. They simply could not answer the questions the authors want to answer. The authors, however, draw extreme conclusions from very crude evidence.

Paul Samuelson has said that a Pareto-optimal real business cycle explanation of the Depression is foolish. He said that in the 1998 Federal Reserve of Boston symposium you were involved in. He said it is foolish to think that "at one time in 1929 folks everywhere developed a desire to substitute intertemporally leisure off the job for good paychecks."
Oh, you mean the Great Vacation? (*roaring laughter*).

I have never heard that one. Let's leave it like that and move on. (Parker is still laughing) *Why do you suppose your 1994 paper "Remeasuring business cycles" has not gotten more attention?*
I think part of the reason my paper did not have more impact is that people don't care that much about the dating of cycles any more. I struggle with this myself. Is there something special with what the NBER calls a recession versus just looking at the time series and the quarter-to-quarter and year-to-year movements and things like that? I think that people may just care less about when the actual dates were and care more about whether we have a good time series on what GDP is. Still, I feel that there was something fundamentally right about my "Remeasuring business cycles" paper – pointing out this change in methodology. I think the carriers of the torch for the old NBER methodology, Geoffrey Moore and Victor Zarnowitz, remembered the Burns and Mitchell of the 1940s. I think their instinct was that the early dates somehow had to have been set the same way as the dates after 1940. What I found so interesting was the idea that in fact those early dates, the reference dates, were set first and then all that beautiful analysis was done after. Nobody focused in on how those early dates were set. My vision is that the early dates were sketched down based on the few, typically detrended series they had, and those just kind of got stuck. I viewed that as a really important insight, but I will agree people have not cared all that much. I think it's just mainly that there are statistical procedures now that emphasize continuous data and that is mainly what we look at.

But you were able to dig through their notes and find out how they went from growth rates to levels. You said, "It's right here," but people just kind of

yawned and moved on I guess. There really hasn't been much more said about the paper.
Well, it's a bit sad.

I looked at the literature on the Great Depression in the early 1980s and found it to be a standstill. It was a product of the tired monetarist/Keynesian debate. Moreover looking at Brunner's collection of papers in his 1981 book The Great Depression Revisited, *it was pretty clear that not much forward progress was in the pipeline. What do you see as the breakthrough contributions that have brought us to where we are today in our understanding of the Great Depression?*
That's an excellent question. Bernanke (1983a) showing us that you could do interesting, modern research on this episode certainly reinvigorated things. But I think it's broader than that. I feel that there was something magical about the mid-1980s for macro history; there just was an outpouring of interest, a synergy, something like that. We had a lot of new tools and I think there was a new appreciation for statistical analysis. So much of the previous literature had been books and not inherently statistical or empirical. So I think it's just a mixture of a few papers getting people excited and then a lot of people working on macro history more generally.

But there's also something to the idea that this is the next generation taking a fresh look at the old questions, isn't there?
I think there is. I think it is a new generation realizing that the Great Depression was fundamentally important. I wonder, as we're sitting here pondering this, what role the new economic history played.

Cliometrics?
Exactly. The revolution in economic history analysis that started in the late 1960s. What had been questions we answered just with words, we started to actually get some old data and evaluate empirically and analytically. I think some of what we saw in the early 1980s is taking that philosophy and looking back at the macro economy, not just at slavery or some of the issues that have been so hot in the new economic history.

What are some of the lessons from the Great Depression we have learned or that need to be relearned?
I think we have learned the biggest one, which is that the government is not powerless to stop a major depression. So when I teach my students all the difficulties of stabilization policy, the lags and timing and whatever, I always say just keep this in perspective. If we are ever hit with a major depressionary shock, none of these things are going to matter. You step on the gas any way you can. And I think the lesson from the Great Depression is that it will work.

I think that is what we saw in the mid-1930s. When we did eventually have a big monetary expansion, the economy unquestionably recovered. I think that is a lesson we learned and it was a good one to have learned.

Could it happen again?
Could it happen again? No, I don't think so. When I describe what happened in the Great Depression, it was a sequence of mistakes. We had contractionary aggregate demand shocks, first coming from the stock market crash, then from the financial panics, then we raised taxes, then we raised interest rates. It was cumulative. So part of the reason why it was such a big decline is we had this confluence of very contractionary shocks. Whether we could ever have that confluence again, I'm kind of skeptical. But even if we did, I don't believe we would compound them the way we did. Even if we had a major stock market crash, even if we had East Asia go down and we had huge financial panics, I think we have learned from the Great Depression that we need to do something. Alan Greenspan in 1987, confronted with a stock market crash, didn't say "hmmm ... what should we do?" He was just all over it. I think that is the crucial difference. We could easily face very big shocks, but our tools, even though they're imperfect, are good enough. I think we are smart enough now that we would use them.

That's all I have. Thanks so much, Professor.

Barry Eichengreen

Barry Eichengreen received his Ph.D. from Yale University in 1979 and he is currently George C. Pardee and Helen N. Pardee Professor of Economics and Political Science at the University of California, Berkeley. As any student of the Great Depression is well aware, no inquiry into the causes and nature of the Great Depression is complete without a thorough examination of his 1992 book *Golden Fetters: The Gold Standard and the Great Depression, 1919–1939*. As indicated in this book's first interview, Peter Temin credits Eichengreen's 1985 paper with Jeffrey Sachs for the impetus that led to Temin's research agenda on the relation between the gold standard and the Depression. Although there was previous work that had been done on the gold standard, such as Brown (1940) among others, there is no doubt that Barry Eichengreen is responsible for deepening our understanding of the gold standard and for returning the prominence of the gold standard in explaining the Great Depression to our collective modern consciousness. I spoke with Barry Eichengreen in his office at the University of California on March 9, 2005.

Could you please provide some background on how you became involved with the literature on the Great Depression.
I became interested in economic history as the result of a wonderful course taught by Flora Gill in my senior year. I knew I wanted to go into the field but I couldn't quite figure out how to do it. Between being an undergraduate at the University of California at Santa Cruz and going on to graduate school, I went to the Brookings Institution to work as a research assistant. Brookings has a great library, which I used to absorb the contents of the *Journal of Economic History*. Reading the journals is a good way to understand a field, just as we tell our students. These were also the Nixon and Ford years, which meant that many influential policy economists were in exile at Brookings, and working under their tutelage gave me a desire to do economic history in a way that resonated with the concerns of policy makers. The literature on the Great Depression was and is an obvious place for economic historians and policy makers to meet. The rest is history, as they say.

Are we any closer to learning how economic policies and economic policy

leadership come to be changed and how policy mistakes are more quickly recognized and reversed? Or does it take utter crisis and catastrophe?
Policy makers certainly learn from crises, as your question implies, but they also learn in more normal times. The conduct of US monetary policy in the last 20 years is a good example. There were episodes of great excitement, for example in 1987 and 1998, but ultimately these don't qualify as full-fledged crises. The progress made in the conduct of US monetary policy – and I think it is considerable – was not made in an environment of crisis. You can see this in emerging markets as well. The crises of 1994–95 and 1997–98 were catalysts for reform and learning, but officials there have continued making progress in strengthening policies and institutions in less turbulent times.

You have said in the past that you see the first year of the Depression as the place where much of the debate still lies. Is the first year of the Depression still that much of a mystery and if so what is left to explain?
I have just finished lecturing the first-year graduate students on the Great Depression. Their reaction – perhaps not unprompted – was that the onset of the Depression is still the phase that is the hardest to understand. My argument is that looking at the monetary tightening of the late 1920s in a global context and considering the implications of US monetary tightening for the rest of the world gets us some way toward understanding why the downturn was so severe. But I would acknowledge that my story about how monetary tightening in the US induced monetary tightening in other countries because of how it was superimposed on a fragile pattern of international settlements and transmitted internationally through the gold standard may not be the entire story. This is why economic historians like Christina Romer continue to look at factors like the stock market crash and others look at events like the Smoot–Hawley tariff.

I was also interested to read your 1989 paper "The political economy of the Smoot–Hawley Tariff" and discovered its impact was mainly through its disruption of the international financial system through the redistribution of gold reserves, one more mechanism for the failure of the gold standard. You said previously that the focus of the last 20 years on money and finance has been real intellectual progress and other matters are ultimately beside the point. Is the Smoot–Hawley tariff one example of issues that are now beside the point?
I wouldn't go as far as to say the Smoot–Hawley tariff was beside the point. But the Depression was fundamentally a macroeconomic event; it was fundamentally about macroeconomic policies. This is why I argue that monetary and fiscal policies hold the key to understanding it. I would acknowledge that the Smoot–Hawley tariff had implications for how the Depression unfolded. It made it more difficult for primary producers to export. It made it more difficult for heavily indebted countries to service their debts.

It contributed to financial difficulties and deflationary pressure in the rest of the world. But, beyond that, its effects were mainly redistributive. The main thing the tariff did, in other words, was to redistribute the burden of the Depression from the United States to the rest of the world. Hence, if we're trying to understand the severity of the global depression and not just its national incidence, I wouldn't focus on the tariff. Another way of putting the point is that economists, including myself, instinctually dislike tariffs because of inefficiencies they introduce – because of how they disrupt the rational allocation of resources between sectors and activities. But the Great Depression was fundamentally about underutilized resources. Putting those resources back to work at almost anything and in almost any sector would have been an improvement. There may have been allocative inefficiencies, in other words, but it takes a lot of Harberger triangles to fill an Okun's gap.

In your "Still fettered after all these years" paper, the way that you linked the timing of the peripheral countries and how they went down along with Germany and so on, ahead of the United States, I think is a very compelling point as well. The gold standard ties those all together.
I wasn't first to make it. You can see the point in the *Economic Surveys* of the League of Nations published in the 1930s. One of those surveys contains a wonderful table listing the years when different countries began experiencing the downturn. It shows how the business cycle peaked in a number of other countries ahead of the United States. When you look at that table you're immediately led to question US-centric views of the Depression.

Peter Temin credits your 1985 paper with Jeffrey Sachs as the catalyst that sent him off on the gold standard path in the 1980s. I looked at the literature on the Great Depression in the early 1980s and found it to be at a standstill. It was the product of a tired monetarist–Keynesian debate. Moreover, looking at Brunner's 1981 book The Great Depression Revisited *it was clear that not much forward progress was in the pipeline. What then do you see as the breakthrough contribution that has brought us to where we are today in understanding the Great Depression? Maybe we should say it was Eichengreen and Sachs (1985)?*
I don't think there was a single breakthrough; that's not how economics and economic history develop. Charles Kindleberger's book *The World in Depression* was very important to my own thinking. It's too bad that Charlie's discursive style has led that book to be neglected by economists. But Kindleberger understood the role of financial factors in the Depression, something that otherwise dropped from sight in the 1970s. Ben Bernanke's 1983a paper on the nonmonetary effects of the Depression was important for restating those arguments about financial fragility and financial instability in a way more accessible to economists. I do like to think that the paper I did with

Jeff Sachs, for which he deserves an awful lot of credit, was important for showing how a comparative framework that looks at the experiences of a number of countries in a systemic way can shed more light on the event and for developing the argument that you have to think of the Depression as a global phenomenon and not just as an event spreading from the United States.

You look at the literature now and a lot of it is a comparative framework approach. Bernake and Carey (1996) and Cole and Ohanian (2004b) all look at a multitude of countries.
That's right, but, as I said, a number of people had already done this. There was Kindleberger in his narrative way, the League of Nations studies I just mentioned, and the work of William Adams Brown for the National Bureau of Economic Research in the 1930s and 1940s. Still, this kind of comparative, open economy work had largely receded from the research horizon, partly because economies after World War II were more closed, and partly because most economic theory was closed economy theory. Friedman and Schwartz's (1963) book was the template for studies of the Depression, and theirs was basically a closed economy model. While international factors appear in their book here and there, fundamentally theirs was a monetary history of the United States. It oriented most of the work done from the 1960s into the 1980s toward US experience and US data. The way Peter Temin reformulated and attacked their thesis in *Did Monetary Forces Cause the Great Depression* (1976a) is representative of the intellectual reaction.

Do you agree with Michael Kitson (2003) who said that the causes of the Great Depression are one thing, but the extent of the Depression is due to the operation of the gold standard?
As I said earlier, I also think that the gold standard was important for the first phase – the onset – of the Great Depression. But the gold standard story really comes into its own when we analyze the depth and duration of the Depression. To be sure, the gold standard is not the only relevant variable; financial structures and policy responses other than those directly connected to the gold standard mattered as well – limits on bank branching in the United States, for example. But it won't surprise you that I think that focusing on the role of the gold standard does shed important light on a number of those responses.

Are Kitson's assumptions concerning the gold standard also correct or are they stated more strongly than they need to be? First, it assumes the global law of one price. Second it assumes that the demand for money is stable. Third it assumes that monetary authorities do not intervene to prevent increased gold reserves from adding to the money supply. And fourth it assumes that the burden of adjustment would be borne by prices not quantities.
All of Michael's assumptions are stronger than necessary and stronger than I

would make. The key element of the gold standard is the commitment on the part of central banks and the societies of which they are a part to peg the domestic currency price of gold. This then has implications for prices, money and credit conditions and all the things that flow from them. But the key implications will follow in a world where the law of one price holds only loosely, where the demand for money can shift, and where other conditions posited in textbook models don't hold.

Assumption 4, where the flexibility comes in prices versus output. Is this not where your story about the emergence of labor comes into play?
Before the First World War adjustment was smoother and less painful because wages and prices could adjust more easily. Labor markets were not as structured as they became subsequently. Tamim Bayoumi and I did some work together in 1996 attempting to recover the slopes of the aggregate supply and aggregate demand functions before 1913 and in the interwar period for a number of countries (Bayoumi and Eichengreen, 1996). Our analysis does suggest that labor markets were more flexible before the Great War than they became after in both the US and UK. Flexibility declined in the US because of the emergence of personnel departments in large corporations, in the UK because of the adoption of unemployment insurance, among other things. In my view, this is one of several differences between the prewar period and the interwar period that made the interwar gold standard more fragile and difficult to operate. Others include the spread of political democracy, the development of explicit theories linking monetary policy to the trade cycle, and the level of unemployment had implications for the credibility of central banks' commitment to the gold standard. Those changes were, if anything, as important as changes in the structure of labor markets and product markets.

You said in Golden Fetters *that "there was little perception that policies required for external balance were inconsistent with domestic prosperity" and also "[t]he policies required to defend it proved inconsistent with economic stability." Do you also agree, given your statements above, that the gold standard was structurally flawed and ultimately doomed to failure and the attempt to preserve it was what produced the Great Depression, as Peter Temin has said?.*
Absolutely.

OK, we'll move on. Your comment in the 1988 Contemporary Policy Issues *paper viewing the interwar gold exchange standard as a "non-cooperative game in which rival countries engage in a competitive struggle for available reserves" was very descriptive of what went on and is very well written. In this and many other papers we see the seeds for* Golden Fetters. *Were you working on the book at the time you wrote the 1988 paper?*

People write books in different ways. *Golden Fetters* was a book that I had thought vaguely about from the time when I got my Ph.D. in 1979 until the middle of the 1980s. My work with Jeff Sachs was important for helping me figure out how to structure the argument. I then worked on the manuscript about half time from 1985 to 1990, partly by writing articles that helped me sort through issues. But I thought then, as I think now, that articles and books serve different purposes and should speak to different audiences. So the articles that led up to *Golden Fetters* contain more technical material than the book itself. But they were important for helping me to frame the issues in a broader way that speaks to a larger audience.

That book must have been a massive amount of work.
I certainly appreciate all the nice things you're saying about it. It's the scholarship that I'm proudest of.

I have a quote here from James Hamilton I would like to read for you: "[t]he most important element in the success of any national gold standard is the public's confidence that the government's fiscal soundness and political imperatives will enable it to pursue indefinitely a monetary policy consistent with long-term price stability and continuous convertibility. By this criterion, returning to the international gold standard during the mid-1920s could not have come at a worse time or for poorer reasons. Clearly, the gold standard was reinstated precisely because *the fiscal and political chaos since 1914 had made it impossible for many governments to reform their monetary policies in the absence of a gold standard." Additionally, "It sometimes is asserted that a gold standard introduces 'discipline' into the conduct of monetary and fiscal policy where none existed before. Indeed, this was the primary reason that the world returned to an international gold standard during the 1920s. I can not think of a more naive and more dangerous notion. A government lacking discipline in monetary and fiscal policy in the absence of a gold standard likely also lacks the discipline and credibility necessary for successfully adhering to a gold standard. Substantial uncertainty about the future inevitably will result as speculators anticipate changes in the terms of gold convertibility. This institutionalizes a system susceptible to large and sudden inflows or outflows of capital and to destabilizing monetary policy if authorities must resort to great extremes to reestablish credibility." That is in a companion paper in the same issue as yours in the 1988* Contemporary Policy Issues.
Jim Hamilton is an important contributor to the literature on the gold standard and the Great Depression. Maybe because *Contemporary Policy Issues* is not the most prominent journal in the field or because Jim doesn't have my habit of publishing the same ideas more than once, his contribution doesn't always get the credit it deserves. Another explanation for why he is not always cited

is that his *Contemporary Policy Issues* piece doesn't entirely spell out the argument. The way I would put it is that the prewar gold standard operated smoothly because there existed an overriding commitment to monetary policies adapted to the maintenance of convertibility. Activist fiscal policy was not something on the radar screens of governments and societies. World War I then upset the apple cart. Monetary and fiscal policies were subordinated to the war effort. They were redirected toward other goals. This provided a rationale for interest groups to then attempt, following the war's conclusion, to redirect them once again, to still other social goals. As a result, the idea that monetary and fiscal policy was subordinated to the maintenance of convertibility was turned on its head. The result was that the interwar gold standard exhibited the same fragility as all subsequent pegged exchange rate regimes. This kind of arrangement can work only if the authorities place the maintenance of the currency peg above all other goals. But in democratic societies, doing so is not always possible. So in 1931 countries discovered that there was a conflict between the monetary austerity needed for the maintenance of the gold standard and the monetary accommodation needed to stabilize the banking system, address the unemployment problem and get the economy going again. This looks an awful lot like the situation in Argentina at the beginning of the present decade.

While you may be correct in your "Still fettered" paper that it is not universally agreed that the structure and operation of the gold standard explains the sharp downturns in the early 1930s, it seems that the overwhelming evidence is that its abandonment was the single greatest factor in shaping the recovery, as shown by Choudhri and Kochin (1980) and also in your Figure 1 in Eichengreen and Sachs (1985). This seems to be one of the strongest empirical macro relations we have in all of economic history. Are you comfortable with that?
Absolutely. I appreciate you reminding me of Choudhri and Kochin. It is clear they were onto the same ideas and, if anything, that they were onto them earlier. I was actually unaware of their article until Michael Bordo brought it to my attention ten years later. But I should have known it.

Your Figure 1 in that paper is overwhelming. It graphs the relationship between exchange rates and industrial production and it's like one wants to say "Eureka, I think I've found it."
I show it to the Ph.D. students every year on the grounds that a figure is worth a thousand words. Jose Campa has a nice article in the 1990 *Journal of Economic History* (he was a graduate student at Harvard when I was there) that does the same thing for Latin America, where the same relationship fits even better. And his graphics program is even better! Actually, you can find the same story in words once again in the League of Nations publications of the

1930s. But I remember presenting the paper for the first time to the Cliometrics conference in 1983, and the reaction to the figure was much stronger than the reaction to the theoretical and econometric analysis that followed. Given that we had ten data points, a simple visual analysis is not inappropriate. I remember that the Cliometrics conference includes a ceremonial banquet with the award of satirical prizes. As a first-time presenter I received the Peter Temin Award for "drawing the strongest conclusions on the basis of the least data." I was honored. Yes, Peter was there.

What is the nature of the "veneer of disputation" regarding the explanations of the Great Depression, as you coined the term? Are people talking past one another, is that your meaning? "Different elements dominated in different countries" as you said, and all parties can make a contribution to a complete explanation of the worldwide Depression.
Do you have a little more of the context of that comment?

It is from your "Still fettered" paper.
Obviously scholars continue to debate the Depression, as they should. They continue to question the applicability of general arguments to the experience of individual countries, as they should. But I think there has developed an understanding of the fact that the Depression was a macroeconomic phenomenon and that in order to understand it you have to focus on macroeconomic policies. And to understand those policies you have to look at the institutional context within which they were formulated, which means the gold standard broadly defined. So one of the things that Peter Temin and I argued in our piece in the Balderston (2003) book is that you have to think about the gold standard not just as a set of monetary arrangements and institutions but also more broadly as kind of a mind frame within which policy was formulated.

The mentalité as you coined it.
Yes, as a mind frame and not simply as a convertibility rule. In addition, you have to think about the Depression as something that unfolded globally. I think most of that has been accepted, notwithstanding the veneer of disputation.

You have been saying for a long time now that "arguing that one international factor played an important role need not imply that another is invalid. Similarly arguing that international forces contributed to the severity of the Depression need not preclude a role for domestic factors in the US and elsewhere." You said that in 1988. And in Golden Fetters *you said that the gold standard is one of several factors contributing to the Great Depression. I mean it is not that one person is right and the other is wrong, is it?*
The new literature emphasizing the importance of the gold standard builds on

earlier contributions that focus on national policies and national cases. There is no incompatibility. In some cases, some of those national policies and cases can be understood better when they're related to the influence of international forces. In other cases they can be thought of independently. For example, there is the debate over the role of fiscal policy in the US and Hoover's "confidence-restoring" tax increases in particular. At one level those are purely US policies that one can try to understand in terms of US politics. On the other hand they were viewed as necessary for maintaining confidence in the dollar's gold parity. You can look at episodes and events like this one both from this international perspective and purely domestically.

Milton Friedman has said in my book and has said recently in a 2004 Cato Journal *article that if he was going to write the chapter "The Great Contraction" all over again he would give a greater role to France. Isn't this what you have been trying to say for 15 years and is this not progress?*
Here I would also give credit to Bob Mundell, an important early scholar who appreciated the role of the international system and of France in particular. He advised a Yale Ph.D. student in history, H. Clark Johnson, who wrote a book, *Gold, France, and the Great Depression*, that made this point. And there is the historian of the Bank of France, Kenneth Mouré, at the University of California at Santa Barbara, who has long emphasized France's role. If you want to think about the role of Asian central banks in the current international system, you have to think both about the Bank of Japan and the People's Bank of China. In the interwar period, similarly, you have to think about both the Fed and the Bank of France.

You have said "[i]n the 1930s providing large amounts of liquidity to the banking system almost certainly would have violated gold-standard statutes; doing so would have raised questions about whether the authorities attached priority to the maintenance of the exchange rate peg relative to other economic and social goals." That was in your "Viewpoint: understanding the Great Depression" paper that your "Still fettered after all these years" paper morphed in to. Is this the same thing as saying that the lender of last resort function for the Fed was severely constrained and is this why you think the Fed failed to act as the lender of last resort?
Yes, I do believe that the Fed felt constrained. A narrow formulation emphasizing the shortage of free gold would focus on 1932. No one questions that there was plenty of free gold in the United States in 1930, or that the cupboard was bare by 1933. The debate therefore centers on 1932. Again, people like Peter Temin and I would emphasize the broader mindset that said that even if you have the free reserves to back some additional provision of money and credit to the banking system, doing so was not the right way of going about a central bank's business. Michael Bordo has emphasized in a

number of publications that before 1913 it was possible to suspend gold convertibility temporarily and let the currency go to a discount and, in that context, to provide additional liquidity to the banking system, since everyone knew that commitment to gold was strong and that convertibility at the pre-war rate would eventually be restored. This kind of temporary suspension and liquidity creation were precisely what was not possible in the interwar period because the credibility of the commitment to go back to gold at the prewar parity was in question. Central banks did not want to do anything that raised questions in the minds of investors.

So it was out of the question then?
Temporary suspensions were out of the question for good reason. Their infeasibility reflected changed political realities and the diminished credibility of the monetary authorities.

Here is one figure that I have been particularly impressed with from an article by Steve Cecchetti in 1998, "Understanding the Great Depression: lessons for current policy" (I show Eichengreen Figure 2 of this paper). This is discounting behavior from 1919 to 1935 and I want your impression of it. Would similar discounting behavior in 1920-21 have even been possible during the Great Depression? One of his arguments is that the Fed failed to be the lender of last resort and he offered this graph as a demonstration of that. Would it have been possible to do what they did before?
Conventional discounting policies would not have been possible because the supply of commercial bills was drying up. To be sure, Friedman and Schwartz and others make the point that there were other devices that the Fed could have utilized had it been serious about providing more credit to the financial system. It could have engaged in open market operations, purchasing government bonds and bills. It could have purchased foreign exchange. This debate is a lot like the debate over what the Bank of Japan could have done to counter deflation in the mid-1990s. A central bank serious about deflation can do a variety of things to inject money and credit into the economy. But in the United States in the early 1930s, as in Japan in the mid-1990s, that wasn't regarded as the appropriate way for a central bank to go about its business.

Because of the gold standard mentalité?
Yes, but in addition because of what my colleague Brad DeLong would refer to as liquidationist ideology. And because of what Allan Meltzer would call the Riefler–Burgess doctrine. These were two forms of the argument that the Fed should only provide as much credit as was being demanded for regular business transactions as opposed to speculative business. The gold standard was a part of that general mind frame, but the attitude was a larger one. It implied that central banks should follow mechanical rules and be largely

passive in meeting the demand for money and credit, not that it should manage the economy in the manner that we expect today.

Am I correct in saying that I hear elements of the Austrian credit boom/overinvestment story as well as Moses Abramovitz's (undated) long swing story of the Depression in your "Viewpoint" paper and also in your 2004 Research in Economic History *piece with Mitchener "The Great Depression as a credit boom gone wrong?"*
Both Moses Abramovitz and the Austrians influenced my thinking(Mo for a long time, the Austrian School more recently). The story of the Great Depression is not complete without a role for technology and long swings, a point long emphasized by Abramovitz. Other scholars like Michael Bernstein, a classmate of mine in graduate school, whose book *The Great Depression* came out at about the same time as mine, emphasized technology and real factors.

Isn't there also a new book by Perez (2002)?
Yes, Carlota Perez's book has resonated with people in financial markets because of their sense that the interaction of technology with financial dynamics was important in both the 1920s and the 1990s. In periods where new technologies, like radio in the 1920s or the internet in the 1990s, are first commercialized, financial markets tend to overestimate their immediate potential. This is part of the backdrop to the stock market boom of the 1920s. It took me a long time to appreciate how much of this story had been anticipated by the Austrians. The 2004 piece that I did with Kris Mitchener in *Research in Economic History* was initially commissioned by the Bank for International Settlements for a conference where they asked us to think about the lessons of history for the current debate over whether central banks should react preemptively to asset booms and bubbles. I hadn't thought a lot about the issue from that point of view, but it led me into the work of the Austrian economists, whose contribution I appreciate more now than before.

You discuss how difficult it is to identify bubbles, but can bubbles have particularly nasty consequences if they happen in a deflationary economy? It seems to me to be where the nastiest parts come from. We had bubbles in the past and will have again, but in an inflationary economy. Could it be that it is deflation that set them off to be as bad as they were during the Depression?
Rather than referring to a deflationary environment, I would emphasize the combination of price stability with very accommodating money and credit conditions – which is what we saw in both the 1920s and the 1990s. Subdued inflation and at the same time a willingness on the part of central banks to provide as much money and credit as the financial markets require is what allowed stock markets to react as vigorously as they did to optimism about the

commercial potential of new technologies. In the 1920s it was the Fed's tightening that set the stage for the bubble to burst and then its inaction that led to the deflation and the Depression.

Do you think then that the central bank has a role to be an arbiter of security prices? Is there some limited role there for them?
I hesitate to recommend pre-emptive action in response to movements in asset prices because of the well-known difficulty of identifying when asset prices are out of line. We are much better at identifying "unsustainable" increases in asset prices after than before the fact. But I do believe that central banks, when they look at inflation risks and form their inflation targets, should define the price level broadly to include not only the prices of goods and services but some real and financial assets as well.

The secret meeting of central bankers on Long Island in 1927, where did you dig that fact up?
Your question reminds me that our conversation wouldn't be complete – indeed, that it shouldn't have gotten this far – without mentioning Stephen Clarke's book *Central Bank Cooperation 1924–1931*. Clarke documented that episode on the basis of the Fed's archives and the Harrison Papers at Columbia University. Clarke's book was fundamentally about the international aspects of monetary policy. But it is another one of those books that is very dense in terms of detail and that demands a lot of the reader. It isn't assigned often in graduate courses, which may be why it doesn't have the citation count it deserves.

Why do you think the US did not follow the United Kingdom off the gold standard in September 1931?
For one thing, until Britain went off the gold standard in 1931 there really hadn't been a country that had voluntarily taken that step. The UK was driven off, and only at that point a number of other members of the sterling area chose to go off voluntarily. After a year or so it became clear that they hadn't suffered the devastating economic consequences or the shock to confidence that had been predicted – quite the opposite. But back in September and October of 1931, it wasn't clear that the consequences would be so benign. The title of my book is taken from a newspaper article written by Keynes right when Britain went off gold. He concluded that the consequences would be positive on balance, but he was still cautious. And he was very much in the minority.

Your piece with Temin in Balderston (2003) explains the counterfactual of what would have happened if the US and Germany had followed the UK off gold, rather like what you had in mind in Eichengreen and Sachs (1985). Is

that not correct?
What we are saying is that these counterfactual observations would fit right on the regression line relating exchange rates to economic recovery in Eichengreen and Sachs (1985).

I asked Temin and now I ask you, since you two have the best multinational credentials: does it not follow from your counterfactual that it could be the case that without the Great Depression there is no World War II?
What did Peter say?

He said that sounds right to him.
Peter has worked more on the connections between the interwar period and World War II, so I defer to him. Certainly we can say that less economic distress would have done less to discredit mainstream politicians and contribute to the collapse of the Weimar Republic. But would the course of the 1930s have been that different in the end and would World War II have been averted? Answering that question requires a braver user of the counterfactual than I.

The work of McCallum (1990), Fackler and Parker (1994), Bordo, Choudhri and Schwartz (1995) and the recent paper by Christiano, Motto and Rostagno (2003) contain counterfactual experiments that ask "how would the Depression have been different if the Fed had kept the money supply growing at the rate it was growing in the 1920s?" Do you see these as useful and informative or are they ahistorical exercises?
I see this work as ahistorical in the sense that a constant money supply growth rate is hard to motivate or reconcile with the institutions of the time. I would start with different assumptions about the rate of growth of the global gold stock and derive different results about the rate of growth of the money supply from that. And I would make different assumptions about the willingness of central banks to accumulate and maintain foreign exchange reserves and use that as the basis for deriving counterfactual monetary policies.

The multiplier of the world money stock would be one of those quantities, correct?
The multiplier would depend on the state of confidence, on the stability of banking systems, and on the willingness of central banks to supplement gold with foreign exchange. All of those things depend in turn on deeper variables and parameters. Starting with an assumption about the outcome, the rate of growth of the money supply, is too much of a simplification.

I have to ask you, since you spoke of it in Golden Fetters: *do you think the Fed saw 1929–1930 as a repeat of 1920–21 and thus saw no reason for alarm?*

The contrasts and similarities between these two periods to me are interesting and I would like you to expand on them, please.
1920–21 was the only previous downturn in the Fed's intellectual portfolio, so it was natural that they looked back on that episode. Unfortunately, they didn't realize the extent to which circumstances had changed. They had changed domestically as a result of growing financial fragilities. And they had changed internationally, since after 1925 other countries were yoked to the United States by the gold standard.

But if they looked at it and said "you know we have been through this before" and acted the same, they were just asking for trouble, were they not?
Right, both because the resiliency of the economy was now less and because the synchronization of business cycles was now greater.

I would like to know your evaluation of the Hsieh and Romer (2004) paper. They claim that capital was immobile during the interwar period while your "Still fettered" paper says that capital mobility was anything but low. Which is it?
You're not trying to sow dissension within the halls of the Berkeley economics department? (*laughter*).

Not at all, nothing I say is hostile and if you construe it to be you have made a terrible mistake (laughter).
In fact, Chang and Christy also argue that capital mobility was relatively high. Our disagreement is over the extent to which the Fed was constrained in adopting and pursuing expansionary monetary policy in the Depression. As I said, there are three key episodes where the Fed could have done something, in 1930, in 1932, and in 1933. The question is whether or not it was constrained by the scarcity of free gold. We agree on 1930. The US had plenty of gold and the Fed was not constrained. To the extent that it didn't respond, this was for other reasons. We agree on 1933. The Fed was tightly constrained by the exhaustion of its free gold reserves and the run on the US gold standard. But we disagree on 1932, when the Fed began to initiate expansionary operations in response to Congressional pressure. Then in August something changed. Perhaps Congress adjourned, as members went back to their home districts to campaign for re-election, relieving the pressure on the Fed. Perhaps the loss of gold reserves that had occurred over the summer of 1932 had come to so alarm Federal Reserve policy makers that they abandoned their expansionary open market operations. Maybe both factors contributed to the policy shift. That's the debate.

Do you think that the Fed could have taken unilateral action in 1930?
I do. In 1930 the Fed still had leeway to inject more money and credit into the

financial system and reduce deflationary pressures. In 1930 it was not the gold standard, narrowly defined, but the gold standard mentalité, the liquidationist viewpoint, the real bills doctrine, the Riefler–Burgess doctrine, or whatever you want to call it that convinced the members ofthe Federal Reserve Board that aggressive action to counter the Depression was not called for.

There have been some questions that you had about the volume of activity in the forward market and how those forward quotations were constructed in the Einzig (1937) data. Has there been any progress on answering those to your satisfaction?
I would value further research that shed light on the operation of the forward market in the interwar period. Einzig's book, published in 1937, is notable mainly for an appendix that contains not only weekly spot exchange rate quotations but forward exchange rate quotations as well. But we still know very little about the volume of transactions, the representativeness of those quotations, and how the forward foreign exchange market worked in the interwar period. If there's no forward discount, does that really tell us that the majority of investors believed in the stability of the gold standard and were not worried about a devaluation of the dollar? Even when you get up into early 1933, when the writing was on the wall, Einzig's forward discount quotations do not suggest that there were significant expectations of dollar devaluation. So I would like to see more research on the depth and liquidity of the market.

In the paper you and Temin wrote in Balderston (2003) you have a salient sentence, "The choice between deflation over devaluation was the most important factor determining the course of the Depression." "Devaluation did not become a respectable option until much later – until after an unprecedented crisis had rendered the respectable unrespectable, and vice versa." I would just like to tell you I think that is a very powerful sentence, very clear in its meaning and with a simple elegance.
I wish I could remember which one of the co-authors wrote it *(laughter)*.

We'll just have joint custody, how about that? You have said the heavy lifting of explaining the Depression has been done. However, the work of Cole and Ohanian (2000, 2004a,b) and Prescott (1999) indicates that they consider the Great Depression to still be a rather large puzzle. What is your assessment of the research findings that they have recently been producing and publishing?
I applaud their continued use of international comparisons as a way of testing hypotheses more rigorously. It's easy to construct a story for one country. It's harder to develop a story that stands the test of many national experiences. I applaud their readiness to challenge assumptions that people like Temin, Bernanke, Romer and myself take for granted. But they have to work very hard to reintroduce elements like a high degree of wage and price flexibility and

then still to be able to begin to account for the Depression. I see them as descendents of Lucas and Rapping (1972). Recall that this was one of the very first new-classical calibration exercises. What Lucas and Rapping basically did was to assume a neoclassical economy, subject it to a large shock and see whether it could reproduce the Great Depression. Their conclusion was no, it couldn't. The scholars you name have essentially been adding complications to that model – additional rigidities, additional disaggregation, and modest externalities of various sorts – in order to reconcile a well-behaved neoclassical model with a very poorly behaved macro economy. As that research program continues, they will converge to pretty much the same place as people starting from the other direction, who don't assume well-behaved markets and symmetric information.

Do you see any role for debt deflation in propagating the Great Depression?
I think Bernanke (1983a) made that case convincingly for the United States. Bernanke's article has two components, one which emphasized the disintermediation caused by bank failures and the other one which emphasized debt deflation. It's regrettable that the second of the two components, the one about debt deflation, received less attention. Richard Grossman and I wrote an article that appeared in a 1997 book that Forrest Capie and Geoffrey Wood edited that tried to apply the mechanism to other countries. We found that while debt deflation is important for the United States, it seems to have been somewhat less important for other countries. There are good reasons why debt deflation probably matters more for the United States. Deflation was greater here than in most other places. The US had a more developed financial system than many countries, so there was more debt, more household debt in particular. Rick Mishkin's (1978) piece on household balance sheets in the Depression, which I read as an important contribution to the modern debt deflation literature, was an early effort to make this point.

What are some of the lessons that have been learned or that have to be relearned from the Great Depression?
For me the fundamental lessons have to do with the importance of a coherent policy framework. This is something that countries must grow at home. It cannot simply be imported from abroad through the adoption of a particular exchange rate regime. A well-defined policy framework requires not just central bank independence but also a clear definition of the central bank's objective function and clear identification of the channels through which policy affects the economy. Those elements were missing in the 1920s. The gold standard was viewed as an adequate substitute. We learned in the 1930s that it was not. This same lesson then had to be relearned, often at considerable cost, by Latin American, Asian and even European countries in the 1990s.

What ended the Great Depression?
The reorientation of policy toward stabilizing prices and financial systems ended the Depression, and a necessary condition for that reorientation was abandoning the gold standard. More broadly, there had to be political realignment and a political consensus that government was responsible for ending the downward spiral. Once governments began to do something, they produced results.

Could it happen again?
I like to think that the answer is no, that there has been learning from that experience, and that there are improved policy frameworks in a variety of countries. The chairman of the Federal Reserve Board is intimately familiar with the literature on the Depression. But to the extent that history repeats itself, it repeats itself in different ways. We will have episodes of instability in the future as we did in the past. Schumpeter reminds us that these are intrinsic to the operation of the market system. But the form in which that instability manifests itself will be different than it was in the past. We will have to wait and see whether policy makers recognize those risks and are able to respond to them in real time.

Anticipated deflation caused high ex ante interest rates and deflation caused debt deflation and high tariffs. Deflation and the asymmetry in the gold standard caused the US and France to drain the world of gold. Deflation caused much of the rise in real wages. So deflation is the key to understanding the Depression. Without deflation these things do not happen and deflation happened because of the behavior of the money stock. Thus the Depression can be correctly viewed as a monetary phenomenon. Do you agree with that?
The way you put the question suggests more of a monocausal explanation than I prefer. But there is no denying the importance of deflation to the Depression, and deflation is always and everywhere a monetary phenomenon. Paraphrasing Milton Friedman reminds me of how long it took me to accept the importance of money and financial factors in explaining the Depression. I was trained at Yale where the debate over the Depression was framed by Tobin as a debate between the monetary and the Keynesian views, as in Temin's 1976 book. I was encouraged to think in terms of the Keynesian view. Now I would emphasize that the Depression was the result of a powerful deflation and that one can't tell this story without giving prominence to monetary policy. But monetary policies were made in a particular institutional setting and global context. That is what always brings me back to the gold standard.

Thank you so much, Professor, that is the end of my inquiry.

Stephen Cecchetti

Stephen Cecchetti received his Ph.D. from the University of California, Berkeley in 1982 and he is currently Rosenberg Professor of Global Finance at the Brandeis International Business School. He formerly was a Professor of Economics at Ohio State University in addition to being the editor of the *Journal of Money Credit and Banking* from 1992 to 2001 and the Executive Vice President and Director of Research at the Federal Reserve Bank of New York from August 1997 to September 1999. He recently has published a textbook on monetary theory and policy, *Money, Banking, and Financial Markets*. I spoke with Stephen Cecchetti in his office at Brandeis University on January 25, 2005.

Will you please give us some background on how you came to be involved in the literature on the Great Depression.
I think that for any macroeconomist the Great Depression is like honey for a bear. We are all drawn to it. I believe that you learn more about the economy when you look at how it operates under stress than you learn from studying how it operates during normal times. Normal times are important, but when you see periods of extreme stress then you really learn how the system works. The big thing about the Depression of the 1930s is that it's the first severe episode for which there is really good economic data. It certainly isn't the first depression that is out there, but it's the first one for which we really have a lot of information and it's also the first one for which the institutions that are in place today were there in one form or another. Now, of course, they weren't the same exact institutions as there are today, and the ones there didn't operate as well as we might have hoped. But the point is that we can study that period and, I think, learn important lessons for current policy. If I said that I wanted to study the severe fluctuations in the late nineteenth century American economy, or the severe fluctuations in some other part of the world, I could try and do that, but I believe that I would learn less of use for formulating policy today.

On a more personal level, I think that the economists from the previous generation were drawn to the Depression because they lived through it. The economists of my generation are drawn to the Depression because they heard about it when they were kids. As we were growing up, we heard about it. I may have heard a little bit less about it maybe than some other people because it turns out my parents were in Europe during the Depression. So much of my interest in monetary policy and inflation comes from long discussions with my German grandfather about the hyperinflation of the early 1920s. I spent hours talking with him, trying to understand why he felt that inflation was so horrible. I started with the economist's view that if you really soak up the lessons of the economics that you first get, you sort of say "what's inflation?" Well, inflation is when you wake up in the morning and somebody has moved the decimal point, they moved it for everything, right? So I see it as a path for me and I came to it then as a period that I thought was really going to help me to understand how policy could stabilize modern economies by looking at periods when it failed to do that.

You said in your 1998 paper "Understanding the Great Depression" that the Crash was not caused by the bursting of the speculation bubble and that the fundamentals seemed sound in 1929. Have you seen McGrattan and Prescott's (2004) paper that argues that the market was undervalued?
The market was undervalued.

That's what he says.
So he's buying the Irving Fisher line. I guess I have not read that paper.

So does that surprise you?
It doesn't surprise me and I think that it's still the case that if you look at normal valuation models for that period, there seem to be very big overvaluations of equities in that period.

DeLong and Shleifer (1991) had that paper on closed-end mutual funds that argued there was a bubble.
Right, and I also think that just looking at price–earnings ratios for that period, you're going to get a similar kind of result. There is a paper by Barsky and DeLong (1990) that argues valuations at the time can be explained by people having strange perceptions about the dividend process. Their argument is that the dividend process behaves like the growth rate is a random walk. If the growth rate of dividends is a random walk, then very weird things can happen to your valuation models. But I think if you look at things like the swift run-up in equity prices in that period, it's pretty hard to argue that things suddenly changed to bring that about. Now, you know, this is a pretty dicey business, right? Because we can sit here today and say "What are the values of some companies that are new companies and what's the value of technology that's out there?" There is no way to know. But I still think that there was somewhat of a bubble. If you look at the simple analysis, as opposed to the really complex stuff, I think the most compelling story, and Christina Romer (1990) made this point, is that it was

some time after the stock market crash that you really started to see declines in the overall growth rate. It wasn't early in 1930. She does argue that the stock market could have been a trigger for consumer confidence declines. But even so, it wasn't until late 1930 that we see any macroeconomic action with output growth rates declining significantly. It is true that in late 1930 prices start to fall. But the reactions are not as swift as one might have thought and they are much more pervasive. We think today about stock market ownership as being really pretty highly concentrated. I mean a lot of people own equity but they don't own very much and most of it is highly concentrated. It was even more concentrated then. The wealth distribution is much, much more skewed than the income distribution is, and during that period it was worse, to the extent that we know. So if you see stock prices collapse, the idea that mansions and yachts are going to go up for sale somehow doesn't really worry you too much. My conclusion is that there was almost surely a bubble. Again, do I know anything for sure? No I don't know anything for sure. But I think it was a high probability.

Let me ask this differently. Regardless of what McGrattan and Prescott's (2004) paper says, is it not the Fed's perception of the position of the market that counts and what ultimately made it act as it did? These postmortems are great, but in explaining what happened and why it matters, is it not what the Fed perceived at the time that is most important?
Yes, that is important and I think the question then is whether or not the Fed should have gone about its business the way it did in early 1929. You know the story of the March 1929 imminent collapse of the stock market that was stemmed by lending following a spike in the cash rate. The lending was facilitated by the president of the National City Bank acting together with the president of the Federal Reserve Bank of New York. The Fed, outside of New York, was on the record as saying that they did not want lending, that they wanted the stock market to fall. Then Herbert Hoover came in and said that he wanted the stock market to fall. Those perceptions I think were very important at the time.

I have come some distance in my view of policy reactions to equity and property price bubbles. But I still think that what was going on then was a misconception really of what happened. Policy makers were not reacting to the growth in the bubble in a measured sort of way. Instead, they were determined to stomp it out at all cost. That, I think, was bad policy. The important thing to see, going forward, is that their perceptions led directly to a refusal to do any discount lending in the face of the financial collapse. Looking at the low levels of discount lending in the early 1930s, it's hard to know whether it's demand or supply. You are watching equilibrium quantities. But in this case I think that what it is that the Federal Reserve had been saying led banks to think that there was not going to be any lending made, and there wasn't any lending. They should have been actively encouraging borrowing at that point, borrowing by the member banks, and they obviously weren't doing that. So yes, I agree with you. It's the perception of the policy makers and the policy makers were intent on bringing things down.

You place the blame for the Crash squarely on the Federal Reserve and also blame it for not helping once it occurred. You say two lessons to come from this experience are for the Fed not to let the security prices affect their decision making and for the Fed to stand as the lender of last resort when financial markets come under stress. Do you think the central banks of the world have learned these lessons?

The second lesson I think they have learned for sure. We see a lot of evidence of a move away from punitive lending practices, lending to financial intermediaries during times of stress that is then punished somehow if it's too frequent or something like that. So I think that has certainly been learned. There continues to be a debate over discount lending and the debate is of two kinds. One is whether or not the central bank has a conflict of interest in doing monetary policy, interest rate policy and discount lending policy all at the same time; whether or not it has the tendency to bail out institutions in one way or another. I don't take that too seriously. The second debate over discount lending brings us back to Bagehot's original proposal in the mid-1800s. Bagehot said that the central bank should lend freely on good credit at penalty rates. We interpret "on good credit" to mean on good collateral. The problem is that during periods of financial stress, that is when discount lending is most needed, evaluation of the quality of any security is difficult. To see the problem, look at standard discount lending procedures. A commercial bank posts collateral in the form of securities with a central bank during normal times. The central bank places some value on that collateral in order to make a discount loan. The idea is that if the discount loan isn't repaid they're going to cease the collateral. But, during a period of financial stress, who can say what the collateral is worth? Some people, like Allan Meltzer, argue that it is impossible to actually evaluate the collateral when you really need to. How do you know the price? The whole point is the financial market is not working. Again, I don't take this too seriously. I think it is a problem, we do want to think about it. But we have generally learned this lesson and if we look around the world we see lending.

Now what about equity and property price bubbles? This is a subject about which we are learning more and more as we go on and I've changed some of my views about this.

I've read that recently.

So, on the equity price side, I think that in a modern economy we learned over the last decade that asset price misalignments, bubbles, unwarranted price increases create huge distortions in the economy. I'm not sure we know enough about 1928–29 to make the same statement there. I certainly don't know enough. I can tell you stories about 1998–99 but not from 1928 and 1929. So I can look and say it seemed like there was this huge amount of negative net present value investment going on (*laughter*). I can't figure out what was going on here and the only explanation I have is that the people were able to sell equity at very highly inflated prices and that's a lot like me going into my basement and printing money. I am able to take these shares and go out and buy stuff with it. And it looks to me that there was a huge distortion that occurred. On the equity side what you see is investment distortion so there is an inefficient allocation of resources cross-sectionally in the economy. We all saw pictures of warehouses with computers just stacked up; this stuff turned into garbage in 2000. These things depreciate rapidly but not that rapidly; a year ago this stuff supposedly had been in service somewhere. On the property side, if you think about property price bubbles, especially on residential real estate, possibly on commercial real estate, the residential side depresses the personal saving rate and causes everyone to think they are wealthier than they are. They raise their consumption level and the income effects are going to swamp the substitution effects with this huge wealth increase.

Hasn't Chairman Greenspan also said that he suspects the marginal propensity to consume from housing wealth to be greater than what it is from equity wealth?
Yes, and that brings us back to the observation I made a minute ago and that was the distribution of equity wealth is very much more highly skewed than the distribution of property wealth. Think of problems posed by liquidity constraints. Most households that are out there face some liquidity constraints. They are unable to borrow against future income sufficiently to smooth consumption today. Those liquidity constraints are going to be eased by a big run-up in the value of their house. This is an asset that can be used as collateral for borrowing. So they are going to have to go for an equity loan or a refinance that they are going to cash out of their house. The important thing there is that it creates another distortion. The first one, the equity distortion, is more of an atemporal distortion, it's more of a distortion of where current investment flows are going. The property distortion is an intertemporal distortion, we have too little saving today and too much consumption so we are not carrying enough forward into the next period. The other thing is that if we think about bubbles and monetary policy, interest rates are going to be much more effective in combating property price bubbles than they are in combating equity bubbles. We also know, looking at the cross-sectional data, that the macroeconomic impact of a property bubble is much bigger than the macroeconomic impact of an equity bubble. There is an IMF estimate that property prices have

something like three or four times the macroeconomic impact equity prices do. And again there are two reasons for that. One of them is that you affect more of the households, more of the population, not just the rich guys. The second reason is that the financial system is much more tied up and their balance sheet is much more dependent on housing than it is on equity. If you think about the collateral that's sitting behind mortgages, you've got a problem when you have property price bubbles. If you think about equity then there is not a whole lot that is collateralized on financial system balance sheets. Most financial intermediaries do not hold equity on their balance sheets.

Do they still hold the bulk of the housing paper? I mean the banks during the Depression held a lot of housing paper.
Yes, they do actually.

Today they do?
Yes, they hold more than you would hope.

I thought that they all bundled up these mortgages and sold them on the bond market.
Yes, but they tend to hold the riskiest remaining bits. That's because of the regulatory failure. If all housing loans have the same capital charge, then what happens is banks end up holding the riskiest housing debt so that they can have the least capital per unit risk. Also remember that these guys have a government sitting behind them.

So, what did we learn from the Depression about bubbles? I'd say that today the lesson I take away is that I want to see measured responses, modest, measured responses. I don't want to see somebody standing up and saying "This is wrong and we've got to do something about it." What I want to do is I want to say this is a threat to stability and I am going to take modest actions against it.

Even knowing what happened back then, it doesn't make you go wobbly?
Even knowing what happened back then. Yes.

Alright. It doesn't make you go wobbly (Parker raises his eyebrow)?
No.

Alright.
I am fine with it.

Very well. In your "Understanding the Great Depression" paper, you discuss debt deflation and say this would not have occurred without deflation and thus this is a monetary phenomenon. Anticipated deflation, as

you showed in your 1992 AER *paper, caused high ex ante real rates, deflation caused debt deflation, deflation caused high tariff rates as Crucini (1994) showed, deflation and asymmetry in the gold standard caused the US and France to drain the world of gold, and deflation caused much of the rise in real wages. So deflation is the key to understanding the Great Depression then, is it not?*
Well it sure sounds like it the way you put it doesn't it? *(laughter).*

Let me just follow this up.
Sure.

Without deflation these things don't happen and the deflation happened because of the behavior of the money stock. You once said to me that you thought the whole Depression was caused by monetary factors. Do you still feel that way?
I do. I do still think that way. I think it's hard to get away from the Friedman and Schwartz (1963) interpretation. It's hard to get away from the conclusion that policy makers were too focused on the monetary base and did not appreciate the distinction between the monetary base and what we would today call monetary aggregates. We might want to cut them some slack, because they didn't compute monetary aggregates. The monetary aggregates for that period were computed after the fact by Friedman and Schwartz. We can't ask people in 1930 to know what we ourselves did not calculate until the 1950s and 1960s. But I think that it was a lack of understanding of the connection between the medium of exchange broadly construed and the price level. It's important to keep in mind that the deflation of the early 1930s averaged 10 percent. So, when people talk about deflation today, again if you want to bring it to the current world, when they continue to worry about Japanese deflation of 0.1 percent or something, Japan has got a problem but the problem there isn't the same order of magnitude it was in the 1930s US. If you have a 10 percent deflation then obviously your real interest rate is at least 10 percent. By any standard that I have ever seen, that's an astronomical number. When we think of equilibrium real interest rates we think of 2, 3, maybe 4 percent at the outside. So the depressing effects that had on investment were surely extreme.

That's your decapitilization story and the changing nature of money that we are going to get to.
So I think that the policy errors started with a failure to understand the connection and to focus overly on the monetary base. Added to that is the fact that the Fed failed to use the tools at hand to prevent the financial system from collapsing. Again, Friedman and Schwartz comment that the money multiplier is collapsing and the money multiplier collapses largely as

a consequence of the collapse of the banking system. There are things the Fed could have done to prevent this. If you understand the importance of the financial system in creating loans, then when it is under stress you have to do something about it.

It's hard to believe that when the banking panics began in early 1931 all of the affected banks were insolvent. We should show our students the movie *It's a Wonderful Life* so that they can see Jimmy Stewart reaching into his wallet and pulling out his last five dollars, but first explaining to everybody that he doesn't actually have their money, it has been loaned somewhere else. What happened instead is that, because of the Fed's failure to aggressively promote discount lending (they actually did the opposite), the mechanism that channels resources from savers to investors, they completely shut down.

Returning to the point about the real interest rate and decapitalization of the economy, this brings us to Bernanke's (1983a) point about increasing information asymmetries that arise when that happens. When interest rates rise it decreases the net worth of borrowers. This worsens information problems associated with attempts to figure out if potential borrowers are credit worthy. Now all of a sudden you've dramatically raised the real interest rate and their net worth collapses in the normal sense that they can't show themselves to be credit worthy anymore. So we are not going to do the lending. You have shut down the lending channels in the economy as a consequence. It always keeps coming back to deflation, in my mind.

And that's a monetary phenomenon.
One would think, (*chuckling*) one would think.

Alright then, you also indicate that Fed behavior was a failure of monetary policy. Discount activity in 1929–31 was completely different from discount behavior in 1920–22, which is shown in Figure 2 in your 1998 paper.
That graph is one of my favorites.

So the Fed failed to be the lender of last resort. Here's my question: where do you come down on the gold standard hypothesis position that this was not a policy failure? The Fed was simply acting in accordance with the gold standard and was constrained in their behavior and this explains why it acted as it did. Could the Fed have acted as the lender of last resort or was it constrained from doing so by the realities of the gold standard?
This is related to a question that came up years ago when I first started thinking about this. That is, why is it that there wasn't exchange rate pressure at this point? My interpretation of the gold standard problem is first of all that what the gold standard did was to export our deflation to other countries. We were actually accumulating gold during this period. So, even within the context of the Bernanke or what I think of as sort of the James

Hamilton view, there was some scope for movement. But you should also ask: what is the responsibility of a government official in a circumstance like this? Is it to defend the gold standard, if this is what you believe, to the point where you destroy your economy? Or is it to provide the reserves – again remember this would have been discount lending so it would have been temporary lending – to allow the system to maintain itself and to possibly even produce small amounts of inflation which then could have put pressure on gold, thereby putting pressure on the government possibly to revalue gold or to go off the gold standard? I mean in hindsight these things are easy to say. Eichengreen (1992) says that this was a political economy problem associated with the interactions of the various governments at the time. We look back and say, "Why did sterling go back on gold at such a high, dramatically overvalued level that clearly harmed the British economy?" I would like to think that a responsible monetary policy authority would be able to expand their balance sheet in a way that would stabilize the macro economy at the expense of putting pressure on those sorts of international agreements and also be able to explain to the international community that they are doing this in order to insure that the world economy is stable and that they will worry about the price of gold later.

So suspend it then.
Well, a question that I think is unanswered in the literature, which I don't have an answer to, is whether the Federal Reserve could have acted in a way that would have put pressure on the Hoover administration to suspend the gold standard.

The question right now it all boils down to in the literature seems to be was the Federal Reserve fettered by gold or not? Did they hit that binding constraint? Were they forced then to defend the exchange value of the dollar because if they had engaged in expansionary monetary policy it would have caused a collapse of confidence, it would have caused a speculative run on the dollar and the Fed would have had to act?
I continue to believe that we need to focus attention on the Fed's discount lending behavior (Figure 2 in Cecchetti, 1998). It's one thing to say that you are going to engage in what may have at the time appeared to be profligate monetary policy. You can see the headlines about risks to exchange rates that were unacceptable, and that would have been increases in the size of the central bank's balance sheet. It's something else to say that you are going to engage in activities that are going to support the domestic banking system by providing them with short-term loans under stress. Remember one of the points of good discount lending policy is that you rarely have to use it. The whole point of it is to say "I'm here to protect you from losses of confidence." Somebody says "I don't need to lose confidence any more

because the central bank is sitting behind my bank, they're always there."
So ask yourself, why would that have been a threat to the banking system in
the early 1930s? In that story, which I think is a plausible one, could the
Federal Reserve have kept the banking system from collapsing during the
first banking crisis of 1930, then early 1931, then the fall of 1931? Could
they have kept things from collapsing through that by offering a credible
discount lending policy? I don't believe that the runs on banks during those
crises were justified by insolvency. Remember going into this period it was
common for these banks to have 25 percent capital. This was not a bank of
2005. The bank of 2005 has 8–9 percent capital tops. These banks had three
times the capital of a modern bank.

That's a point that's seldom made.
Yes. So let's say the Fed succeeds in maintaining the liquidity of the
banking system in the 1930s, avoiding those banking crises. Then what
happens is they don't have to expand my balance sheet, but the financial
system provides the medium of exchange that is necessary for transactions
and continues to do its job of intermediation. That I think is the argument.
This lesson, I believe, drove some modern policy actions, specifically those
in the fall of 1998 (when I happened to be working inside the Federal
Reserve). Recall, the Russian default was in August and Long-Term Capital
Management collapsed in September. In response, the Federal Reserve
reduced interest rates 75 basis points that fall. At the time Bill McDonough
was the president of the Federal Reserve of New York. He said this was the
worst financial crisis since the Great Depression. Now, what was going on
at that point was that the liquidity in financial markets had evaporated
completely. So what's the right action of the central bank at that point?
Well, it's to provide the liquidity. A similar thing, although not as extreme,
happened in the aftermath of the 1987 stock market crash. Alan Greenspan
was new in his job, but he got up and said the Fed would provide the loans
that are necessary to ensure liquidity in the financial system. For how long?
It was for a couple of days with that one. In the case of September, October,
November of 1998 it was really for a few months. In the case of September
11, 2001, it was for a couple of weeks. You have to be ready to do that and
the Federal Reserve was not ready to do that in 1931.

Do you know why?
The only tie that I can find is it's related to this unwillingness to provide
loans that would then potentially be used in the equity markets.

Even in 1931 when the economy failed?
They got used to this. Some thought it was good. They followed the real
bills doctrine, the idea that it was not their job to ensure that the banking
system provided the lending, that the lending would be provided if the

projects were out there, not thinking about the fragility of the financial system. Again, the language that I am using is not the language of the 1930s. This is the language that has evolved during the last quarter century because I'm talking about the information problems, I'm talking about the support for liquidity and those sorts of things. So this is not the language these guys from the 1930s would have used.

Well, then just letting the banks fail because they had to, to support the gold standard, I bet you don't buy that.
No, and today we let banks fail but we do it in a way that is designed not to create panic. A bank failure today will almost be invisible to its customers because it will be done over a weekend, often through a purchase and sale. What happens is that the regulator goes in on Friday afternoon after the close of business and the buyer opens on Monday morning. In fact the name doesn't even change for a while. It looks the same. The same ATM machines, the same building, but it's owned by someone else. The "sale price" for the failed bank may be negative, but it is all done in an orderly fashion. Today we make sure, maybe too sure some people would argue, but we make sure that problems like we discussed above don't happen.

Paul Samuelson has said that it's unrealistic in hindsight and would have been unheard of for the Fed to have acted to increase the base by whatever was necessary to stop the deflation and the falling money supply. After all, the base did not fall during the Depression. What do you think about that?
I think that's a realistic point. Again the question is whether or not they could have stemmed the financial collapse without increasing the base. I continue to believe that the focus on the base as opposed to the focus on the lender of the last resort function ...

You mean the difference between the base and the monetary aggregates that we were speaking of earlier?
Yes, I think that's overblown. To paraphrase Richard Nixon, we are all monetarists now *(laughter)*. I think that it may be unrealistic to think that the Depression-era Federal Reserve could have increased the monetary base to the extent that would have been necessary after the banking system started to collapse. But could they have stemmed the banking system collapse through discount lending? If they had, then the monetary base could have continued to grow at the rate at which it was, consistent with gold stocks and gold reserve ratios that Bernanke and James (1991) and others have emphasized. And that's where we sit I think. I would focus on the lender of the last resort function. People are going to say "you are overly optimistic about the way the lender of last resort would have functioned." But again, I can look at the data on lending and I always come back to the question of why is it that you have severe movements of prices in the early

1920s without the same problems that you had in the early 1930s? The most compelling explanation, I believe, is the difference in discount lending activity.

The liquidity trap is caused by nominal–real confusion. Is that not correct?
Yes.

So then all this talk over all the years about the liquidity trap is a real–nominal disconnect, right?
I think so. I think that once you start to think about the problems associated with deflation, you realize that it's not an issue of monetary policy being ineffective. It's really a question of the real effects of price declines and what the right monetary reaction should be to that.

Once you hit that binding nominal zero rate ...
But then you can still increase the monetary base.

You sure can.
One would think.

One would think, and try to stop the deflation and high real interest rates.
In the modern context, this brings us to the debates over what Japanese monetary policy should have been and whether the right Japanese monetary policy is to announce certain kinds of price level or inflation targets. I think what I would have done at a minimum, which might have been politically feasible, is to announce that you are going to increase the monetary base in Japan until prices start to rise. That's all. I am not going to sit here every week and decide again. I am just going to keep going at some pace until prices start to rise.

OK, switching papers now a little bit. I like the segregation of the main questions of the Depression contained in your and Karras's 1994 Review of Economics and Statistics *paper. You ask why it started? Why was it so deep? And why did it last so long? Can we also add why did it spread so completely and why did recovery come when it did?*
Sure. For the international spreading, there I buy the gold standard explanation, the exporting of deflation and world monetary base declines through the gold standard. Here, I believe the original Choudhri and Kochin (1980) evidence on the cross-country experiences remains compelling.

I've never gotten past what I read originally about the recovery. You know the real recovery comes with the War. You start to get some recoveries in 1937. Then you get this great monetary experiment, one of the cleanest monetary experiments we have ever seen. The reserve requirement increase in 1937 just sends the monetary aggregates back into the dumper and the economy stagnates again. So I have never had anything structured and disciplined to say about the recovery.

So if you want to structure a discussion today and you want to go all the way, you have to answer those two additional questions you mentioned above.

You like the decapitalization story and the implication of a changing nature of money in Cecchetti and Karras (1994). This then all goes to the evils of deflation and nominal rates hitting their lower bound. In fact as you have emphasized, but is seldom said, postal savings accounts put a 2 percent floor on nominal rates, letting real interest rates be bounded only by how high the rate of deflation climbs. So do you see instability in the price level, both up and down, as one of the greatest sources of economic instability in the last century and would you be willing to say that maintaining price stability is one of the key lessons for central bankers to learn from the Great Depression and the Great Inflation?

Yes. That's simple. That's easy. I am willing to have a debate about whether you want price stability to mean 0, 1 or 2 percent measured inflation. But after resolving that, what I would insist on after that for monetary policy strategy is symmetry. Policy makers have to care just as much about down as up. So everybody has focused in the last few decades on problems associated with inflation. For the last year and a half to two years, we have had much more talk about deflation in this country and obviously the Japanese have had talk about deflation. I think that the objective of the central bank has to be to deliver low, stable inflation. Stable inflation is an inflation that doesn't go either above or below the target. There's a danger that if inflation starts to fall significantly, you are going to have real troubles. So when the federal funds rate hit 1 percent people got nervous and inflation looked like it was falling. You start to ask how far can inflation fall? The answer to this is that you can still have a stable economy – this has been Friedman's point for years – even with a steady deflation rate of 1–2 percent. It's at that point that you have zero nominal interest rates and a real interest rate that's around the equilibrium level. So if you look at where the real bounds occur on deflation they are actually pretty low. You are not going to get real interest rates rising above the equilibrium levels until deflation starts to go below about −2 percent. That's the barrier below which things become unstable. At that point real interest rate increases force declines in the size of the economy.

But the primary lesson central bankers have learned is they don't want inflation or deflation. There is one caveat. You may want small amounts of inflation. The small amounts of inflation could be justified either because of nominal stickiness or because you want to reduce the probability of going to the bad negative place. So that's like a risk management thing where you want the probability of hitting the bound where you get into really serious trouble to be sufficiently small that you are willing to raise your inflation target slightly. So if you look at the common inflation targets today, you see numbers like 2 percent and they are all consistent with small amounts of positive inflation where you are trying to stabilize things. You don't want to go way up, you don't want to go way down.

You have emphasized in your writings that deflation is to be "feared" and I think that's the correct word to put on it.
Yes.

You don't want it.
No. So I think I agree with the terminology of Chairman Greenspan when he says that the central bank takes a risk management perspective. And risk management is about making sure that the probability of this really bad thing happening is sufficiently small.

You say in your paper "Understanding the Great Depression" that the behavior of the economy in 1920–22 remains a mystery. Why was there no depression after that sharp deflation, yet there was in 1929–33? Are we any closer to an answer about the difference between those two episodes? Does discounting and Fed behavior explain the difference?
That's one explanation. Another is that the 1921 deflation followed a severe inflation that came at the end of World War I in 1919. There was a sharp run-up followed by a sharp run-down in the price level. That had a different impact from what had happened when you had a relatively steady price level in the 1920s and then a sharp decline. So one possibility is that you are just reversing this increase, so it's not as bad. Yet another possibility, which is the focus of Bernanke and Carey (1996), is that there was a lower level of wage flexibility in the 1930s. In the end, the explanation is likely to be a combination of all these things but I would surely point to the fact that you have this large deflation without a financial crisis. Look at the picture of discount lending behavior.

(Parker raises his voice in a friendly tone) *But why were they so profligate then in 1920–22 but not in 1929–33?*
Different people. Benjamin Strong being alive would be Anna Schwartz's answer.

What about the presence and absence of the interwar gold standard?
It's a possibility. And remember, the Federal Reserve was started as a consequence of the panic of 1907, as a consequence of the failure of the New York clearing houses, as a consequence of the fact that there was no lender of last resort and the realization that the private sector was not going to supply it. Benjamin Strong, acting as the agent of J.P. Morgan, was able

to stem the crisis in 1907. That's what happened then, but we needed to institutionalize this. There is this great comment by Warburg contained in Whitehouse (1989) that in the early twentieth century the US was several hundred years behind the Europeans in their banking system.

Who said that?
Paul M. Warburg, he became a governor of the Federal Reserve Board.

You also stated in your paper "Understanding the Great Depression" that our understanding of deflation is incomplete because the duration of deflation is important. It's different in 1929–33 than in 1920–21. So could you expand on that please.
This is a casual statement really. The statement is that if I am going to get a drop, let's say I am going to get a drop in the price level of 50 percent, which is pretty huge, it matters if it happens in six months or six years. Then somehow quick looks like it might be easier to handle than slow in that sense, once you get over some hump. I don't think we have a good understanding of that. There is a possibility of course that I am just describing symptoms. All I am doing is describing somebody who has a long illness relative to someone who has a short illness. And it is also possible that I am describing something more fundamental and that's what I am referring to there and I think we don't know and I don't know today.

There is a little section at the end of your 1988 working paper "Deflation and the Great Depression." That paper has never seen the light of day.
That's right.

It's never been published. I am aware of it and have read it many times.
I'd have a hard time even finding a copy of that paper

I have a copy of it right here if you want one. But that's where you talk about the timing of deflation in the Calvo (1986) model and so on.
The only place where I really wrote about that was in the "Understanding the Great Depression" paper. And I abandoned that discussion because I thought that the technicalities of that model were beyond my mathematical capacity.

That's no badge of shame.
Maybe one of these days I will have a student who will go back to work it out. But I haven't done it. What did I say?

You were working on the Calvo (1986) model and you said that what happens depends upon the speed of the decrease in deflation and the change in money growth and whether you go to a lower equilibrium where the

nominal rate is binding. But it's never seen the light of day because that paper morphed into your 1992 AER *paper.*
The first part of it did but the last part of it got dumped. It just got too complicated. Well, you know life is long *(laughter)*.

(Jokingly) *I am a professional and this is my business. So I had to ask about it.*
Well, it reminds me of something my late colleague G.S. Maddala once said. I asked him if he had done something, and he responded "Well, you know, I take the Indian view that if you don't do it in this life, you will do it in the next one" *(laughter)*. Maybe, I'll do that in the next life. I'll take more math classes in college next time around and I'll be ready *(laughter)*.

Well, we'll be waiting.
Ah, I don't think so.

Does not the Asian crisis of the late 1990s show that the world really has not learned the lesson that fixed exchange rates are hard to coordinate and difficult to maintain and are a toxic transmission mechanism for real shocks?
I would have interpreted the 1997–98 Asian crisis a little bit differently.

That's one of the points you make in your 1998 paper.
Yes. Today when I look at fixed exchange rates, I see that they encourage complacency in both the private sector and government. In the private sector, people don't hedge sufficiently and so the risk of an exchange rate movement wasn't properly priced. In the government sector there was a conscious decision to hide things some of the time. So, I think that fixed exchange rates with capital mobility, which is what we were seeing also in the 1920s, creates a certain kind of moral hazard. The private agents think that the government is going to bail them out. The governments think they can bail them out or possibly in today's world that international agencies are going to bail them out. In the 1920s nobody had any illusions that the French were going to bail anybody out. And the only international agency that really existed at that time was the Bank for International Settlements and they had a somewhat different job. So, I would say that these things are a problem. There is another issue that has arisen following the Asian crisis and that is the place of capital controls. If your country cannot withstand the pressures of the free-for-all, the international financial system, then should you have in place a set of capital controls and possibly a fixed or crawling peg exchange rate while you are opening up, while you make sure that these things can be withstood? Part of what we have also seen is that you can just open yourself up with flexible exchange rates and capital mobility and you can get crushed.

With flexible exchange rates?
Yes, with flexible exchange rates your domestic financial system can get crushed. So I am not sure that this is the lesson of Malaysia. The lesson of Malaysia could be a little bit different, but it's definitely the case that Malaysia didn't fare badly with the imposition of capital controls and fixed exchange rates. It's also the case that, while there were inflow and outflow controls for Malaysia that were temporary, the Chilean government's capital inflow controls were in place for several years and they seem to have insulated the Chilean economy from severe problems. But if you look and say what's happened in other South American and Central American countries, some of them have been forced to dollarize, some of them have had severe contractions.

Argentina had a currency board.
Well, the currency board was just a fixed exchange rate regime.

Doesn't it also take away the lender of last resort function of the central bank?
Well, when I was sitting at the New York Federal Reserve we figured we were the lender of last resort for Argentine banks because the central bank of Argentina had lines of credit with New York City banks and the New York City banks were ultimately backstopped by the Federal Reserve Bank of New York. It does take away the lender of last resort function. But again, it lulls you into a sense of complacency. You look at that and say "I have a currency board and I am going to be one-for-one with the dollar, I can make all my arrangements and it doesn't even matter whether I use dollars or pesos in my accounting." Well, it does matter. Look at what happened in Argentina. It didn't even matter whether you were the central bank any more. The central bank was constrained by their dollar reserves in what peso currency they could issue but that didn't constrain anybody else. Other governments in Argentina issued money instead. Do you know this story?

Other parts of the Argentine government issued pesos?
Yes. This particular note (Cecchetti points to page 510 of the first edition of his textbook *Money, Banking and Financial Markets*) is a five peso note issued by the government of the Province of Buenos Aires. This is a bond technically. If you read the back it tells you that this bond promises to give you 35 percent interest in five years. So this is a five-year, zero coupon bond at a 7 percent linear rate over those five years. That's what it says on the back. But these were issued and used as payment for the obligations of the provincial government. So, who's constrained by the currency board? Just the central bank and even then pressure can be put on the central bank. My view is if you want a fixed exchange rate, you better dollarize. But dollarization can be reversed as well. So in the end there is nothing that gets

you away from that. What gets you away is you can always have a flexible exchange rate.

The real business cycle people have picked up on a theme of yours. They now want to compare the 1920–22 recession to the Great Depression. So Cole and Ohanian (2000) pick up the theme by comparing the recession of 1920–22 to the Depression. This is how they discount the validity of debt deflation, saying it should have been worse in 1920–22. They then go on to say that since real rates were higher in 1920–22 than they were during the Depression, this casts doubt on the validity of the real interest rate story for the Great Depression. What say you to that?

First of all they have a very limited number of transmission mechanisms available to them in their models. I think that's where we have to come to the question of whether or not the speed and length of the deflation matters. There is only so much investment. If people stop investing for six months, so if we get a spike in the real interest rate and all of sudden we have no investment for six months, that's going to have a pretty different impact from three years of steady, high, not spiked, but high real interest rates that crush investment. Surely everyone would agree, just to make the point, that an instantaneous deflation where we wake up tomorrow and somebody has moved the decimal point to the left instead of the right, one would think that even in their model, they would smooth right over it. That's where I would be looking.

Cole and Ohanian (2000) comment that the total deposits-to-output ratio increases between 1929 and 1932. Thus loanable funds were abundant and this questions whether monetary policy really was a problem.

There you are looking at the ratio of the equilibrium values of two endogenous variables and trying to draw some sort of causal statement from it. What I have been arguing in my comments throughout our conversation is that you have to look at the collapse of the banking system; that you have to look at loan supply. Loan supply affects output. You are looking at a huge decline in loan supply and an even bigger decline in the output. Equilibrium loans fall but output falls even more. Surely it could be just loan supply declining as a consequence of financial system stress.

I learn a lot from thinking about these things in these general equilibrium models. So if you look at Cole and Ohanian (2000) or Christiano, Motto and Rostagno (2003) and you ask yourself, "What do I learn from this stuff?", at the very basic level what you tell your students in the graduate level class is to think in terms of impulses and propagating mechanisms. So what's the shock, what's the forcing process in Cole and Ohanian (2000)? I'm surprised that Cole and Ohanian would focus on these two endogenous variables without telling us much about the impulses and the propagation mechanisms. So what I would say is "How does this tell you about the impulses and the propagation mechanisms then?" because I don't see it.

Would you not say that your decapitalization story could be viewed as a big productivity shock of great importance?
In an equilibrium model it would show up as a large, negative and highly persistent productivity shock. That's the way that you would end up parsing it. The same thing is true if the financial system collapsed because they are all one.

People in the real business cycle literature don't know where the productivity shocks came from and can't explain them. What I'm saying is I think I've got an explanation here.
I think that's right. In some ways you can ask yourself how in a general equilibrium model would you end up parsing the Bernanke-style explanations, the original ones, the sort of loan supply and cost of credit intermediation explanations? Those are going to show up as productivity shocks as well. There are a lot of things we can point to in the financial system that are going to show up ultimately as productivity shocks.

Several of their papers systematically go about trying to totally discount any financial angle at all.
Well, we have different views and that's what makes life interesting (*laughter*).

OK, great. Your JPE *paper on negative nominal interest rates (1988a) must have been a great deal of work.*
(*Laughingly*) No kidding.

But yet I don't see it get cited very often and I'm kind of scratching my head about why not.
I can look at this either positively or negatively. The positive way is to say I actually have a definitive answer to an interesting question and there is not a whole lot left to write about that. There was a puzzle, I found the answer. The answer turns out to be pretty simple once you find the institutional details. That's the more positive way of looking at it. The more negative way is that people are for some reason complacent about data quality. That's unfortunate, but what am I going to do? I don't worry about that too much. So I'm not disappointed. It was a fun paper, but it was a huge amount of work that paid off.

So, debt deflation ...
I have to tell you one quick story about that paper. I sent that paper to the *JPE,* and I got a quick letter back within two months. It was very thin and I

was sure it was just another rejection. I opened it and the letter from the editor was only this long (Cecchetti spreads his hands open about three inches). The letter said "the referee likes your paper, we like your paper and the referee thinks maybe you should think more about the implications of what you are doing. We are prepared to publish a paper with the current orientation, but we wish you would remove section six on taxes," or something like that. Never before or since have I gotten anything like that.

Gee, what do I do?
While it's far from being my most cited paper – in fact my most cited paper was maybe my most rejected paper – this paper was the easiest to publish.

Which paper was most cited?
The paper on magazine prices (Cecchetti and Ball, 1988) which was rejected by a fair number of places. Also, I handled it badly because I was a very young assistant professor and didn't really ask for the right kind of advice.

So, debt deflation. You don't think it holds much water, do you?
Well, I think I have a different mechanism in mind. I think this is a problem with loan demand and loan supply. I look at the history and I see deflation, I see investment decline, and I see apparent problems in financial intermediation. Is it because borrowers are less credit worthy because their net worth has fallen due to deflation? Or is it because their projects have to reach new, higher hurdle rates? It's very hard to know. I would just say that in the decapitalization argument, technically the way I thought about it, I didn't build imperfect information or adverse selection problems into the model. I could have been built it in as a risk premium that was increasing or something like that. I don't think I ever wrote that I thought debt deflation per se was the wrong explanation.

No, you didn't say it was the wrong explanation. You said it didn't happen in the 1920s when the conditions should have been much worse for it, but yet it happened during the Depression and after all, this is a deflation problem, so it's a monetary problem. What you have to do is show substantial accumulation of medium- and long-term debt. So Jim Fackler and I have just published a paper this month (January 2005) in Economic Inquiry *about debt deflation and the accumulation of medium- and long-term debt.*
So, what do you think?

Well, I think it's part of the story.

It's hard to dismiss these things, but I think ... you know we keep coming back to the deflation and then really in a policy sense you want to ask yourself what is the source of the deflation and how can you avoid it?

I would agree with that.
That's what we keep coming back to.

OK, we've just got plum questions left now. What ended the Great Depression? I think you told me it was World War II.
In the absence of the 1937 reserve requirement increase, I think we probably would have done a lot better. We wouldn't have set the economy back into the dumper. It is the case that I think that rapid monetary expansion had the potential to bring us out of the Depression, but it didn't successfully do that.

You mean bring us back to the pre-1929 level?
Yes. It had the potential to do that. Although, the political economy of this is quite complicated because what you've got is a change in the structure of the economy and a change in the government. It is a critical change in the federal government that's come about with more centralized power, a bigger government, and the question is what you are going to get. You've got a fundamentally different economy from the pre-1929 economy and one with a lot more government intervention in it.

Any remaining important questions yet to be answered?
That we haven't been through? No, I don't think so. I still think that, again, there is this 1921–22 vs. 1930–32 comparison that's important. But I would say I'm not prepared to devote a lot more time to going back and rehashing this myself because I think that, from a central banking policy perspective, most of what I think we can learn we have gotten out of this. Whether the deflation caused the economy to collapse for reason A or reason B is of less interest to me as a monetary policy advisor than the mere fact that the deflation was the problem.

Fair enough. I always ask everybody, could it happen again?
Ah, anything can happen again. I think that the risks right now are that fiscal policy is on an unsustainable path. The risk is of a high inflation together with a collapse of the economy. I guess the answer is I don't see us having a 30 percent deflation and a 30 percent decline in output, 10 percent a year each for three years. That seems pretty hard for me to imagine right now. I think we learned that lesson. Could we have a very sharp collapse in the economy together with a very high inflation as a consequence of fiscal policy problems? Yes, and what would come along with that would be, again, a very high real interest rate.

OK, just some contemporary questions. Something you've been writing recently. You have a fiscal policy piece in the Financial Times *where you provide a modest proposal to keep tax revenues at a 40-year average of 19 percent of GDP and the debt-to-GDP ratio at 50 percent. Have you had any takers on this yet?*

There's been a movement, a very modest one, inside Congress to try and go back to some of the fiscal restraints that existed before the Bush administration, the ones that were put in place in the late 1980s to try to recover some of that discipline. It is interestingly coming from people like Senator Leiberman, someone I think of as the fiscal conservative in the Democratic party, and I think that they picked up on trying to put limits on fiscal expenditure that would make clear the sustainability of the path or things like that.

A more forward-looking fiscal policy.
Yes, to try to do more forward-looking budgeting.

Where did you come up with the 50 percent number?
(Cecchetti answers right away) I made it up.

That's all I wanted you to admit (laughter).
It's below the 60 percent Maastrict treaty threshold for the European economies. It's hard to pick a number. You know zero is lower than you need and you know it's the debt-to-GDP ratio that matters so you can have a permanent deficit, if you want. You know that numbers like 100 percent, 125 percent and 150 percent, where the Japanese are, can generate unsustainability all on their own, for sort of Brazil kinds of reasons. Where in that range should you fall? Should it be 50 percent, should it be 60 percent, should it be 70 percent? I don't think I care what number you pick, but you should pick a number and stick to it. What it does is it creates an anchor for expectations and creates a discipline on the fiscal authority to remain responsible.

So, then, the 19 percent of GDP, that's the 40-year average. That plus the sustainable deficit is what we have to spend.
Right, that's what we have to spend and that's the forward-looking, disciplined way to look at it and the debate should be over how big you want the government to be and how we should pay for it.

That's all I have, Professor. Thanks so much.

James Butkiewicz

James Butkiewicz received his Ph.D. from the University of Virginia in 1977 and he is currently Professor of Economics at the University of Delaware. The recent archival research he has conducted on Federal Reserve Board Governor Eugene Meyer deserves our consideration as these documents have heretofore received little attention from economists. Moreover, besides Allan Meltzer, perhaps no active scholar has a greater wealth of knowledge about the real-time inner workings of the Federal Reserve System during the interwar era than Professor Butkiewicz. I spoke with James Butkiewicz in his office at the University of Delaware on May 10, 2005.

I understand you have looked at some archives regarding Federal Reserve Board Governor Eugene Meyer that may shed some new light on the events during the Great Depression.
Eugene Meyer was a central figure who has been ignored and Ithink there is an explanation for that. Meyer's biography, written by Pusey, comes out in 1974. Also, Meyer provided an oral history interview with a man named Albertson and the transcripts are deposited at Columbia University. I checked with Columbia University and until 1974 the Albertson transcripts of the oral history were restricted and you had to have the approval of Katharine Graham, one of Meyer's daughters, to see them. The Meyer papers also are deposited in the Library of Congress in 1974. So Friedman and Schwartz (1963) and Wicker (1966) looked through the archives and they used what was there. Meyer's stuff wasn't available, generally, to anybody. My interpretation is the family held it back until Pusey's book could be written. Once his book was written they released it. But they wanted his interpretation of events to be written.

In your 1980 paper with Anderson you are one of the few, other than Field (1992), who has paid any recent attention to the role of the housing market in propagating the Depression. What's your take on the role of any real estate bubble back then?
Well my interest has been rekindled largely because of the work I've done on Eugene Meyer. Because Meyer felt it really was a real estate bubble that spilled over into the stock market rather than the other way, and I'm curious to explore his ideas more, for a lot of reasons. For our paper, that was

something that we put into the model because I guess we felt that we couldn't ignore it. It was something in our paper that we never pushed very hard after that. But now, when I read what Meyer says, I've become a lot more interested in going back and exploring that. And also your first book, *Reflections on the Great Depression*, sort of reminded me that it was one of those questions that was left hanging. The other thing is Christina Romer's argument about the decline in spending on consumer durables, the stock market and so forth. But durable expenditures are also highly correlated generally with housing because when you buy a house that's only the first step in the whole process, and we all know that. What's the relation between housing and consumer durables which Romer argues is so important? Is there something there? I don't think she ever explored it. I think that's a connection worth looking at. And Meyer always argued in his explanation that there was sort of a housing bust from about 1912 to 1922. There wasn't enough housing being built. Then he said from 1922 to around 1926 the demand was being met. After that it became more speculative, and then he said it spilled over into the stock market. So for housing, there may be more there that needs to be explored and I sort of left it hanging 25 years ago. It doesn't seem like that long ago does it?

No, it's not that long. Let's not count. We'll just talk about the paper and not the year. How about that?
OK.

You have a story (in Butkiewicz, 1999) to tell regarding the Reconstruction Finance Corporation (RFC). It is a tale of Michigan, the gold standard and the panic of 1933 and the story is rather like helping heroin addicts, but under the condition that their names get splashed in full color in the newspaper. Won't you please brief us on this experience of the RFC.
The interest in the RFC was stimulated by Friedman and Schwartz when they said the RFC seemed to help. And a lot of people in their writings said the RFC seemed to help. I said OK, I'll certainly take that as a working hypothesis but let's see if it really did help. In reading some of the stuff that Eugene Meyer was talking about late in his life, he was saying how much it hurt and other people were saying that it really didn't increase failures so much as it just stopped helping. And that's sort of what I felt the data suggested to me. The RFC was helping through July of 1932. When the names of the banks began to be released in August, banks appeared to be reluctant to borrow much more. Meyer did say many banks were afraid to show any bills payable on their books because it was a sign of weakness. John Nance Garner clearly had political motivation too. He was running for president. There was a three-way tie at the convention. He shifted his support to Roosevelt in exchange for the vice presidency, which he held for eight years before he turned on Roosevelt in 1940. So Garner did not want to see it work, obviously. It seemed to be working. It seemed to be providing some relief. Casual empiricism suggests

that it did and then when I did my empirical work that also supported the notion that it did up through July and then after that the effectiveness diminished. Then I got interested in the second issue which was did the publicity increase bank failures and that's when I started to look at the July through February period. And I just didn't see it. Although a lot of people say that bank failures were mounting and so forth, it really looks like the Michigan situation was a spark that set off a conflagration that wasn't really happening to that extent before. People want to debate whether bank failures were increasing or not. It just wasn't dramatic. After Michigan it was terribly dramatic and I think Michigan was a crucial spark that really led to the final crisis. And I'm curious because some people don't talk about it very much. There's a 1973 book by Susan E. Kennedy, it's been well known and widely cited for years and she has a chapter that is just titled "Michigan."

It's her book on the 1933 banking crisis.
Yes, and anybody who reads that book should know what she means by that title "Michigan."

They had a bank holiday, right?
Well what happened was, and it's interesting when you really go back through the archives, all these banks that were in trouble were in trouble for a year or two before they ultimately met their Waterloo. The Union Guardian Trust was the bank in Michigan, as I recall now, and it had deposits of about $28 million and it made a lot of real estate loans and it was in trouble. They wanted to close the bank, pay off the depositors, and operate as a trust business. The RFC ultimately was going to close the bank. Lincoln's birthday came on Sunday. This was a time when Lincoln's birthday was a federal holiday and so the banks were closed Monday the 13th. They met over the weekend and they wanted to resolve it. James Couzens, who was a senator from Michigan, got wind of this. Couzens had once been Henry Ford's partner but now they were arch enemies. And Couzens, who had been sort of investigating the RFC and was interested in the RFC's activities, came to Detroit and said "If we're going to lend this bank $28 million to pay off its depositors, Henry Ford is going to subordinate his deposits," which were about $7 million of the $28 million. Henry Ford said, "I'm already the largest tax payer in the United States, I'm not giving the government any more of my money." I got the microfilm from *The Detroit Free Press* and there's a picture on the day that it was announced of these two old guys, they were about ready to choke each other. I mean you could just see it in the picture – the animosity and the anger and the hatred – and basically they couldn't resolve the situation between the two of them. The Governor of Michigan declares a bank holiday and all of a sudden panic starts to spread. Immediately you see people saying "Well Cleveland's going to be OK." You know when they start saying things like that it's not going to be OK and it spreads to Ohio and it spreads to Maryland. Two weeks later, by the end

of February, the week preceding the Saturday inauguration of Roosevelt, every day on page six, *The New York Times* had a table, a whole page describing the banking situation in every state, who had limited withdrawals to 5 percent and 10 percent, who had declared holidays, who'd been suspended. It had become a nationwide phenomenon in two weeks, and I think and Elmus Wicker (1996) thinks that Michigan was the spark that led to that. What I really set out to look at was did the publication of the identity of the RFC loan recipients cause a real problem? And I sort of felt no, it didn't cause a real problem, but that it was really Michigan that set off the spark. I saw it in a lot of things. I looked at the data – the stock prices of Michigan banks, because I had the microfilm from The Detroit Free Press; you just didn't see any anticipation of crisis. The other thing that's very interesting is you didn't see it in the dollar. Before Michigan the dollar was within the bands and afterwards the dollar was shaky and there's a real break at that point in the exchange rate. And people all of a sudden, the speculators, are starting to bet against the dollar. Well they hadn't been up to that point. So whatever happened at Michigan at that time, Monday was a federal holiday and on Valentine's Day they announced the bank holiday at one in the morning and all of a sudden things changed. And I think that was a real spark that led to the last banking crisis.

Calomiris in his 1997 paper with Mason said that the RFC was the only entity charged with helping avoid the insolvency of individual banks. At this time Federal Reserve banks did not view the prevention of bank insolvency as their mandate.

This is all tied together. Meyer said that the Fed did not feel much obligation to help the nonmember banks. That's why he created the RFC. Actually, my interest in Meyer began with the question "Why did the Governor of the Federal Reserve Board create the RFC? Why did he feel it was necessary and why did he make it look like part of the Fed?" The RFC offices were located in Fed buildings and Fed officials did double duty working with the RFC.

The RFC is often criticized as being too stringent with its lending policy. It took much of a bank's good collateral, leaving it less liquid.

Yes it did, and often took 150–200 percent of the loan value. Later in his life Meyer said the RFC could be criticized for not being more liberal. But at the time the RFC was tight with its loans because Congress wanted it that way. In the Senate hearings for the RFC Meyer testified that he had been told by individual Senators and Congressmen that it would be alright for the War Finance Corporation (WFC), which Meyer ran in the early 1920s, to lose money, but Meyer said he didn't think that was a good policy and the WFC didn't lose money. Senators at the hearings made it very clear that they didn't want the RFC to lose money.

Meyer's wife tells a great story in her diary. It's a Sunday in July 1932 after the Chicago bank crisis in June. Meyer's health is becoming a problem so he sat all day in his dressing gown talking with George Harrison, both drinking whiskey, and prohibition was still on. Harrison urged Meyer to make more "Dawes loans", referring to the very liberal loan made to save Dawes' bank in Chicago a few weeks earlier. Meyer's wife wrote that if they did that "Congress would have a day of reckoning." The RFC was tight because of the political pressure it faced.

Let me ask you for your impression of Figure 2 that shows up in Cecchetti (1998). The figure shows Federal Reserve discounting from 1919 through the Great Depression.
Well there are a couple of things. First of all, the high level of discounts during the War and the immediate post-war years was the preferential lending rate that the Fed had for government bonds, which was really a Treasury policy. And basically the Fed was put in the position of having to discount these bonds at a rate below the rate that they were paying. Now if you're a bank and you're getting say 4.5 percent on a liberty bond and you can discount it at 4 pecent, you're going to take a lot of that action because that half-point spread is pure profit and you can just go out and buy more of them with what you've discounted and keep doing the same. So there was really a war-financed inflation there. And then when the preferential policy ended banks didn't have the same incentives because now the discount rate may have been above what they were getting on their assets instead of below. So I think a lot of that has to do with the preferential discount rate, number one, and then, number two, in the 1920s they discovered open market operations and so they began to substitute that for discounting. In fact at that point the Fed wants to move away from discounting as a policy. Once the Fed discovered open market operations and understood how they worked, there is a change in their approach. And they move away from the original model to a different model. So yes, in that sense there was a regime switch but it's not just that they discouraged discounting. I think you have to look at the high level of discounting as war-financed inflation and what happened afterwards as more normal but also the discovery of a new policy tool.

Christina Romer has called the US decision to stay on the gold standard perhaps the biggest policy error of the Depression and calls the Depression a result of failed policy. On the other hand Temin told me that after 1931 "the Fed had picked their side" and thus their actions should not be construed as policy failures. Their behavior was not a shock or inept but a continuation of the path that they had chosen. What do you say?
Well, once again, having done all this work on Eugene Meyer I know the thought of leaving the gold standard never crossed his mind. It's taken as a given. We were a gold standard country. He was asked several times by Congress about this. He said he'd never considered leaving during the whole period. That I think, at least to Meyer, was never a consideration. He was

always defending the gold standard. He felt that was one of the things that just came with the job. And even after we left the gold standard his comments on Roosevelt were very critical. I think we retrospectively look at these things and talk about policy choices. I'm not sure people at the time always saw the same menu of choices that we see today. It's like the British debate where Keynes clearly saw a different menu of choices than other people. Everybody says, "Oh sure it was pointless to come back to the gold standard at $4.86 per pound." That was a mistake but, as I understand it, the issue was never the rate, it was only the timing. I mean you have an empire all over the world that's centered on you as a financial anchor. You've got to establish the old rate. I think today we look at that and say "of course you don't" but I think at the time a lot of people said "of course you do." That's not really a choice. I think in the United States, and I don't know as much about Herbert Hoover or Andrew Mellon or Ogden Mills or any of those people, but for Eugene Meyer, who was the Governor of the Board from 1930 to 1933, leaving the gold standard was not a choice. It was not a choice.

So you want to defend the exchange value at all peril?
Yes. For Eugene Meyer, I don't think there was ever a question in his mind. Leaving the gold standard was never an option. In the 1950s when Meyer was talking to Sidney Hyman (who in 1976 wrote a book on Marriner Eccles) and in the oral histories recorded by Albertson, he was very upset about the devaluation of the dollar and leaving the gold standard. He felt that was totally wrong.

He still felt that in the 1950s?
Yes.

Hsieh and Romer (2004) rely on the Harrison papers to investigate whether the Federal Reserve was concerned about expectations of devaluation or a speculative attack on the dollar as a result of the open market operations of 1932. What is your understanding of what was happening inside the Fed at this time?
That's an interesting question because Meyer really never says anything about it, although he was always worried about the French. He was worried about the French before he became Governor. His brother-in-law was in Paris in early 1930 and he asked him if he could learn anything about French intentions. When he came to the Fed he was very concerned about all the foreign deposits in the New York banks and he wanted to get them out, and he urged reductions in the discount rate in 1931 to do it. And he was worried about the French in October 1931 when he wanted the discount rate in New York increased and it was increased twice. Then in 1932 he didn't say anything about it. But I found some other sources that suggest that gold really was the issue. One of the key pieces of evidence I found is a letter from Russell Leffingwell to Carter Glass.

Leffingwell was a senior partner at Morgan Bank at this time. He later became the president of Morgan Bank. He succeeded Thomas Lamont as president. Glass was a Senator from Virginia who had been Secretary of Treasury for Wilson when Leffingwell was the Assistant Secretary. Leffingwell wrote to Glass in 1933 and he said that when the gold drains started in May and June of 1932, he feels that's when the Fed officials lost their nerve and that's when they stopped the open market operations.

Then I went back to the New York Fed archives. It turns out that the key person here is Randy Burgess. W. Randolph Burgess was the Deputy Governor of the New York Fed and he was the person in charge of the execution of open market operations. In his papers in New York there are letters from some of the reserve bank governors saying that they were running low on gold and that they were concerned about making any more purchases. At that time each Federal Reserve bank had to take a certain percentage, an allotment of the open market purchases. They could only do so based on the amount of gold that was available. Most of the banks had reserve percentages in the neighborhood of 50 percent. A couple were under 50. Several were over 50 and approaching 50. From these letters you get a sense that 50 percent was as far as they wanted to go. The reserve requirement was slightly under forty but they just didn't want to go below 50. The two banks that had a lot of gold were Boston and Chicago. They were the most opposed to the open market operations. There was some discussion about changing the allotments, but they knew Chicago and Boston wouldn't go along. It seems as though they just stopped.

Also, on June 8 New York Governor Harrison wrote a letter to the other governors. In his cover letter to Meyer he said that he had so many calls about the gold issue that he thought it was important to write a more or less all-inclusive explanation of what was happening. Harrison argued that since most of the French funds had been withdrawn or were going to be withdrawn, he thought the gold drain was coming to an end. There was a lot of concern within the system. The archival evidence clearly demonstrates that a lot of people there were worried about gold. Meltzer (2003) talks about how New York's reserve percentage went under 50 percent. Even they were worried about losing their gold, and so they quit making purchases. So I think gold really was a factor.

So free gold was the issue?
It was and it wasn't. In 1931 Meyer was not concerned. Meyer had decided, at least by June if not earlier in 1931, that gold inflows were being sterilized by currency hoarding and that the Fed needed to do something about it and he tried to make his case. This is at the August 11, 1931 meeting of the Open Market Policy Conference; the minutes don't say very much but it's well known, that Meyer wanted to make 300–400 million dollars in open market purchases. Charles S. Hamlin, who was a Board member, in the testimony to the Banking Act of 1935 said that Governor Meyer went in, and at this time the

Board had no real operational authority, they only had approval authority, so Meyer could only suggest and urge and recommend. And he said Governor Meyer for two hours argued a case very strongly that nothing short of a bold stroke would work. Meyer wanted "to strike a bold stroke" and the other governors basically said no. Harrison was more supportive and Black of Atlanta was always more supportive but the others said no. Governor Caulkins from San Francisco said, "How do you other Governors and your Boards of Directors feel?" and they went around the room and most everybody said no. About half of them either directly or indirectly alluded to a free gold problem. That was when the free gold gauntlet was thrown down, that's when they said free gold was a constraint. Now that wasn't the first time that free gold was discussed. The Board began measuring free gold in 1927, and had daily measures of free gold, although there were three different ways they computed free gold. And I think the crucial aspect of free gold is that it delayed Meyer's efforts to expand and the economy was that much worse in 1932 than it was in 1931. Had he been able to pursue his policies in 1931, maybe they would have worked faster.

Meyer claims that he was the one who wanted Section III of the Glass–Steagall Act.

Glass–Steagall of 1932.

Yes, that was the one he was really involved in. Section III was the provision that allowed the substitution of government securities for gold or eligible paper to meet the Federal Reserve's collateral requirements. Meyer said he got his friend, Carter Glass, who was a pretty strict proponent of the real bills doctrine and got his insight from H. Parker Willis who was a very strict proponent of real bills, to pass the RFC "and now I have to go back and ask him for something else he is opposed to and that is to allow the substitution of government bonds for gold and eligible paper to meet the collateral requirements." But they passed Glass–Steagall. Meyer had said in February/March of 1932 the Fed had never been in a stronger position and they were ready to begin the open market purchases. They still did not pledge the government securities as collateral. The Federal Reserve Bank Governors asked Meyer if they were going to do it right away and Meyer said no, not until they had to. I think you can see the reason why in the testimony for the Banking Act of 1935; you can see Carter Glass is mad. He said he wanted on the record that he never would have reported that bill, that is co-sponsored the Glass–Steagall Act, had he known it was going to be used. He was told it was only for psychological purposes. Meyer waited as long as he could before using Glass–Steagall because, I am sure, it was Meyer who promised Glass it would not be used. Although it may have been through Harrison since Meyer was busy with the RFC and had left it to Harrison to lobby Glass for the Glass–Steagall Act.

Anyway, back in August of 1931 Meyer asks Emmanuel Goldenweiser, director of research at the Federal Reserve Board, if they have enough free gold to expand. Goldenweiser replies "We have $800 million, some individual banks may have a problem, but for the system as a whole there's enough free gold to expand." By the next March it is down to $370 million if you don't count government securities. Every day on a 5 x 8 sheet of paper (I found this only in Meyer's archives) Meyer got a report (I think it was from Edward Smead, the Board's Chief of Bank Operations) of the free gold position of every reserve bank and the system as a whole. He saw how it dwindled and then by early May it was down to $170 million or something like that. That's when he said they were going to use government securities as collateral so they could keep going.

And they did keep going.
Yes, there was a directive sent out on May 2 and May 5, 1932, was the first day government securities were pledged as collateral and free gold was no longer an issue. So in 1932 when they were ready to expand, Meyer felt that they were never in better shape and were ready to pursue an expansionary policy when they did.

Why did they quit it then? Was it just the loss of gold?
(*Butkiewicz takes a deep breath and sighs*) I think there are some things that are very clear. The Reserve banks never wanted to do it, except for Harrison and Eugene Meyer. Meyer was basically pushing them to do it and it was resented. George Norris, Governor of the Philadelphia Fed (who in his memoirs never mentions Meyer by name but from the period it is clear who he is talking about) said "during this period the Board sought more authority for themselves and made themselves an operational entity instead of an approval or regulatory entity" and he very much resented what was happening. Meyer himself says the main problem was Chicago. He never mentions James McDougal by name, but he did say "the Governor of the Chicago bank was a first-class accountant, I guess, but not a good central banker." You know, damning him with faint praise. And this too comes out in Marriner Eccles' testimony for the Banking Act of 1935. Meyer said the Board of the Chicago bank was dominated by George Reynolds, who was the head of the Continental bank group in Chicago. Reynolds had been on the Chicago Fed Board since the day it was started. When they started the Chicago Fed it was announced that there was going to be a governor who was going to be the executive officer. There was debate among the Chicago leading bankers about whether it was more important to be Governor of the Chicago Fed or president of one of the leading banks and they decided that the important job was to be president of one of the leading Chicago banks. Governor was a subsidiary position. Meyer said that Reynolds dominated the Chicago Fed and he was one of the nine members of the Board of Directors, the class C members who had the votes.

Reynolds and his people always wanted higher interest rates and any time there was a move to make open market purchases or lower rates, they were against it. But Meyer said there was also hostility among the other banks as well. Then too, in the press by May, *Time* magazine had Meyer's portrait on the cover of the May 30, 1932 issue and inside they talked about how the open market purchases weren't working because banks weren't making enough loans.

So the governors of the Reserve banks were increasingly hostile and some of them had stopped participating because they said they didn't have enough free gold. The governors were upset, the press was saying it wasn't working, and it was considered extremely radical at the time. The scale of the open market purchases in 1932 was far greater than anything that had ever been done. They bought over $1 billion of securities in an economy that at that time had a nominal GDP of $50-some billion. It was some kind of an open market operation. Today we think this is what they should have been doing all along. But you can find contemporary publications in the *Journal of Political Economy* and the *American Economic Review* saying what they were doing was really out of the ordinary.

By August of 1932, Meyer's health is not good and he is mostly out of commission for two and a half months. When he comes back, given the increasing hostility of the Reserve banks, I think he realizes he is running out of gas and that Hoover would lose the election and he would be gone. At that time the Governor of the Board served at the pleasure of the President, and Meyer and Roosevelt wouldn't mix. By the end Meyer and Hoover were at odds over everything. Meyer's wife wrote in February 1933 that he hated going into work, and he was a self-proclaimed workaholic. He seemed to be beaten down, and his wife described him as being on "death's doorstep" when he finally left. He resigned in March but stayed on through May at FDR's request.

We also need to remember that unlike today, where Alan Greenspan is considered next to God and God may have to schedule an appointment and the Board is all-powerful, back then the Board was not respected. The Board was in some sense viewed as a retirement home for Federal Reserve officials who had served their usefulness and were sent to the Board. The Board was the least of all parts of the system. The Reserve banks felt that they were in charge. Friedman and Schwartz, and here is where I have to part company with them, talk about the Federal Reserve System. It was not a system. There were two systems. There were the district banks, which felt they were in charge and that they should initiate policy. And then there was the Board and the Reserve banks were jealous of their independence and always wanted to strike off in another direction.

In fact, if you look at the Banking Act of 1935 testimony, one of the things Marriner Eccles really rants about is how open market operations are the most important policy tool we have and one group initiates the policy, another group approves it, and a third group gets to decide whether to carry it out or not and can veto the decisions of the other two. And he said to get policy enacted you have to convince 108 members of the Boards of Directors (nine times twelve), the Board of Governors, and the Governors of the 12 Federal Reserve banks and he said this is wrong.

We need to remember someone like Eugene Meyer had to walk the tightrope between getting the governors of the district banks to do what he wanted and Congress to do what he wanted. The independence that today's Federal Reserve Board of Governors enjoys did not exist back then. There were lots of people and lots of interests and lots of folks saying "this is what should be done." When we look at where we are today, or even in the 1960s after the Treasury–Fed Accords of the 1950s got the Fed out from under the Treasury's thumb again, back then it was not the Federal Reserve as we know it. To look at it today and retrospectively say "they should have done the same thing back then," you don't really appreciate how different life was. I think that is sometimes not given enough emphasis.

There is something else I don't think that's been played up enough. The long period between the election and Roosevelt's inauguration was the last long interregnum. The 20th Amendment had just been adopted to end the period between the election and the inauguration in January rather than March. Hoover wouldn't do anything unless Roosevelt agreed. Hoover wanted Roosevelt to agree to it on Hoover's terms, and Roosevelt wasn't going to agree to do anything that had to do with Hoover.

And I don't blame him.
So they were paralyzed. And in this period the financial structure of the country collapses. Friedman and Schwartz say there's no policy in January and February and it was true.

Hsieh and Romer (2004), in reference to the Glass–Steagall Act of 1932, say that perhaps the avoidance of the Great Depression was "a simple legislative change away." If it had been enacted in 1930 perhaps we wouldn't be talking about the Great Depression right now. What do you think about that?
(*Butkiewicz shakes his head*) I think that those things would not have been possible legislatively in 1930–31.

Why?
It wasn't desperate. Orthodoxy wasn't only Eugene Meyer, Andrew Mellon, Ogden Mills, George Harrison and Herbert Hoover. It was also Carter Glass, Henry Steagall and a host of others in Congress with a lot of say. Congress back then, as now, was a very eclectic group with people of all stripes and colors and its own collection of nuts and flakes, two of them were named Brookhart and McFadden. They all had an agenda. What was possible in 1932 wasn't necessarily possible before that. For example, Meyer said he felt the need for the RFC even before England left gold. But he didn't think it was

possible to get it. After England left gold, it was possible because it had become that bad.

Friedman and Schwartz claim the Fed's purchases in 1932 were stimulated by the Goldsborough bill and as soon as Congress adjourned they stopped the purchases because the pressure was off. What can you tell us about what contemporaries had to say in this regard at the time?

Goldsborough said that himself during the hearings for the Banking Act of 1935. While the purchases were being made he was very complimentary to the Fed. But of course, when they ended it was Goldsborough, long before Friedman and Schwartz, who claimed those purchases were only made under the pressure of his bill and once it was defeated the purchases stopped. But everybody left from that period denied it in Congressional testimony. Adolph Miller denied it, Hamlin denied it and most of all Emmanuel Goldenweiser got really irritated. Everything I've read suggests Goldenweiser was a soft-spoken, mild-mannered man. But he said he was tired of the assertion that "we didn't do anything," because we tried. And he said the purchases were not tactical. The problem is, and there are several aspects of the observational equivalence problem here, Meyer clearly told the Governors that there was this legislation pending in Congress which would make them do worse things, that is, the Goldsborough bill. But was he afraid of the Goldsborough bill or was he using it to hit the Governors over the head? Was he manipulating Goldsborough or was he manipulating the Governors? He did tell his biographer that the purchases were useful in fending off things like the Goldsborough bill. While I have no evidence of this, I firmly believe Meyer knew that bill was not going to get by Carter Glass. Harrison said at the time that Glass would kill Goldsborough's bill.

Now, the Goldsborough bill was passed by the House. But it had to get through the Senate. It was never going to get through the Senate unless Carter Glass approved it because Carter Glass dominated monetary legislation in the Senate. He was a key member of the committee, and Carter Glass wasn't going to approve anything that explicitly called for that much inflation. Meyer had to know that Glass was never going to let this bill out so he couldn't have been afraid of it. I mean, I don't know that for a fact but I have to believe it. He was a sharp, sharp guy.

Why did Meyer oppose the Goldsborough bill?

I think that there may have been a little bit of the fallacy of composition. Meyer said you can not control the price of a product unless you control its production, and he just saw an index of 376 commodity prices as the sum of its parts. He didn't see it as the aggregate price level. He said unless you can control the production, you're not going to control the price. At least that's what he said. It's possible he was dissembling. He just didn't want to do it, so he said it couldn't be done. Meyer was a firm, firm believer in discretion. He did not like rules. He didn't want a monetary rule. He said every time there's a problem it's something different than the last time. He didn't feel rules should constrain you because there were new issues, new problems, and you should be free to respond as you best see fit. He would never want to be tied down by a rule for policy. He didn't like the real bills doctrine. He said you should allow people to make loans on good collateral, whatever they feel is good collateral, not be specific. He said H. Parker Willis' definition of the real bills doctrine was purely technical. They were looking for a certain type of loan and anything that fitted that technical definition was eligible and nothing else was. Meyer said make good loans from good collateral.

Why was Carter Glass against the Goldsborough bill?
Because it was inflationary. It called for an increase in the price level back to the 1926 level. As Meyer said about Glass and H. Parker Willis, "their theories belong in a museum." They saw inflation everywhere in a country that was dead from deflation. Glass was a strict adherent to the real bills doctrine, so getting the Glass–Steagall Act through and getting him to sponsor it was a huge accomplishment. Glass didn't want it. He didn't want a bond-backed currency, which we had. It should be backed by real bills.

What ended the Great Depression?
Oh, gosh what ended the Great Depression? I certainly think that World War II had something to do with it. I think the gold inflows and the monetary expansions were helpful. Also, I wonder how much the RFC and the Federal Deposit Insurance Corporation (FDIC) were to blame for the slow pace of the recovery? This is an item on my research agenda, so I really don't want to go out too far on a limb here before these things are investigated. But Jesse Jones, head of the RFC under Roosevelt, if he didn't like the way a bank was being run he'd cut the bank officers' salaries or remove them because they were buying the preferred stocks in the banks. Banks also had to meet FDIC criteria. I'm wondering if these agencies made the banks reluctant to lend. And if there really is a credit channel to monetary policy, one of the unexplored items that I want to look at is, and I think that this is partly archival and partly statistical, what effect did these organizations have on banks' lending policies?

So the FDIC through greater or more scrutinizing regulation dissuaded banks from loaning more than they already would because of the Depression, is that the thesis?
It's something that I want to investigate. It's the visible hand of government.

I see. Alright.
And how much did the visible hand affect the recovery?

I got it. And then there's the golden avalanche that you just mentioned.

Yes, and I think they all helped. But when the government starts hiring everybody, everybody has a job. When everyone is getting a uniform and a gun, there's a lot of employment there.

Could it happen again?
No. I think we've learned from our mistakes. All the things that went wrong aren't going to go wrong and we are not blindly committed to the gold standard. There was no consideration that I can see before Roosevelt of leaving the gold standard. We talk about that as a policy choice. I don't think it was either seriously discussed or contemplated, even after Britain left it. Moreover, I think the Federal Reserve System was truly dysfunctional. Friedman and Schwartz (1963) put a lot of emphasis on the shift to the Open Market Policy Conference from the Open Market Investment Committee. When you read the end of the chapter "The Great Contraction," in the end I think that is what they focused on as much as anything for why policy failed. I think they don't put enough emphasis on it. I'd put even more emphasis on it because of the tensions within the System and it was no longer the Board against New York. Meyer and Harrison worked together, and they opposed deflation.

How do you vigorously defend the gold standard and oppose deflation?
Good question. There were really two different causes of deflation. If deflation followed from a defense of the gold standard that was OK, because defending the gold standard came first.

The other reason for deflation is what Meltzer calls the "industrial equilibrium" school. Here deflation was the necessary sequel to inflation. After the stock market speculation of 1928–29, deflation was necessary to restore equilibrium. Meyer and Harrison were opposed to deflation for this reason. Both testified that what was needed was reflation of commodity prices. They didn't call it inflation. The connotations were too negative, so they spoke of the need for reflation of prices. It was an internal–external balance thing. Deflation may be required to maintain external balance, but it was never needed for internal balance. Only the "industrial equilibrium" school felt that deflation was needed for internal balance, the "liquidate everything" philosophy. I think this was much better understood at the time. There were the "deflationists" and those that opposed deflation, but always for internal balance.

That's all I have. Thanks so much, Professor.

Michael Bordo

Michael Bordo received his Ph.D. from the University of Chicago in 1972 and in 2006–07 he is a Fellow of Kings College and Pitt Professor of American History and Institutions, Cambridge University. He is the Director of the Center for Monetary and Financial History and also Professor II, Rutgers University. If you are looking for the world's foremost authority on the history and mechanics of the classical gold standard and interwar gold exchange standard, Michael Bordo is a man you would want to talk to. I spoke with Michael Bordo in his office at Rutgers University on May 11, 2005.

Would you give us some background on how you got involved in the literature on the Great Depression.
I'm an economic historian and I have been interested in monetary history through my whole career. I wrote a thesis under Milton Friedman on the effects of the sources of change in the money supply on the real economy. I compared how money was injected into the economy in three different institutional eras in US history. So the Great Depression just comes about automatically from my interest in US monetary history and I have been teaching courses in economic history and monetary and financial history for a very long time. A key part of what I focus on in the courses I have taught has always been the Great Depression and I have always come at it from the Friedman and Schwartz perspective, as a student of Milton's and a colleague ever since 1970 of Anna Schwartz. So I guess that's how I got into it. I got directly into it when I wrote an article for a festschrift compiled in honor of Anna Schwartz in 1987. I wrote a paper on Friedman and Schwartz's *A Monetary History* and what the legacy was for that book in economic history. A good deal of the literature survey that I did was about the Great Depression. In fact before that I wrote a paper called "Explorations in monetary history," which was a review article for *Explorations in Economic History*. And again it was sort of a survey of the literature. A very significant fraction of the literature in the early 1980s was on the Great Depression and specifically the debate between Friedman and Schwartz and Peter Temin. I then began doing some original research with Anna Schwartz and Ehsan Choudhri and we wrote a paper around 1995 to see whether, if a Friedman-type money growth rule had been followed, the

Great Depression would have been avoided. We followed this with another paper a few years later that looked at the question whether the Fed would have been constrained from following these policies because of the limitations of its gold reserves and specifically the free gold problem. We constructed a model of a large open economy with limited capital mobility. We showed that the Fed had sufficient reserves to have dealt with any of the problems that could have come up in 1931 and 1932.

We are going to get to that.
Also, I guess I have always been interested in the issue of financial crises. When you talk about financial crises, you get to the Great Depression and the gold standard, which is probably my main source of research. Again, you can't really talk about the gold standard unless you stop in 1914. But once you carry it forward then the interwar gold standard becomes a key thing that one has to look at.

You have a piece in a web outlet called The Concise Encyclopedia of Economics *about the gold standard. In that encyclopedia entry you list statistics about the gold standard that are somewhat startling. Comparing 1879–1913 versus 1946–1990 the coefficient of variation for real output was 3.5 versus 1.5, prices were 17 versus .8, and unemployment averaged 6.8 percent versus 5.6 percent. Eichengreen in* Golden Fetters *has said "The policies required to defend the gold standard proved inconsistent with economic stability" and Hamilton also said to me that anytime there was an increase in the relative price of gold for whatever reason, that was going to impose deflation on all countries on the gold standard. So any of the non-cooperative events during the Great Depression that increased the demand for gold relative to its supply was going to transfer that volatility to a country's aggregate price level. We look back and it seems like a rotten system. Can you help today's student of the Great Depression try to understand the allure of "the Midas touch"?*
The classical gold standard was a very special time. It was a period when you had minimal amount of government intervention and when prices were pretty flexible and the adjustment mechanism to adhere to gold involved price levels rising and falling. Also, there wasn't that much to worry about from the real economy, it was an environment of minimal nominal rigidities so the real output fluctuations associated with the adjustment mechanism weren't that significant. Even if they were considerable compared to today, people didn't worry about them as much. So I think it was a different time than today. The Great Depression took place in a different environment. The Great Depression is in the environment of a gold exchange standard which was set up to economize on gold. So in a sense the gold exchange standard was more fragile than the gold standard. Secondly it was a system where the primary goal of policy had changed. Under the gold standard the

primary goal of policy was to defend the parity and let the domestic economy adjust. During the interwar they already came to a view that Eichengreen talks about, which I think is correct, that people began to worry about domestic economic stability. So they had two objectives. Once you have two objectives and one instrument you've got a problem, Mundell's assignment problem, the external imbalance problem. So that in itself meant that the gold standard wasn't going to work the way it did before World War I and that there were going to be situations where countries were going to make decisions to defend the domestic economy, which would mean that adhering to the gold standard could be a problem. Or if they went with the gold standard the domestic economy would suffer. Also during the interwar nominal rigidities were much greater than in the pre-war due to the rise of labor unions and other institutional changes in markets. This then meant that deflation would be associated with depression. In the pre-1914 period deflation was primarily good, that is, prices fell but the real economy grew quite rapidly. So the environment was different then, there was no maladjustment issue. I am reading Meltzer's book *A History of the Federal Reserve, Volume I* right now and something that he gives a lot of play to, which I think is correct, is that the principal belligerents after World War I went back to gold at misaligned real exchange rates. The pound was overvalued, the franc was undervalued and the dollar was undervalued. The US and France both followed pro-gold policies, France especially. The US followed a policy of sterilizing gold inflows because they were worried about inflation even though it was an environment of deflation. So this is why the gold standard created problems which contributed to the Great Depression. I don't buy the view that the gold standard caused the Great Depression, I think the Great Depression was caused by bad monetary policy largely made in the United States. The gold standard had one other feature which worked fine before 1914 but didn't in the 1930s, which is that it transmitted shocks between countries. If you have an adjustment mechanism that works, where a deflationary shock is transmitted from one country to the other, what happens is that prices fall. But if you have nominal rigidities output falls too. So the US, through its poor monetary policies, through its tight monetary policies in the run-up to the Depression and then for not offsetting the banking crises after 1930, transmitted a shock, a negative shock through the balance of payments, through the fixed exchange rate gold standard, to the rest of the world. So that's why the gold standard gets a bad rap, because it wasn't really run like a pure gold standard. Now I'm not advocating a pure gold standard because I think, along with a lot of people going back to Irving Fisher and others, that the gold standard did not give us perfect price stability and it had considerable variance in prices. It led to a certain amount of short-run price level uncertainty and we could have done better by adopting some kind of rule like Fisher's compensated dollar plan or Marshall's tabular standard or even a fiat money standard which follows a Friedman rule or another type of fiat rule. So even though I thought the gold standard was great before 1914 for the reasons I mentioned, I don't advocate it for now.

Michael Kitson has said that the gold standard was "simply structurally flawed" and could not have survived even with coordination and cooperation. What does Michael Bordo say to that?
Well I don't know. I wrote a paper in 1998 with Barry Eichengreen in which we asked "what would have happened if we hadn't had the Great Depression?" What we said was if we hadn't had the Great Depression there is a pretty good chance that the gold exchange standard would have survived for a long time, and that some of these issues would have been worked out. Assume that the Fed did not make the mistakes that they did and/or second that there had been some cooperative solution to the misalignment problem. Given those two assumptions, we then showed that the gold exchange standard would have actually survived through the 1930s. We calibrated a model of the gold standard showing the adjustment mechanism in a closed economy or world gold standard which highlighted the effects of falling price levels on gold production. We showed that deflation would have continued and the gold exchange standard could have survived. Indeed even if they had done what was done in World War I and the US Civil War, and suspended it in World War II and we had gone back to it, it could have continued for quite a long time. I think that there was a lot of belief in gold. Eichengreen and Temin have written about this gold mentalité and I think that people did think that the gold standard was the way of the world and had the Great Depression not come about through the various shocks that did happen, especially the bad policy shocks, I'm not convinced that it would have just blown up by itself.

Peter Temin has said that it is the adherence to financial orthodoxy and the attempt to preserve the gold standard that produced the Great Depression. What does Michael Bordo say to that?
I don't buy it. I think that the Great Depression was caused by the Federal Reserve. The Federal Reserve by failing to stop the banking panics and the consequences thereof in the United States was what turned a serious recession into the Great Depression. I think that the real bills doctrine probably was more important than the gold standard in terms of why the Federal Reserve just didn't get their act together and follow the right policy. And I think that it's the model or the theories that were driving the Fed and the primary theory was the real bills doctrine. The gold standard was also important, but the Fed didn't pay that much attention to it really. I mean they sterilized gold flows in the 1920s and they really were trying to follow primarily a domestic monetary standard. So I don't think that is the main reason for the Great Depression coming about. I don't say that it didn't

matter, it mattered a lot. It took the huge shock of the Great Depression to get rid of that financial orthodoxy and for the US to switch to a reflationary policy. I think that the Treasury did that and I think that what they did was great. But I think that financial orthodoxy really has to be defined more carefully.

Alright then, let me just continue on this theme. Eichengreen in his paper "Still fettered after all these years" seems to me to be saying that there's a role for both domestic policy mistakes and the gold standard and Romer has for many years admitted that the gold standard plays a prominent role in understanding the nature and spread of the Great Depression. So, is there much of a debate left? Romer admits that 1931 and 1933 were beyond the Fed's control, and Eichengreen said to me that the Fed could have done more earlier on. The debate seems to be on 1932 and whether more expansionary policy was feasible. So my question is first, is there much of a debate left, and second, was the Federal Reserve fettered by gold at any time during the Great Depression?

I think that on the big macro issues there's pretty well a consensus. I mean everybody believes that the gold standard was important, especially for other countries. I completely buy Eichengreen's story about golden fetters for all the small countries that were locked in to fear from following expansionary policies which they needed to do to deal with their banking crises and their depression. The case of the US is where I disagree with him. Anna Schwartz, Choudhri and I published a paper on this in 2002 and Hsieh and Romer (2004) have also written on this subject. We really think that the Fed had sufficient gold reserves throughout that whole period, even in the critical period right after Britain left the gold standard. They had the ammunition to follow expansionary policies and in 1932 the policy was working and the Fed bailed out. So I really think that the US was in a special place, it had the power to stem the Great Depression.

So you don't think they were hitting their gold constraints or the psychological effect of hitting below 50 percent in the summer of 1932 or anything like that?

There are a number of issues here. There's the issue of did they ever hit the limit or would they have? Now, we show in our simulations that they would have been a couple of percentage points, in the worst case scenario, above the weighted average minimum gold reserve. People have said to us, "yes, but once they get close to that then adverse psychology is going to take over and people are going to assume it's going to collapse and you'll get a speculative attack." In response we estimated speculative attack models on this period and they did not show that. So, we're doubtful about that outcome, but it's possible. But then there's a second line of defense which Friedman and Schwartz (1963) made and Meltzer (2003) stresses in his new book, which is that they had fail safes. In the Federal Reserve Act you could suspend the gold reserve requirements and they did do this in 1915. Because it had been done before, it could have been done again. The gold standard could have been treated as a contingent rule as I have discussed in my work with Finn Kydland. So the thinking that as soon as they hit the limit they just couldn't do anything is just not true. There was precedent for temporary suspension in US history and precedent for it in the histories of other countries.

If you break the Depression down and segregate it into a series of questions, I think it goes like this: what started it? why was it so deep? why did it last so long? why did it spread so completely? and why did recovery come when it did? Is there any of one of those segregating questions that you think remains a mystery today?
Not really. I think that the interesting work that's going on today on the Great Depression is the approach that's been taken by the real business cycle people, Cole and Ohanian at UCLA and Prescott and others. I think they've raised some interesting questions about real shocks and the real side of the economy. I don't completely buy it, but I do think that's the direction we need to go. I think that there is a consensus now between me, Eichengreen, Temin, Calomiris, Romer and others which is that it is both US domestic policy and international considerations that were responsible for the Depression and the weights that we attach to these two views differ between us.

So then I'm right. There's not a lot of debate left.
There isn't a lot of debate left, but there's this other view that's coming out now, the reinterpretation that's coming out of Minnesota that either needs to be refuted or maybe it will become the new consensus.

Well let's just go to that right now.
OK.

What's your take on the recent flurry of real business cycle papers on the Great Depression? I observe that you wrote a comment with Erceg and Evans on Cole and Ohanian (2000) in the 2000 NBER Macroeconomics Annual. If we thought that we had the Depression explained before, they present a whole new set of questions. Ohanian indicated that the whole line of research basically addresses the question "what is preventing people from working and producing more?" So let me ask you, what are we learning?
In that comment with Erceg and Evans on their paper at that NBER conference a few years ago, we were pretty skeptical of the story they told for the Great Depression itself. The numbers just didn't add up. We went

back and looked at the data on wages and prices. They argued that the wage rigidity story didn't hold up and we looked at different data and showed that wage rigidity was a problem. So that's what that debate was about. But where they do have something which I think is really important isn't in 1929–33, it's the recovery. They have done a great job, building on a 1981 paper by Michel Weinstein, and they showed Weinstein was right. It was the supply-side constraints imposed by the New Deal and the NIRA and then later by other stuff like the Wagner Act which really did impede recovery. So I do believe that is good work which is not in any way contradictory to the Friedman and Schwartz story.

But for 1929–33?
I just don't buy it. The arguments that there was a negative productivity shock is hard to believe. The logic of the model is just pretty hard to accept and secondly the data they looked at is doubtful. In fact there's a paper that I discussed (Bordo, 2003) by Christiano, Motto, and Rostagno which is a nice modern attempt, which encapsulates the more recent Minnesota approaches to macro in a believable narrative on the Depression. It is grounded in a maximizing model, but it throws in the kind of rigidities and the problems with the banking sector which are stressed by Friedman and Schwartz and Bernanke and others and I think that is a good way to go. So they are bringing in the disincentives on the real side that are discussed by the Minnesota people, but they're integrating that with the nominal rigidities that are coming out of Bernanke's work and the Friedman and Schwartz story of the bank failures and failure of lender of last resort. So in a sense that's an integration of the literature that I think is very, very good and very promising.

Do you think the comparisons of the 1920–21 recession to the Great Depression are pushed too hard while explanations for their differences are ignored?
In the NBER version of our 2000 *AER* paper, Erceg, Evans and I had a section comparing 1920–21 to the Great Depression which I really liked but which we had to delete from the *AER* version of the paper. The comparison was extremely interesting because the deflation was very severe in 1920–21 but the decline in output was not nearly as large and the recovery was much faster. The difference we argued was due to the fact that the degree of nominal rigidity was greater later on in the 1930s and also, and this is probably a more important difference between the two periods, so were expectations. We argued that people expected that the US would go back to gold (in fact the US did not formally leave the gold standard during World War I, it imposed an embargo on gold exports from 1917 to 1919), that the Fed was going try to get the price level to be consistent with what the real price should have been and that people understood this. So expectations

were anchored by the gold standard. For the later episode, the gold standard was already not doing very well and expectations did change a lot. So not only was the difference in the anchoring mechanism of expectations but also in rigidities and that's why we thought that episode is important.

Peter Temin has said that counterfactual experiments asking what would have happened if the Fed had increased the money supply by what was necessary to maintain its 1920s growth path to avert the Depression are ahistorical approaches. There was no credible discussion taken seriously outside of the gold standard mentality. Do you see the work of McCallum (1990), Fackler and Parker (1994), and Bordo, Choudhri and Schwartz (1995), where there are counterfactual experiments assessing what would have happened if the Fed had managed money growth differently, as useful and informative exercises or are they ahistorical?

Well, I think you know what I am going to say. I think they're useful exercises. I think that what we learn from the new economic history has always been that if something is important let's assess how important it is by conducting a counterfactual. Now the question is did we conduct the right counterfactual? Given that we assumed a Friedman-type rule, would this be reasonable given that they didn't talk much about the monetary base or given that nobody talked about money supply much in that period even though Irving Fisher and Laughlin Currie did? Is that a reasonable thing to say? Yes it is reasonable because that's ultimately what central banks do. I mean, even though they didn't do a very good job at measuring the monetary aggregates, ultimately the way things work in a monetary economy is that the money supply changes and, regardless of the control technique you are using, changes in the money supply do impinge on prices and the real economy. So that's why we asked that question. Now, if I were doing it today I might think of possibly implementing a different rule. It's possible that I could even do a Taylor rule as Taylor (1999) has done for historical episodes like this and maybe model the Fed's reaction function a little better. So I don't think that it's an ahistorical exercise. I think that the counterfactual approach has to be taken with a grain of salt because any counterfactual has a big stretch to it. I think the way to conduct a good counterfactual is to write down the assumptions which people who read the paper who don't really have strong priors would look at and say "Yeah maybe, you know maybe." When I gave the paper I did with Eichengreen on the gold exchange standard that appeared in 1998 in the book *The Defining Moment* at Harvard, Temin was there and he said to me, "You know there is one big problem with your paper. You're assuming away the Great Depression and then you're imposing World War II on it." He said "Now why would World War II have happened if the Great Depression hadn't happened? Because if the Great Depression hadn't happened Hitler wouldn't have come to power." Obviously there really is no answer to that.

You have to make these assumptions and then people have to come away from what you do by saying, "You know, that's interesting" as opposed to "No, that's total science fiction."

Temin told me after 1931 the Fed had "picked their side" and, as he has said in the past, their actions should not be construed as policy failures. Their behavior was not a shock or inept but was a continuation of the path they had chosen to defend the exchange value of the dollar. What say you to this?
It's true. They did. But they also did one thing else. They forgot their Bagehot's rule. Bagehot's rule says when faced with an external drain and a banking crisis you lend freely at a penalty rate. They got the penalty rate part of Bagehot right but they forgot the lend freely part. Bagehot's rule was financial orthodoxy as it existed back then. Fed officials even talked about it. Meltzer documents in his book how many Fed officials would quite often cite Bagehot. In fact they cited Bagehot in 1931 but they got Bagehot wrong. They got half of Bagehot right. So Peter is dead right about that, but that's not to say, had they followed Bagehot's rule, they could have done it. That is, they could have charged a penalty rate, lent freely and, given the gold reserves that they had then, and they did in September and October of 1931, they could have prevented the banking crisis from getting worse.

(Laughingly) *I don't mean to get you riled up, Mike.*
No problem, this is fun.

Do you have any familiarity with the Einzig data that Hsieh and Romer (2004) use in their paper and how it is constructed? Eichengreen doesn't seem to think that it is very informative in the debate on 1932.
I'm on the side of Romer and Hsieh on this one. It was the best data available and the data, to me, was very convincing. I mean that plus the rest of their paper which complements my 2002 paper with Choudhri and Schwartz. And I think that Barry is acting in a very defensive manner on this. A lot of people use the Einzig data and it was the best data available. I mean, sure, you know maybe if it was today the data would be better. But I found their results very compelling.

Why do you suppose that the gold standard was not suspended nor was deposit convertibility at this time and why didn't the US follow the UK's lead in 1931 and leave gold?
Because, as Temin told you, they really were wedded to gold standard orthodoxy. The Fed was based on the gold standard and the real bills doctrine, and they were really opposed to giving either of those things up. They really believed, and mistakenly so, that the Great Depression came out of an asset price bubble, the stock market boom, which in turn was

precipitated by mistakes made by Benjamin Strong of the New York Fed, in helping the British out by lowering the discount rate in 1927. And so the Fed didn't have any problem with the gold standard. Oh no, they were gold standard advocates to the bitter end. Then when Roosevelt was talking about devaluing the dollar in 1933, they weren't too keen on that. They were more worried about the problems within the Federal Reserve System, like the fact that when New York's gold reserves were running down and they turned to the Chicago Fed bank and said, "Could you lend us some reserves?" Chicago said "Sorry, we've got our own problems." Those were the kind of issues they were concerned with. And I think that the British leaving the gold standard was a big shock to them too. They left the gold standard because they were shot out of it. It's not because somebody sat around and said, "Gee, you know the gold standard is really not a good rule. Let's just leave it and go to something else." It was events that kicked them off the gold standard. Once they were off they looked around and said, "Gee, you know, maybe we had better live with this world." But it took them a while to think about that. At the 1933 World Economic Conference, the main assumption was that the world would go back to gold. Even the British were willing to do it if it was at the right exchange rate. The French wanted to go back in any circumstances. In the US, the Federal Reserve people, Harrison and others, the people that went on that mission, they were working on the assumption that they were going to restore the gold standard.

In 1933.
In July 1933 at the London Economic Conference. Roosevelt was the one who did, into 1933, believe in the gold standard. Even after he took the US off it, he didn't say that we would never go back to gold, but he changed his mind during the World Economic Conference. At that point he said no. We need to attach primary importance to domestic economic policy, the gold standard is incompatible with that, we don't want to go back to it. But it was only after that point, July, when the US finally pulled the plug. Then they abrogated the gold clauses and did all the rest of the stuff that followed. It took much of a whole year before Roosevelt changed his thinking. He was being pushed by people like Frank Warren and many of the New Dealers who wanted to get off gold. But he hadn't made up his mind yet.

So the Fed was wedded to the gold standard is what I just heard you say.
The Fed was wedded to the gold standard.

But you go further then and say but they had discretionary powers that they didn't use and that's why it was a policy failure.
Right.

Is that right?

That's right. Because the gold standard was a contingent rule. I've written several papers with Kydland (1995, 1996) and a lot of people have picked up on it. The gold standard was a contingent rule. If you're hit with a big emergency, given that you've been credibly following it, you can bail out of it and then you can come back in. And if the Great Depression wasn't a big enough emergency, I don't know whatever was.

What is your impression of Figure 1 in Cecchetti (1998) on discount lending? Does this not show the failure of the Federal Reserve to act as the lender of last resort, and thus should we not let them off the hook so easily? Even if they were on gold as the graph shows, little was done before Britain left gold when all agree the Fed had some room to do something and the first and second banking panics passed with discounting barely even registering a pulse. Why is it so different in the 1920s than it was later on?

Right, well this is again one of the major themes of Allan Meltzer's book. The story was they followed something called the Riefler–Burgess doctrine which said that you look at two things. You look at member bank borrowing in New York and whether it's greater than 500 million dollars and you look at the level of nominal short-term interest rates. If member bank borrowing was below 500 million dollars, the way the Fed interpreted things in the 1920s and 1930s was that it was a state of monetary ease. They believed that member banks only came to the window when they really needed to. They didn't go there to make profits. The Fed looked at member bank borrowing in 1930 and 1931 and they said, "Gee nobody's coming to the window. I guess things are good." I mean really, that's the key point.

The Fed looked at borrowing and said everything must be OK.

Everything's just fine. They said, "Nobody's coming to the window. If they're not coming to the window, we don't need to deal with it." The problem was that they were locked into this stupid doctrine. That was the problem, that they did not have the smarts to look out the window and see the breadlines and say, "Gee, you know, maybe we should be doing something about it."

So if I were to say to you that "providing large amounts of liquidity to the banking system almost certainly would have violated gold-standard statutes; doing so would have raised questions about whether the authorities attached priority to the maintenance of the exchange rate peg relative to other economic and social goals" you wouldn't buy it to explain that graph, would you?

No, I mean look, they could have done it. They didn't and the gold standard isn't what prevented them from doing it because the gold standard tells you that when you have a crisis you lend freely. You provide liquidity and this is what they didn't do. You can do this if you have credibility, that is, if you've been on gold for a long time, then the markets understand what you're doing and they're not going to blow you out of the water.

Let me read something to you from Calomiris (1993): "Borrowers or bankers who have already suffered large losses due to increased debt burdens and costs of financial distress will not regain lost wealth as the result of subsequent open market operations. Their balance sheet positions have changed. Moreover, the effects of policy-induced deflation and inflation are asymmetric; that is, too much leverage is penalized by the capital market by more than too little leverage is rewarded, and costs of financial distress incurred in states of low net worth have no counterpart in states with high net worth. Thus, according to the new view, even if Friedman and Schwartz and their supporters were entirely correct about the importance of monetary shocks in precipitating the Depression, it does not follow that open market operations to restore the money supply would have had offsetting effects in promoting recovery from the Depression."
Well in a sense what I think he's saying is that you have to distinguish between liquidity and solvency.

That's correct.
And so he's saying if you don't act, if the central bank doesn't act to deal with liquidity problems to the extent where banks which would normally be solvent become insolvent, then monetary policy is not going to solve the problem. He's right. Once they'd made the mistake, they weren't going to refloat the banking system because the banks were already dead. So then you need a restructuring. The whole literature on financial crisis talks about crisis prevention, crisis management, and crisis resolution. Calomiris is talking about crisis resolution. The RFC was set up to do that but didn't have quite the teeth to really accomplish the job. They'd already figured that out, but you need to have an expansionary environment. In other words, if the Fed had expanded the money supply even if it wasn't going through the insolvent banks, and they'd injected the money in different ways, it still could have stimulated the economy. To assume that the only way you can reflate the economy is through the banking channel I think is too narrow, and this is the story that they're telling. But it's really true that there was a huge bank structure problem which had to be dealt with by restructuring the banks and recapitalizing them. Had the RFC had the kind of capital and had it had the credibility, which it lost by publishing the names of the banks they were lending the money to, had they done that, they could have helped a lot.

So once the macroeconomy crashed and started making banks insolvent, monetary policy is limited in trying to resurrect the banking system.

Right, and look at Japan today. In Japan today there are two issues. There is the banking solvency issue, which requires restructuring, you know, setting up a good bank and a bad bank and selling off the bad assets and recapitalizing the good ones. And secondly, there is monetary policy. You need monetary policy to deal with deflation and macro stability. So monetary policy is going to give you the growth of nominal income that you need. The banking structure story has now become a real story. You need to restructure the banks to restore economic growth and to get the financial intermediation process going. That's the long-run story. Once the banking system is shot, expansionary open market operations are not going to get you out of it, but in a sense look at what happened. In 1933 and 1934 there was a huge reflation that came about both through expansionary open market operations and through gold inflows and they did restimulate the economy. Why? Because we had a banking holiday. The banking holiday got rid of the bad banks. So we restructured in a way the Japanese have never been able to do. We said yeah, there's a huge mess, one sixth of the nation's banks are under water. We eliminate them. Bang. They're gone. The new banks that survive don't have the problem that Calomiris talks about and monetary policy does work.

So use monetary policy to reflate the economy and end deflation and then microeconomic policies to restructure the banking system.
Right.

Do you not see the evils of deflation whether anticipated or unanticipated as the greatest villain in the story of the Great Depression, and thereafter the freeing of the economy from the deflationary vortex that existed being the greatest engine bringing on recovery?
I don't buy that. I don't think the evidence backs it up. It's unclear. The only evidence we really have is the evidence in Bernanke and James's paper in 1991 on deflation and the debt deflation story. The empirical evidence that they've put together is only circumstantial. It's very, very, very descriptive. They don't have a really tight bunch of evidence to show that deflation was that much more sinister. I do believe that the deflation working through the deflation channel definitely exacerbated the banking crisis. But I'm not sure if deflation was that much more the cause than all the other stuff that was going on. So I don't know. I think that's an area that we need more research on.

A 33 percent fall in the price level? What is the transmission mechanism then that you have in mind?
No, I'm saying that falling P and falling Y are symptoms of the same thing, a collapse in aggregate demand. It is unclear whether P has a separate effect in addition to this, another separate effect by itself, that is, either coming

from the debt deflation story of Fisher which is based on unanticipated deflation, or whether it is expected deflation operating through real interest rates. The evidence is not clear on how different that is from the aggregate demand channel. That's what I'm saying. If I had to pick a story that I believed I would believe the real interest rate story. But the real interest rate story is part of the channel of transmission.

That depends on anticipated deflation.
Right.

And you're saying that it is unclear which one of those stories ...
Right, it's a debate. It's Cecchetti (1992) on one side and Hamilton (1992) on the other. And both papers are very good and I don't think you can really say which one is going to convince you.

Can't they both be right? I mean some of the deflation was anticipated and some was unanticipated and they both help explain what was going on?
They both could be right. It could be. But I see the deflation story as tied in with Fisher. No one has ever written down a model of Fisher's debt deflation.

Well let me ask you differently then. Would you say that maintaining price stability is one of the key lessons for central bankers to learn from the Great Depression?
Definitely. Because price stability is macro stability and that's what central banks can do, and that's what they're supposed to do.

And if they had done that in the Great Depression and not let the deflation happen maybe we wouldn't be having this conversation?
If they had done that in the 1930s we wouldn't have had the Depression *and* the deflation (*Bordo emphasizes the word* and). So you've really got to tie those two things together.

But they are *tied together* (*Parker emphasizes the word* are).
Right, but if you have zero nominal rigidities and price expectations are anchored, then the price level is not going to have any real effects.

No, that's true. That's true. And if everyone had rational expectations in 1929 as well, maybe we wouldn't be having this conversation.
    OK, one of the lessons of the Great Depression Ben Bernanke has pointed out is that fixed exchange rate regimes can be dangerous and destabilizing. Given the experience of the Great Depression and the Asian crisis of the late 1990s do you think that fixed exchange rate regimes have much to recommend them? From your writings in the 1995 paper "Is there

a good case for a new bretton woods international monetary system?" I bet your answer is no.
Right, I agree pretty well with Ben Bernanke on this. I think there isn't much use for fixed exchange rate systems except for small open economies that can't conduct stable monetary policies themselves or if they are highly open. Then they should follow fixed exchange rate/currency board types of arrangements tying themselves to some other larger, more successful country. But for advanced countries, I think what we learned, not just from the Great Depression but also from Bretton Woods and from the EMS crisis in 1992, is that fixed exchange rates don't work.

Why did Argentina bail on the currency board?
Because they didn't follow the fiscal policies consistent with a currency board. I mean a currency board ties down monetary policy. So the premise for doing it was "it will be able to prevent us from having a central bank that will print money, because our history has been high inflation." Great, they did it. We can adopt a gold standard. We are going to go back to the convertibility law of 1900. They did it. But there's one problem. They did not anchor fiscal policy. And so they began running fiscal deficits, in the provinces especially. There was no constraint on them spending money. Then the markets began to think "Gee, you know they're running up big deficits. How are they going to service this debt?" And once the doubts started to come up, then they started charging high interest premiums. The high interest premiums in turn meant that more and more of the government deficit was devoted to paying the interest, which meant that they kept borrowing more from abroad to pay the interest on the previous debt and then the dynamics of unsustainable debt took over. So it was a debt crisis. And once the debt crisis happened then it meant that something had to give. They had to let the exchange rate float. They could not run a currency board. That's what happened. They didn't follow the rules. Because the rules say a currency board means G = T and it means no central bank and they violated the fiscal side of it.

What are some of the other lessons from the Great Depression that have been learned or need to be relearned?
I think what we learned from the Great Depression is that all central banks have learned to try to avoid banking panics. I think they've really learned that lesson well. They may have learned it too well. They're erring on the side of bailouts. So, I think that lesson has been learned. I think they've also overreacted on deflation because, by thinking of the Great Depression and thinking of the debt deflation hypothesis and the standard view that comes out of some of the literature that we've discussed, they're unwilling to follow price level targeting because of the fear of deflation. Just last year the Fed was following much too loose a policy because of this concern

about deflation and the zero nominal bound. OK then, it actually stimulated the economy and that's why they're following this tightening right now. So, I think that they learned these lessons really well, but they over-learned them. They forgot about the distinction between good and bad deflation.

Talk to us briefly about that.
Well the story there is that if you have a deflation that's driven by a productivity advance, driven by a big innovation like computers or the internet or something like that, that allows the real economy to grow at a faster rate. That means, other things equal, that unless you accommodate it by more expansionary monetary policy, and unless velocity changes to offset it, prices are going to fall and people are going to be content with holding cash balances. The real cash balances will rise to reflect the fall in the price level and you'll be in an equilibrium, assuming that this deflation is anticipated. Milton Friedman wrote a famous piece in 1969 that's been picked up ever since, "The optimum quantity of money", which said that indeed a low deflation of maybe 2 percent per year may be optimal in terms of the fact that paper money does not bear interest and that deflation is a way of paying interest on money. So, it would make money holding efficient. So in that environment, you can have long runs of deflation and positive growth and it's not a problem. It wasn't a problem before 1914. We had deflation. We had quite a bit of it in the nineteenth century associated with rapid growth. Now I should cover myself a little bit, because it's not to say that people back then were always happy about deflation because not everybody did adjust to it. And some groups felt that they had lost out, and they took out their concerns in the political process. So the period of the 1870s, 1880s and early 1890s in the US was a very, very rocky period politically with the debate over greenbacks and free silver. In Europe deflation was a big issue with France, Germany, and the UK. The French and the Germans reacted to deflation by saying it was coming about through falling commodity prices coming from commodities exported by the United States, and they imposed tariffs to protect their agriculture. Even though the reason why prices were falling was because the price of ocean shipping and other transportation was going down in the world, and North America, Latin America and Australia were being converted into one big wheat farm (*laughter*).

Alright then, Barry Eichengreen has said that the focus of the last 20 years on money and finance has been real intellectual progress and other matters in the literature on the Great Depression are ultimately beside the point. Do you agree with that?
Basically I agree with that, but I really would like to see some more believable research on the real side because I really think that the Minnesota approach, especially the work they've done on the 1930s, is important. And

money alone can not explain the sluggish performance of output in the US and other countries. One of the papers in the series edited by Prescott in the *Review of Economic Dynamics*, the paper by Beaudry and Portier (2002) "The French depression in the 1930s", shows the effects of the French New Deal policies.

There is a whole series of papers there on many countries.
Yes, but the one that really hits you in the face is what France did. They imposed short workweeks, all the stuff they still do. They went crazy in terms of helping out the labor market.

Yes, they cut the workweek and raised the wage in order to try and increase employment.
Right.

And they're still doing that (laughter).
They still do. But it started really with Blum in 1936 and that had the same effects as had occurred with the NIRA in the United States.

So there is still a lot to learn there.
I think there's a lot to learn there. I think that work is really important. I think another important direction of the overall Depression research agenda, again coming from the Minnesota people who, as you see, I have great admiration for, because their philosophy is pretty close to mine; I'm just not crazy about some of the modeling they do. But their work on the stock market, the paper by McGrattan and Prescott (2004), I think that it's pretty interesting stuff. I do think that maybe the stock market boom might have been a real boom and not a bubble and that the Fed killed it.

Whether it was a bubble or not, does that really matter? Or is it the Fed's perception that mattered the most and how they acted on it?
What mattered then was the Fed's perception and that's what killed it. The Fed followed the real bills doctrine and lending to finance speculation was anathema to them. They assumed that speculation in stock markets, pushing up asset prices, would automatically feed into goods market inflation. That was the view that everybody had back then and that goods market inflation would inevitably be followed by deflation. There was no way you could prevent deflation. They didn't think deflation was a consequence of their policy. They thought deflation was necessary because of the inflation.

OK then, the standard questions I ask everybody. What ended the Great Depression?
What ended the Great Depression was Roosevelt. It was the bank holiday, the devaluation of the dollar, the following of expansionary gold policy by

the Treasury. It wasn't the New Deal. The New Deal and the fiscal stuff I don't think mattered too much. And the Fed definitely became more liberal in its open market policies. But I think that it's primarily a Treasury story. The Great Depression was ended by Treasury policy and the Fed never got its act together.

The Treasury and the gold flows.
The Treasury and the gold flows. And the first part of the gold flows story is the Treasury story. The second part is a consequence of Hitler.

Could it happen again?
I don't think so. I think that the Great Depression was a very unique event brought about by a confluence of a lot of issues. I think that Temin's 1989 book is very interesting and so is Barry's *Golden Fetters*. Temin's book talks about World War I and the imbalances that came out of World War I. That meant that the gold exchange standard was going to be a problem. It meant that, in a sense, the way the world worked before 1914 was not going to be repeated. And the political instability, in Europe especially, I think really did add to the mix. Then you throw into that the central bank. The Federal Reserve was a new operation. It was just learning how to operate as a central bank. It had major flaws coming from its structure. It had the basic problem of people learning how to be central bankers. It had the real bills doctrine. All of these things together created a mix of trouble. So the international dimension, with the misalignment and the problems with the Federal Reserve itself meant that, in a sense, the tightening that started in 1928–29 led to a series of cascading events around the world. The first shocks came about from other countries as Eichengreen (1992) points out. The first downturn occurred in other countries in the spring of 1929 and then fed back to the United States. And what was going on was when the Fed raised interest rates to kill off the stock market boom, what it did was it attracted funds from the rest of the world into Wall Street. This meant that monetary conditions in the other countries kept tightening and so they reacted, the Bank of England especially because it was one of the weakest of the four countries, it reacted by raising the discount rate. This precipitated recession there and the stock market turned down in England a month or so before it turned down in the US. So the pressure came from around the world. And then you had another issue, which was not caused by the Fed, but another issue that made things worse. Some people attach more importance to it than I would, but it was the collapse of commodity prices.

So I think those issues are important but I think that the monetary policy nexus, the monetary policy plus gold standard nexus, was so unique that I don't see that happening again. Other things could happen. We can tell all the doomsday stories you like. I was at a conference over the weekend where they were talking about the dollar falling and the Asian countries selling off their dollars. You know all this stuff happening, cascading declines in the exchange rate feeding into inflation, the Fed tightening causing a serious recession, causing the asset price/housing price boom to stop. But I just don't see anything, any of the scenarios you could paint, that is going to lead to 1929–33. I see the world pre-1929 as much more relevant, for the business cycles it had. The real business cycles in the 1920s and the nineteenth century, because they were real business cycles, have resonance for the world that we're in today. I see it as primarily a real business cycle world and as countries move toward maintaining stable money and inflation targeting or price level targeting the recessions are going to be primarily not caused by the central banks but by real shocks (however there is still a risk that the Fed could make errors by raising the federal funds rate when the economy is already contracting, as in March 2001, and lowering it long after the economy is awash in liquidity and it should be higher).

For example?
A war is a good one. Oil price shocks are another one although I view those as endogenous. You know, political crises, the things that happen that can have big effects. I see the tech boom and bust as a shock. That's a negative shock and it's going to take a long time before we have completely adjusted to that. And we may have a housing price correction which may be part of the next wave of adjustments.

Do you think that there's a housing boom right now?
(*Bordo chuckles*) Well, I don't know what the prices are in your part of the world but up here in New Jersey they've been going up pretty high, as is the case in some other parts of the US, like California.

Lee Ohanian told me that it's very difficult to attract assistant professors to UCLA now given what they're paying compared to what housing prices are doing.
Correct.

Alright, thanks Professor.
It was great.

Charles Calomiris

Charles Calomiris received his Ph.D. from Stanford University in 1985 and he is currently Henry Kaufman Professor of Financial Institutions at the Columbia University Graduate School of Business and a Professor at Columbia's School of International and Public Affairs. His extensive knowledge of the history of banking and finance together with his recent focus on the causes and consequences of banking distress and failures during the Great Depression make him a natural for our list of scholars on the economics of the Great Depression. I spoke with Charles Calomiris in his office at Columbia University on May 12, 2005.

Would you please provide some background on how you got involved in the literature on the Great Depression.
I came to the subject of the Great Depression from my graduate training at Stanford in both macro/monetary economics and economic history. As an assistant professor at Northwestern I was teaching both graduate and undergraduate monetary economics and I was also teaching undergraduate and graduate American economic history. The Great Depression is a pretty important event not just to macro economists but to understanding American economic and political history in the twentieth century. Many people were beginning to see a need to revisit the macroeconomic history of the 1930s around the time I was in graduate school in the early 1980s.

In your 1993 Journal of Economic Perspectives *piece you talk about the different implications of the Friedman and Schwartz hypothesis. One of them was that money shocks will have larger impacts if they occur at times of high leverage or in an economy with a poorly diversified or a geographically fragmented banking system. That's certainly easy enough to understand. One of the arguments that you make that I would like to pay particular attention to is what you say about the power of open market operations. In Calomiris (1993) and also in your 1995* Journal of Financial Services Research *paper you talk about how it may be hard to undo a financial collapse with stimulative open market operations. So, along with the two pieces you did with Mason that showed up in the 2003* AER, *the policy implications matter regarding the sources of bank failure. If it's a fundamental versus a liquidity crisis, the policies are going to be different. Could you speak on that, please.*

There are several different strands running through the question that you ask. The last one was about how a crisis that's a liquidity crisis would play out in the banking sector and beyond. That's related to, but a little distinct from, the broader question which you referred to in the *Journal of Financial Services Research* and the *JEP* papers. What I was emphasizing in those papers is the irreversibility associated with the way monetary shocks mattered in the 1930s. The basic point is that suppose all these firms get highly levered and you have a depression or deflation. Now these firms are insolvent. Well, now you've got all these firms in financial distress and they have had to make irreversible, real decisions regarding their investments, their hirings, etc. Now, if the next day the Federal Reserve announces that it's going to restore the money supply to where it was before, those firms don't go back to where they were before. Most obviously, some of them have even gone out of business or gone bankrupt, and the transfer of their assets to other owners is unlikely to be neutral from a macroeconomic perspective. You've disrupted the economy at the micro level. You've put firms into different situations as a result of the financial consequences of that monetary shock. This discussion all goes back to Irving Fisher, Keynes, and more recently Ben Bernanke, all of whom emphasized the need to think about the Great Depression from a corporate finance standpoint, thinking about what happens to a firm when its balance sheet goes through the Great Depression. In addition to financial irreversibilities, I think the financial perspective on the Depression also illustrates nonlinearity in the relationship between shocks and outcomes. Financial propagators matter more in extreme circumstances. As things get worse and worse, more and more firms and banks are going to pass over the threshold where they are forced to take irreversible financial measures.

For example, even if a firm's economic fundamentals are sound, if its level of debt is unmanageable in the new environment, then it is in trouble and unable to undertake what might be positive net present value investments. Similarly, with the banking system, if shocks destroy banks and their equity capital, there is no magic wand to wave to bring those banks back into existence. Some of my research with Joe Mason suggests that bank distress had significant effects in deepening and lengthening the Depression. So if you shrink the money supply and in shrinking the money supply you cause fundamental problems that destroy banks and force firms into financial distress, the consequences can be profound and long lasting. And of course, the responses of firms and banks feed on each other because the firms borrow from the banks. When the firms are hurt, they hurt the banks and when the banks are hurt they cut credit off to the firms. You can't snap your fingers, restore the money supply and have everything be the way it was before because you've created real consequences in the financial plumbing and the entrepreneurial plumbing of the economy through the destruction and financial weakening of firms and banks. That insight, which was fundamentally Fisher's and Keynes's initially, is also the insight that Ben Bernanke brings to his influential 1983a paper. His "cost of credit intermediation" is sometimes misinterpreted to be a measure only of bank distress. But if you read his paper it is broader than that, to encompass balance sheets, too. The whole idea of monetary neutrality, at least within time horizons of a decade, is silly in a world in which people have nominal financial contracts and nominal shocks are large. That is possibly the most important lesson from the Depression for macro theorists.

So that shows then that simple open market operations to try and restore money growth aren't going to get you back to where you want to go and may not be the correct policy to address that situation.
Well, it depends on what date you are talking about. If you're asking whether open market operations by themselves could have immediately reflated the economy back to its prior level, I think that the answer is no. I would also mention that there's another issue regarding whether the Fed was free to do enough open market operations under the gold standard to the extent that would have been necessary.

We're going to get to that.
With respect to the first question, my point is that as of March 1933 even a very aggressive restoration of the level of the money supply would not have immediately restored the economy to full employment. Too much water had gone under the bridge in terms of the financial destruction of 1929–33 to be able to restore production and employment to pre-Depression levels by just increasing the money supply. So far, I have made no mention of the devastation to expectations, which is a separate reason for that irreversibility. Monetary shocks undermined the "new age thinking" that dominated the economy around the middle of 1929. While expectations may have been too optimistic in mid-1929, and thus bound to change even without the shock of the Depression, I think it is likely that expectations became unduly pessimistic as a result of the shocks of the Depression, and that those expectations would not have reverted to normal in response to open market operations. This adds another reason to believe that the shocks of the Depression were not easily reversible. The Great Depression illustrates the pitfalls of simplistic monetary neutrality thinking.

You have said that macroeconomically bank distress could have been mitigated if the collapse had been avoided. But there was little that could be done on a microeconomic lender of last resort level to arrest the bank failures before 1933 and indeed you go on to say that short of a bank bailout not much could have helped on the microeconomic side.
I think that's true. That is not to say that lender of last resort policy could not have been better, and that making it better wouldn't have helped a little. Also, I would point out that there was a bit of a bailout, subsidized through the

Reconstruction Finance Corporation. Starting in 1933 RFC support was made effective by expanding the RFC program to include preferred stock purchases rather than just debt purchases. So we did actually do a little something there and one could have decided to do a bank bailout on a much larger scale earlier, whether through stock injections, likely RFC post-1933 injections, or a variety of other measures. But lending by the Fed and even by the RFC in 1932 for the most part was lending from a senior creditor against good collateral. That is a good way to deal with a bona fide liquidity crisis, but it can actually make runs against banks worse if they're suffering from large fundamental shocks. The reason is that the such lending can reduce the asset backing available for deposits. That is, you subordinate the deposits to the senior lender of last resort. The lender of last resort gets to keep the best collateral. So what does that do to depositors' incentives? If a bank pledges its better than average assets to get a loan, then the remaining depositors might look at that and say, "Well, compared to our position before that loan, we're worse off." This is what people were saying in the 1930s about why the RFC's initial policies weren't working. If you were, however, in a situation where there was only a liquidity shock, let's say of the unrealistic extreme form of people just suddenly waking up and deciding that they needed more cash because they wanted to buy more today, then such senior lending would be enough to solve the problem. But that is not the story of the Depression. Large fundamental shocks were at the core of the problems of the banks.

How does that point relate to the question of panics?
A "pure" panic might be defined as an adverse exogenous shock to liquidity demand or supply unrelated to the fundamentals determining the value of assets. If you think that's what's going on then a classic lender of last resort policy, lending freely against pretty good collateral, will help. But, we know now from microeconomic empirical analysis of banking problems during the time, that for the most part, prior to 1933, that isn't the right story. There were a series of adverse economic shocks, not just one shock, and these shocks affected incomes and asset values, and differed across locations and times, and cumulatively produced significant deterioration in banks' creditworthiness. The deposit outflows from particular banks largely reflected rational perceptions of fundamental weakness that were not universal across all banks but that were located at particular points and particular places. In this regard, Elmus Wicker's insights and criticisms of Friedman and Schwartz are important. Wicker (1996) was not saying that Friedman and Schwartz's focus on the money supply was wrong, at least I don't think that that's what he was saying. He was saying that the shocks often had different magnitudes in particular regions, at particular times, and that the complexity of the Great Depression partly resulted from our unit banking system, which connected the fates of banks in particular regions to the borrowers in their particular location. And that matters a lot for the way the Great Depression played out in the

United States as opposed to other countries. The industrial organization of banking mattered a lot. Regional disaggregation helps us empirically to trace the impact of these shocks. If Joe Mason and I had wanted to analyze bank distress by location in Canada in the same way that we did for the US, we couldn't have done it because credit supply wasn't local in Canada because you had nationwide branch banks.

That's true.
While there may have been panic elements at particular spots that worsened the financial situation, it's largely a story, prior to 1933, about fundamental shocks that were sometimes nationwide, sometimes region-specific.

So bank bailouts would have been the remedy and not simply saying that the discount window should have been lending.
I'm not saying that more bank bailouts should have happened, but I would agree that such a policy would have been needed to accomplish the objective of keeping banks from failing. Some have said that the Fed failed and that it could have solved the bank failure problem with freer use of the discount window. I don't agree. If you believe that bank failures had irrational origins, then it makes sense to call them a Fed failure. I see it differently. It is expecting too much of the Fed as a liquidity supplier to have solved the insolvency problems of 1930–33 with discount window lendingto banks. Of course, the Fed could have done a lot to prevent the Depression and the bank failures from occurring through sound monetary policy. But, holding constant the time path of the supply of money, a greater willingness to assist banks with more discount window lending probably would not have had a large effect in preventing the bank failures that occurred. I want to emphasize that if the Fed had, through open market operations and discount window lending, kept the money supply sufficiently high in 1929–33, then that would have removed downward pressure on nominal income, asset prices, and debt burdens of borrowers. That could have avoided bank failures. But that is not the same as saying (wrongly, in my view) that Fed unwillingness to lend to banks (holding constant its aggregate money supply policy) was a primary cause of bank failures. And expanding the money supply aggressively in 1929–33 and going off the gold standard to help do that would not have kept all the bank failures from happening. There still would have been large regional shocks that would have caused many bank failures.

With respect to monetary policy failure, I agree with Friedman and Schwartz, and Brunner and Meltzer, and others, that it was bad thinking about monetary policy that made monetary policy procyclical.

The real bills doctrine.
Yes, and more generally focusing on the net free reserve measure and looking at interest rates. Wheelock (1991) has done some good work on this and so did

Meltzer (2003) and I think they're right. The Fed was looking at the wrong indicators. Some of what they were looking at made sense if you were a central banker on the gold standard. You have to look at gold outflows. Meltzer and Wheelock pointed out that they did do so. But they also focused on indicators that gave false signals.

Getting back to your earlier question, bank bailout policies have a lot of negative side effects, so saying that bailouts could have made a difference is not to say that more of this should have been done. Moral hazard costs of bailouts need to be considered. The reason RFC policy post-1933 was fairly successful in not creating very bad moral hazard consequences is that assistance was selective, and was accompanied by discipline to limit the use of funds. The RFC provided assistance to banks that were on the margin, and probably worth saving. And they gave discipline along with assistance through involvement in the board of directors, RFC veto power, restrictions on dividend payments, making banks devise a capital plan.

And would a massive bailout program by the Fed not have been beyond contemplation at the time?
It was not viewed that it was the Fed's job or anybody else's job to keep insolvent banks from failing.

I've heard you say that before and Peter Temin has said that to me too and I've got a question about that. Did you read that somewhere?
I know that from what I haven't read. The point is what you read is what people are saying their policy goals are. They're not thinking about monetary policy in those terms and furthermore people like Franklin Roosevelt and the Fed and Treasury officials at the time when deposit insurance was coming up, I know from that discussion they were very cognizant of moral hazard problems that came from deposit insurance, which is a form of ex ante protection, probably with less negative moral hazard than ex post protection.

Yes, I was surprised when I read that, that you said Roosevelt was against deposit insurance.
Yes, and I'm not the one who came up with that. You can find other papers to document that. Go back to the whole history, not just in the United States. How did central banks deal with problems in banking systems? I am working on looking at the period from 1870 to 1913, around the world. I haven't found a central bank or government between 1870 and 1913 that thought that its policy toward the financial system should be to bail out insolvent banks. So, it's not part of the thinking of this time period.

Isn't that why the Fed was created though, to be the lender of last resort and support the banking system? Help me here.
According to Bagehot's rule, if you go back and read *Lombard Street* or even

before that with Lord Overstone and the debates back in the 1840s having to do with the Bank of England, nobody is saying that the policy of the central bank should be directed toward stopping insolvent banks from failing. Rather, it should be directed toward keeping the economy stable, and preventing solvent banks from failing. Now, it is true that if you look at the 1890 Barings crisis, the Bank of England provides assistance to prevent the failure of Barings. But here's what's interesting. It provides assistance in concert with the private banks and only as a backup to the private bank consortium that had decided that if Barings went down it was going to send a bad and incorrect signal about all of them. The banks, and the Bank of England, decided that rather than having an unwarranted run on all the banks, they would help Barings, and thereby help themselves. The Bank of England agreed to back up the consortium of commercial banks who were providing collective assistance to Barings. That is effective as liquidity assistance. Why? Because certainly the consortium of all the commercial banks in England is solvent. This is very similar in spirit to the way the Russians provided lender of last resort assistance in 1900 and the way the Mexicans did it in 1908. Central banks were willing to provide limited backup to bolster confidence in the banking system, but not to bail out obviously insolvent financial institutions. Dealing with insolvency was handled differently. Bankruptcy codes were created. We had general debt moratoria, going back to the nineteenth century and we had agricultural debt moratoria in the 1920s. But we didn't have policies of governments bailing out insolvent banks, or government taxpayers bailing out insolvent bank creditors. That is quite interesting and it's not just the US, it's everywhere. In other words, bank bailouts were not the purpose of central banking, or of government policy more generally. That's why Bagehot's rule is to lend freely on pretty good collateral at a penalty rate. Those were the three pieces. It's not just lend freely, but on pretty good collateral at a penalty rate. Those last two conditions distinguish liquidity assistance from bailouts.

So they didn't see it as their job.
And it wasn't their job and it shouldn't have been their job. When we decided that we wanted to have a lender of last resort that crossed the line a bit to provide some assistance that resembled bailouts we did so on a limited basis after 1932, via the Reconstruction Finance Corporation. It took us about a year to get it to be effective by allowing it to be a holder of something that was junior to deposits. Its assistance, however, was still limited to pretty healthy banks, and was provided under strict rules that prevented large-scale bailouts, or bailouts of deeply insolvent institutions. It helped banks that were on the margin of insolvency.

Well then simply, what's the purpose of the lender of last resort?
To deal with liquidity crises, not solvency crises. Now when I say that it makes it sound like I think that liquidity crises don't have a solvency component. Of

course they always do. People are hit with a shock and then the question is how hard have they been hit? If you go back and read the papers that I and others have written about the pre-World War I banking panics, they were liquidity crises involving uncertainty about the magnitude of loss in the financial system and who was likely to ultimately bear the loss. They happened at cyclical downturns. They resulted from adverse shocks, but they were liquidity crises in the sense that the runs reflected uncertainty about the incidence of losses more than the actual underlying losses. That is to say, people knew that losses were large enough that it was possible for one large New York bank to fail. But people also knew that the New York clearing house as a whole would remain solvent. That's why the clearing house could bring its members together and provide liquidity assistance to the whole market. And that's why, in the Barings crisis of 1890, the Bank of England was comfortable backing up the London banks in that same way. And that goes back as far as the Emperor Tiberius in A.D. 33, when he lent to the Roman banks during their suspension of convertibility.

In the Great Depression, the bank insolvency problem in the aggregate was much worse than during the pre-World War I panics. You had a negative net worth of failed banks over those years equal to something like 4 percent of GDP. During every major banking crisis in the late nineteenth century that ratio never got up above 0.1 percent of GDP. Of course, today we're in a different world, where insolvency costs make the Depression look small, because of problems of moral hazard resulting from generous bank bailout policies. Indonesia, for example, had a resolution in the late 1990s costing 55 percent of GDP. So it's a completely different world. But that's a separate discussion.

No, that was very good with the modern percentages there that you just discussed. It puts it all in the proper context. So the Fed's big mistake was to let the macroeconomic situation deteriorate in the first place.
Absolutely.

OK, Romer has called the US decision to stay on the gold standard "perhaps the biggest policy error of the Depression" and calls the Depression a result of failed policy. On the other hand Temin told me after 1931 the Fed had "picked their side" and their actions should not be construed as policy failures. Their behavior was not a shock or inept but was a continuation of the path they had chosen to defend the exchange value of the dollar.
Well, now we seem to be talking about definitions of policy. Within the confines of staying on the gold standard Temin is saying that they really didn't change policy, and I think that when you look at Wheelock (1987), his Ph.D. thesis, he shows that the same reaction functions are being used by the Fed. That gives some credibility to what Peter's saying. But that's not inconsistent

with the notion that staying on the gold standard was a major policy error, and I'm sure Temin would agree to that. So I don't see a contradiction.

So why are people knocking heads so badly over this?
I don't know. Part of it perhaps is people still are disagreeing about the extent to which the gold standard was a marginal constraint on monetary policy. I think the gold standard was a constraint. If I know that I'm going to hit a constraint at some point then I have to run my policy today in light of that. So I do think in some sense it is not so relevant whether on the margin at every moment in time the gold standard constrained the Fed. What's more relevant is whether the Fed was effectively constrained, in a forward looking way, from expanding the money supply by the existence of the gold standard. If we had not been on the gold standard in 1931–33, monetary policy would have been more accommodative. Not just because of some mechanical analysis each moment in time of whether the constraint mattered, but because of a forward looking view of how you set policy if you know that you are living under a certain world of constraints.

You have said previously, "One can lament poor policy in the 1930s, and it's true that some criticized the Fed at the time (thus wise advice was available, in principle), but one cannot expect the Fed to have learned the lessons of the Great Depression before it happened."
I think that is true. At the same time, you can legitimately complain about US policy in 1931 because some countries went off the gold standard and we didn't.

That's my next question.
I don't think you can blame the Fed. That has to be a decision that's made not just by the Fed, but by the US government.

Why do you think they didn't do it?
Well, now we're being very speculative. The gold standard is a rule. You don't give up rules easily. You shouldn't give up rules easily because those rules, as we know from the work of Bordo and Rockoff (1996) and others on the gold standard, had benefits in terms of credibility. I'll give you an example of the benefits of credibility. I looked at the Russian crisis of 1900 and the Mexican crisis of 1908, both of which were banking crises that resulted from shocks that didn't originate in those countries. In Mexico it originated in the US. In Russia it originated in the developed part of western Europe. But what's interesting is that because those governments, Porfirio Diaz's Mexico and the Czar's Russia, had credibility in their monetary policy and their fiscal policy and their commitment to staying on the gold standard, these sovereigns were able to access international capital markets. They used that access to provide limited liquidity assistance to their banks. How different from our current emerging

markets situations, where sovereigns have to appeal to the US and to the IMF because they are shut out of markets. I agree with Bordo and Rockoff (1996) and others that the gold standard commitment probably contributed to that access.

The Good Housekeeping Seal of Approval.
Yes. The Czar and Porfirio Diaz had that Good Housekeeping Seal of Approval, although that reflected more than just their commitment to the gold standard, per se. Even in the midst of international financial crises they could borrow, if they needed to, on international markets. So, there are benefits in managing crises that come from adhering to the gold standard. That may explain why countries were reluctant to go off the gold standard in 1931. And, bear in mind that many countries had just gone back onto the gold standard in the mid 1920s. They were trying to restore the stability of the pre-World War I era, which Barry Eichengreen has very nicely pointed out they didn't do, and it was hard to do because the global political economy had changed, among other things. The world was different from what it had been in the mid to late nineteenth century. But sitting there in 1930 and 1931 I'm not sure if I would have gotten that decision right because obviously there was a tradeoff. From the retrospective of 1933, as Eichengreen and Sachs (1985) made clear, countries that had gone off the gold standard fared a lot better. But that's retrospective. You could not know that in 1931. Mistakes are always more apparent retrospectively.

It's hindsight basically?
Yes, it's easier to see in hindsight that going off the gold standard in 1931 was a good idea. Clearly we should have done it but ...

We've had 74 years to think about this.
And maybe even just in two years we would have known. By 1933 Franklin Roosevelt thought it was a good idea. And of course people made decisions based on economic models that aren't as sophisticated as the way modern macroeconomists would think about it.

You have a footnote in your 1998 paper with Wheelock where you say "Although today many of the liquidationist arguments may seem strange, under the gold standard the price level tended to be stationary, and thus, there is logic in the view that an inflation would be followed at some point by deflation, and the greater the inflation, the deeper the deflation." That's one of the nicest ways to explain the liquidationists' ideas that I have come across because I was scratching my head: how could they think that? They were worried about inflation even at the deepest, darkest depths of 1933.

Unfortunately, we only get to look back. When you're making policy and you're doing things, running a business, running a government, running a class, whatever. You only get to look back.

Sure, and hedge funds too. (Parker makes this comment to be funny since Calomiris is involved in managing a hedge fund)
(*Calomiris laughs*) Exactly, you only get to look back. You get to anticipate forward but you don't get to see. If I could only have one newspaper from tomorrow ...

In your 1993 JEP *paper you said that "Anticipated deflation still could have a depressive effect on the economy, but that it would not cause financial distress, since agents anticipating deflation would reduce interest costs to offset the capital loss from the debt deflation." Does this not depend on whether the binding nominal floor of zero is reached for interest rates?*
Yes, it does depend on that.

Does it not also depend on whether small and large borrowers have the same access to financial markets and refinancing opportunities?
Maybe it does.

I don't mean to bust your chops over little footnotes you have in these papers, but that one has always stuck in my head as not being quite right.
Well, I still think it's true that generally speaking an anticipated deflation doesn't have the same costs as an unanticipated deflation. So I'm agreeing that anticipated deflation can also be costly as a theoretical proposition, but that's not a historical statement. That is, I'm not saying that in the context of the Great Depression the nominal interest rate floor was a big deal. I can agree with you that in theory you have to qualify that in that way. But whether that's of practical relevance to the Depression is a separate question.

Alright then, given the accelerating inflation of the 1970s and the bad record we have from that, would you not say that maintaining price stability is one of the key lessons for central bankers to learn from the Great Depression and the Great Inflation?
Absolutely. Both are important lessons, but in the 1960s and 1970s they slipped into inflation and they should have seen it coming. In a paper in 1998, Wheelock and I argued that that slippage was unintended but it was something that was avoidable; after all, it was government policies that were pushing inflation higher. Whereas during the Great Depression I think you could say, as in that quote that you read from Peter Temin before, that deflation resulted from a coordination failure internationally, as well as a procyclical monetary policy mistake by the Fed – perhaps some combination of the two. But the deflationary policy errors of the Depression don't have the same degree of ex

ante blameworthiness, in my mind, as the inflationary policies of the 1960s and 1970s. If you go back and read the Federal Open Market Committee minutes there are governors in the 1960s who are blowing the whistle, saying "Hey guys, what are we doing?"

What is your take on the recent flurry of real business cycle papers on the Great Depression?
I think that the real business cycle approach has been useful for getting people to focus on productivity and thinking of productivity itself as a random variable and not as some constant or smoothly adjusting variable. Perhaps that's the main contribution of those papers. The problem is that because the models tend to be nonmonetary and representative-agent models, they really can't help us very much empirically in understanding the Great Depression as a historical phenomenon, because the Great Depression was largely a response to monetary shocks, and because it is not well understood in a representative-agent context. Stories about particular industries matter a great deal and so do stories about particular regions and particular times. In my 1993 *JEP* paper I pointed to the fact that you could learn a lot about productivity disturbances and understand some of the Schumpeterian changes that were going on during the Great Depression by looking at industry studies. I pointed to Bresnahan and Raff (1991) as one of those examples in the automobile industry.

It is useful to keep in mind the large historical literature on the way that technology is diffused, including Schumpeter's idea of beneficial shakeout during recession. There's a distribution of technologies within each industry. During cyclical downturns certain firms drop out and certain firms enter. And that process contributes to technological progress.

Real business cycle models remind us not to think of technological change as constant or smooth, which was the presumption of the macroeconomics that I was taught at Yale in the 1970s. Technological change is not necessarily low frequency. But the real business cycle models that have been written about the Great Depression with which I am familiar are not serious models of the Great Depression and I infer from the lack of depth of those models that the authors lack a real interest in understanding the Great Depression. I think that they are really involved in a methodological exercise. That's how I interpret their contribution, as a methodological contribution to help spur future research that would be more realistic. The papers that I've read often have been oversold by their authors and I think that they're not taken seriously, except by macroeconomists who don't know any better.

You've also made the point about aggregate demand having long-term and persistent effects. That they are not simply transitory. So it's not like a Blanchard–Quah methodology where aggregate demand shocks phase out but aggregate supply shocks persist.

We talked about it earlier. There are important, but fragile, state variables in the economy. The health of the banking system and real credit supply are among those variables. In fact, this is why I like, from a methodological standpoint, the real business cycle approach. It allows us to model the financial sector as part of the production function of the economy. Of course, it helps to include money in the economy, which allows monetarypolicy to affect those real variables.

So this is the path dependency that you talked about.
Yes. Technology is endogenous to the path of shocks, not just because of exit and entry within an industry affecting the distribution of productivity within an industry, but also because the financial sector of the economy is part of our technology. When you transfer wealth from creditors to debtors or vice versa, especially when some of those creditors are banks, you see effects on the technology of credit supply. Those are real effects. Demand shocks have long-term effects, in part, because they affect the distribution of wealth, which is a state variable that affects financial technology.

What ended the Great Depression?
First you have to define what you mean by the Great Depression. We have two definitions out there, maybe three. We've got one definition where 1933 is the end. We've got another where 1939 is the end, and perhaps we've got another one with 1940-something as the end. Let's answer your question for each of those defined endings. If you define the Great Depression as the free fall during the period from 1929 to March of 1933, because we know that March of 1933 is when industrial production starts back up, I think it's pretty clear that going off the gold standard and having Franklin Roosevelt inaugurated were the two most important events in March 1933. Some of that timing reflects an expectations reversal, "We have nothing to fear but fear itself." But a lot of it I think is the change in monetary policy away from a gold standard regime, which underlay the expectations shift. Not just the money supply at the time, but the reasonable forward-looking expectation about the money supply process being changed. So I agree with Peter Temin and others who argue that was a real watershed event.

If you define 1939 as the end, clearly there are other elements that have to do with industrial growth and the coming of World War II. Which is the right definition? I would emphasize something that people don't point to a lot: if you look at the period from 1933 to 1937 before the 1937–1938 recession, you see a period of very high investment, and high growth. At the same time the Depression persisted beyond 1933 in terms of the depressed level of economic activity, and I believe the financial sector had a lot to do with that, the irreversibilities we discussed before. When you think of the Great Depression in terms of rates of growth it seems to have ended in 1933. When you think of it in terms of level of activity the end is 1939 or later.

Well that's how I answer it too by the way. It depends on what you mean by the end.
Right.

Could it happen again?
I don't think so, not in the US. I think we know too much, I think the ideology of policy is different, not entirely for the better, but on average for the better. That is, our way of thinking is probably on average better. We would be much more interventionist much sooner. So no, I don't think it could happen the same way. I think we have a social safety net mindset, which has its own costs. But one of them is not a very high likelihood of a Great Depression.

OK, thanks Professor.

Allan Meltzer

Allan Meltzer received his Ph.D. from the University of California, Los Angeles, in 1958 and he is currently the Allan H. Meltzer Professor of Political Economy at Carnegie Mellon University. In attempting to point out some of the highlights of his long and productive career, I printed out his professional biography available on his web page. It is 30 pages long. Perhaps it will suffice for our purposes to say that I consider Allan Meltzer to be the unofficial historian of the Federal Reserve System given his vast undertaking to document and understand the history of the Federal Reserve System contained in the books *A History of the Federal Reserve, Volume I* and *Volume II*. For this and many others reasons, he is a key economist with ideas on the economics of the Great Depression that we need to hear. I spoke with Allan Meltzer in his office at the American Enterprise Institute, Washington, D.C. on Wednesday, November 9, 2005.

Alright, so here we are with the great Allan Meltzer. I have saved the best for last.
Thank you.

So if you would, Professor, I'm going to ask you a series of questions and you just tell me what you've got on your mind.
OK.

I looked at the literature on the Great Depression in the 1980s and found it to be at a standstill. Moreover, looking at your friend Karl Brunner's collection of papers in 1981, The Great Depression Revisited, *it was pretty clear that not much forward progress was in the pipeline and in fact he used the word "nihilism" to describe some people's approach to answering research questions. What then do you see as the breakthrough contribution or contributions that brought us to where we are today in our understanding of the Great Depression?*
I think the main thing is that people have gone back and looked at it again. I mean Bernanke's 1983 paper and in my book *A History of the Federal Reserve, Volume I* , I have quite a long chapter on how we got into the Great Depression and how we got out of it. And then of course Eichengreen's book on the gold standard. He spends a lot of time on the Great Depression. So I

think people have gone back and looked at it. Then there's the research at Minnesota where they've been working on the Great Depression, looking at productivity change and how productivity growth may explain what went on in that period. So I think people have come back, which is often the case, with new tools and thoughts.

So every generation has its look at the Great Depression then?
I think so because it's an extraordinary economic event. In the history of the Federal Reserve there are only two big major events. One is the Great Depression and the other the Great Inflation.

That's the theme of this book. I'm going through every generation for their look at the Great Depression. My first book talked to the generation of economists that lived through the Depression. This book now speaks with the next generation. Historians have told me that to have an honest evaluation of history there has to be a generation removed from the event.
Probably.

So that's one of my ideas here.
And the tools have improved. Economic theory now is very different from what it was a generation ago. People want to go back and say "Well here is a cataclysmic event. Can we use our tools to explain that or do we need something else?"

You think, do you not, that Friedman and Schwartz's claim about the death of Benjamin Strong causing the inaction of the Fed is not the best explanation of Fed behavior at the time? Would that not be correct?
That's correct.

Wasn't he a staunch supporter of the gold standard?
Yes he was, as was most everybody at that point. But yes, he at one point has a conversation with the great Irving Fisher and Fisher says to him something about Fisher wanting Congress to adopt price stability as a guide for monetary policy. Strong says to him, "Well, we have the gold standard, we don't need that." Fisher said to him, "You're going to be gone at some point and how will we be able to implement this policy?" Strong said, "My people will know how to do it because I've been instructing them." But he believed, as did many people at that time, that once you're on the gold standard there wouldn't be any great cataclysm.

And you also said in your book that Strong would have had to convince others to go for another round of speculative credit creation early on in the Depression at a time when they were worried about inflation.
That's correct.

And he probably couldn't have got that job done.
See, they were worried about inflation because they had a very different
definition of inflation. They were real bills doctrine people. Prices were not
rising. Prices were actually falling very little, but falling. But they were real
bills people and the Federal Reserve Act is written on the basis of the real bills
doctrine. So inflation to them meant that they were monetizing non-productive
credit.

Speculative credit.
Speculative credit. Yes, the stock market, and that's what worried them
throughout 1928 and 1929.

And even in the 1930s.
And even in the 1930s.

*They were talking about it in 1935 as they were worried about the next great
inflation.*
That's right.

Even when the economy was burning to hell.
And prices were falling (*both chuckle lightly*).

On the sixtieth anniversary of the bombing of Hiroshima the Wall Street
Journal *wrote an editorial and suggested it's important to remember what
people thought about the bombing at the time that it happened. I find that not
enough scholars take this view of looking at what the Fed did during the
Depression mindful of what they were thinking at the time. In deference to this
line of inquiry I don't know if there's a better individual with whom we could
ask questions of what the Fed was thinking in real time. So, there are many
things that you identify as the problem with the Federal Reserve during the
Great Depression. Please chime in at any time if you want to amplify these
statements. The framework that guided the Fed's actions or mis-actions during
the Depression was a reliance on the real bills doctrine.*
Yes, I think people see the world through the glasses they put on, and that's
what they wore. We all do that. I mean, that's not unique to them. They saw
the world in the real bills doctrine and so they tended to look for things which
supported that and discarded things which didn't fit with that.

The purging of speculative excesses.
Yes.

The inability to distinguish between real and nominal interest rates.
Yes.

Deflation as the inevitable consequence on inflation.
Yes.

The focus on the level of market interest rates to indicate tightness or ease leading to the belief that they'd done all they could to prevent the collapse of the monetary system, and it was the natural result of the previous credit inflation.
That's correct.

Their failure to act as lender of last resort.
Yes.

All of these things drove the Fed's actions during the Great Depression.
Yes. It is implicit in that but what deserves to be explicit is that they believed not only that they had done everything they could do but that if they did more it would be inflationary. Many of them believed that and there's a wonderful line which I quote where, when they are talking about engaging in open market operations, Norris, Governor, as they were then called, of the Philadelphia bank said the Fed would be putting out credit when it isn't needed and it will have to be withdrawn when it is. And what did he mean by that? He meant that under the real bills doctrine they should wait. You see, they were designed as a *passive* institution (*Meltzer raises his voice and emphasizes the word* passive). The gold standard took care of the long-term price level. The real bills doctrine took care of what was happening now. They didn't have to make decisions except to move the discount rate up and down and when banks came in to borrow they could lend. If banks didn't come in to borrow then they were absolved of the responsibility for what happened. That was the way they explained it to themselves.

So policy is totally endogenous then.
Right. That's right. It depends entirely on the market. If the market doesn't want to borrow, then you just have to wait for things to collapse even more until you get to the point where they will. It really is amazing to think what a revolution there is in economics on the role of government in business cycles. They didn't have much of a role at that time.

In reading your book what really caught my attention was when you indicated that if they had simply followed the rules of the gold standard which were known, or followed the knowledge from the nineteenth century according to Thornton or Bagehot, they could have avoided the slump.
That's right, that's why I put that chapter in. It wasn't that we were asking them to do things that were unknown. They were known, but they were ignored. And it's interesting because time after time they refer to Bagehot and they say, "You know we're following Bagehot." But they weren't.

The story of the Depression is really a story about not doing something about, and indeed ignoring, deflation and even believing that, while it would take time, "deflation was the correct solution to the mistakes of 1928–29."
That's correct.

It's all about the misbehavior of the price level and not doing something about it.
Right. They believed that Benjamin Strong had influenced them to help Britain in 1927 and that that had been the source of most of the problems that followed. And even though they all voted with Strong at that time, they later accused him of having made these mistakes and being responsible for what happened.

What are your views on the different price level targeting proposals that were talked about during the period? Do you not think of these as potentially fruitful and what were the Fed's major objections to them? There's not a lot of attention paid to the Goldsborough bill or the Strong bill.
They regarded those bills as highly inflationary.

That was the point though, right?
It was to restore the price level back …

To 1926.
To 1926, which is to stabilize it. That's what Goldsborough had wanted to do. But no, the Fed was against it and he got very little traction in Congress.

But the Fed's major objection was because it was inflationary.
Yes, they regarded it as inflationary.

So, what was the major objection?
Inflationary meant we would be buying Treasury bills, I mean the thing they do as a matter of course now.

Right.
(*Chuckling*) It's really kind of interesting how the world has changed in that respect.

And they would have considered that, what did you call it, liquidating loans versus non-liquidating loans?
Right, they were going to liquify government credit. Remember that the Federal Reserve couldn't buy mortgages and national banks weren't allowed to buy mortgages. All of that was speculative credit. While they eased it a little bit in 1927–28 at the time when they made a permanent charter for the Federal Reserve, they retained the real bills notion throughout and only gave it up very

slowly in the post-war period because of the Full Employment Act.

What was the major objection of Carter Glass to the Goldsborough bill and other such legislation?
Carter Glass was *the* (*Meltzer emphasizes the word* the) most extreme real bills person in Congress. I mean he believed, without entirely being justified in believing it, but he believed that he had written the Federal Reserve Act. It was his bill and this was his great contribution to American economic policy. The Goldsborough bill, by his definition, was a terrible thing, inflationary. He did not criticize the Federal Reserve for what it had done during the Great Depression on grounds that it was too deflationary. Not at all. He badgered them about the fact that they didn't do enough to prevent speculative credit from rising. He never could understand that you couldn't tell what the use of the credit was by the assets which the bank came in and used to borrow. When people tried to explain that to him he just did not want to hear that.

So there are important things to learn about these price level targeting proposals like the Goldsborough bill.
I think that they are a very significant part of American economic history and the source of great error and as you pointed out the main reason why I object to Friedman and Schwartz's and Irving Fisher's explanations of the role of Benjamin Strong in the Great Depression. There are two steps there. One is that Strong had to figure out what it was that had to be done. He was a bright man and he might have done that, but then he had to convince the others to do it. And that seems to me to be almost impossible and implausible under the circumstances.

Alright, you said that not adopting the Strong of Kansas bill in 1926–27 was a missed opportunity.
Yes.

You sure are right. The deflation would have been avoided ...
(*Meltzer interrupts*) Alan Greenspan wobbles on that.

On that point?
Yes, he says it in the Foreword to my book. I said if they had adopted that bill there would not have been a Great Depression or the Great Inflation, assuming that they would have followed that logic. Greenspan kind of steps away from that, he doesn't want to acknowledge it.

Well maybe he didn't want to be known publicly as an inflation targeter explicitly and that's why he was shying away from that.
Maybe.

You'll forgive me. I skipped the Foreword and went straight to the meat and potatoes of the book.
That's OK, I certainly can't complain about that.

Do you not see the evils of deflation, whether they are anticipated or unanticipated, as the greatest villain in the story of the Great Depression and thereafter the freeing of the economy from the deflationary vortex that existed being the greatest engine bringing on recovery?
Well, yes to the second. On the deflation, I think the deflation was terrible, but in my book I have a deflation in 1920–21, 1929–33, 1937–38, 1948–49, and then in Volume II we will have 1960–61 when there really is deflation. Only one of those episodes was a disaster and the only one that was a disaster was because they cut the money supply faster than the price level fell. So the expectation was that it was going to continue on. That's what made the deflation so disastrous. Deflation may be costly but it isn't as costly as contemporary economists believe because the other four deflations, one of which, 1920–21, was quite a serious deflation, were not particularly harmful. I mean the economy recovered from them just as it recovers from most other recessions.

Is it because of the tyranny of zero on nominal rates during the Great Depression?
No, I don't believe the binding floor of zero story except as a very long-run story. The Fed could always buy assets. There were plenty of assets to buy. In 1937–38 Treasury bills were actually selling at negative interest rates because they had certain option value.

So what was different about those other deflations compared to 1929–33?
They increased the money stock.

And then during the Great Depression the money stock fell faster than the price level.
Right. To a very considerable extent that's what happened to Japan, although not nearly to the same degree. The Japanese also did very little to get rid of their deflation except to talk about it.

Moreover, given the ruinous effects of deflation during the Depression and the dismal record of the 1970s in accelerating inflation, would you not say that instability in the price level both up and down is one of the greatest sources of economic instability of the last century? And would you not say that maintaining price stability is one of the key lessons for central bankers to learn from the Great Depression and the Great Inflation?
Yes indeed. And in fact I believe that for the present they have learned it. Not only have they learned it but in many places they have institutionalized that

learning in inflation targeting and so on. We'll see whether they're going to stick with that. But no question that's really the great lesson of the Great Inflation and how much harm you can do. You know, for the history of the United States up to 1970, all inflations were war-time inflations. That's where the idea comes from that government budgets are the source of inflation because the subtlety of the fact of how the government budget is financed gets lost in popular and even not so popular discussions. The lesson of the 1970s was that you can create an inflation without a war, and that led finally to recognizing that the Fed was really responsible for inflation. And they accept that. I mean in the 1950s and 1960s and many other times, they would not accept the idea that they could prevent inflation or that inflation was something that had to do primarily with them. William M. Martin believed it was budget deficits and Arthur Burns believed it was labor unions.

OK, well hopefully you live and learn.
Yes, that's right.

Cooperation or lack thereof was not the problem with the international gold standard; "countries' objectives were incompatible with the international monetary system they had adopted." Restoring the pre-war gold standard to prevailing exchange rates without the additional adjustment of relative prices of traded goods on both sides of the Atlantic was not going to happen. Do you not think that the gold standard was structurally flawed and doomed to failure and no amount of coordination or cooperation would have saved it?
Yes. That is, countries were not willing to make the adjustments that were necessary to maintain the gold standard. I mean, I like to say that we don't have the gold standard now, not because we don't know about the gold standard, but because we do (*roaring laughter*).

That's a great one. Do you think Peter Temin is correct that it was the resumption of the gold standard and the status quo ante and the attempt to preserve it that gave us the Depression? After World War I the world had changed and trying to put the pieces back together, particularly the gold standard and its mentality, led the world economy down the wrong path.
I think the gold standard had a role, but I don't quite believe it had the role that he assigns to it. I mean the real bills doctrine was vastly more important. The reason I say that is gold flowed into the United States from 1929 to 1931 and it didn't lead to an expansion. They sterilized the gold inflow, so it wasn't the gold standard itself because they were violating the gold standard rules. So when one wants to go and dig a little bit deeper than Temin has and ask "Well, why did they do that?", of course I believe it has to do with the fact that the real bills doctrine told them that they could only expand credit on the basis of borrowing by commercial banks.

Are you familiar with the Bernanke and Mihov (2000) paper?
Sure.

I don't think that paper gets nearly enough attention. They basically said that it was self-inflicted wounds from 1929–1931 and then, after Britain left gold, the international gold standard was done.
And on its way out.

And it was tying the Fed's hands. But they say that it was self-inflicted wounds in the beginning and then the gold standard took over after that. Whether it did or not, I don't know, but that self-inflicted wounds in the first part seems right to me.
That's right. But I would say it was self-inflicted wounds throughout. The argument about free gold, the most you can say is that it had something to do with what the Fed did between November of 1931 and January of 1932 because after they passed the Glass–Steagall Act they didn't need to worry about gold any more. And they knew that. But Harrison himself at one point says free gold was never a problem. And there were lots of things they could have done. They had a lot of notes outstanding that were idle and being held in various banks. They could have canceled those notes or exchanged them through the inter-district settlement fund and then canceled them. They had the legal authority which they had used in 1920–21 to make banks with surplus gold lend to the banks with deficient gold. They didn't do that. I mean, there are just a lot of things that they could have done and it was only a couple of months that they really had to suffer. Once the Glass–Steagall Act was passed they could have expanded without any restriction by gold.

But they just gave it up though, right? They gave it up in July of 1932.
They gave it up in July of 1932, yes. Friedman and Schwartz say that was mostly a political decision. I think that's probably not entirely accurate. The main reason they gave it up was that New York would lose gold, Chicago and Boston would not participate in the open market operations. Banks at that point, reserve banks at that point, had to approve the open market purchases or sales by their banks through their investment committee, that is, through the directors. Chicago and Boston had opted out of the open market expansion or had told New York that they would not opt in for it if there were any more. And New York did not want to lose gold to Chicago and the Federal Reserve Board would not force Chicago to either participate in the open market purchase or lend New York the gold. That's why Harrison quit, principally. The fact that Congress was going home for the summer ...

(Parker interjects) *After they had defeated the Goldsborough bill.*
Yes, correct. It may have contributed to what the Fed did, but it was not the thing that they talked about most. It was mostly Boston and Chicago.

Temin has said the Depression resulted because people at the time held onto a theory too long, and he's talking about the gold standard. You'd agree with that except that you'd say that it was the real bills doctrine that was held onto too long.

No, both, both of them. The gold standard was certainly operating as a deflationary force, and the reason that it was operating as a deflationary force was because the United States and France, which were the countries that received gold, would not inflate. The French sterilized all the gold that they received. The French were unhappy to be on the gold exchange standard when Britain and the United States were on the gold standard, very much like the 1960s. The French wanted to have the gold just the way the United States and Britain did. So they sterilized all the gold so that the countries who were receiving the gold would not inflate, and the countries that were losing the gold had to deflate. That was the mistake in the operation of the gold standard at that time. How would things have worked out? You want to ask yourself, suppose the French and the United States had inflated when they received gold, that is, they responded to the gold standard as they were supposed to. The answer is, in my opinion, there might have been a recession, but there would not have been a Great Depression.

Some of the world leaders at the time still had a desire to return to gold even after they left it, did they not?

Yes that's right. I think I quote the London *Times* in my book criticizing Britain for going off gold in 1931, saying these guys just don't have the guts and courage their ancestors had. Beliefs are important.

Yes, they are and it seems like it takes a lot to let them go too.

Oh yes, oh yes.

Do you think the heavy lifting of explaining the Great Depression has been done?

I think it's been done in the sense that the various things that you've talked about probably give us a much clearer, fuller picture of what was going on. I think that there are probably some things in the Treasury archives that one could get which would supplement that, maybe some of the foreign countries, especially Britain and France, that would supplement that. But I think that we have the general picture of what went on. What we don't have is a very good model. That is, there hasn't been a way of showing that, with or without changes, the model that we have of the economy can be applied to that period.

You mean modern-day theories applied to that era.

Right. I don't agree with them, but that's what I interpret the Minnesota people as trying to do. They're trying to show the real bills cycle ...

(Parker stops Meltzer and points out the humor) *Boy that is a hard belief to shake* (laughter).
(*Meltzer corrects himself*) They're trying to show the real *business* cycle model can be used to explain the Great Depression. I don't agree with that.

Well why don't we just go there? What's your take on the recent flurry of real business cycle papers on the Depression? If we thought we had the Depression explained before, this line of inquiry presents a whole new set of questions. Lee Ohanian indicated the whole line of research basically addresses the question "what is preventing people from working and producing more?" So let me ask you. What are we learning?
From those models?

Yes sir.
Well I don't think that we're learning a lot. I think that we're learning something that we knew before. We now have a model and that's probably a step forward. We knew before that wages did not adjust downward enough. We knew before that unemployment rose and didn't come down, and we knew before that productivity growth slowed. But putting that into algebra doesn't seem to me to add a lot. It may help people to build on what they've done, but I don't think it helps explain much more than what we already knew in words, in the histories we have and what is in Friedman and Schwartz for example. Plus, they have the monetary side which for some reason Cole and Ohanian and others are anxious to avoid. They don't want to admit that the collapse of the banking system had anything to do with the slow-down. I mean, thinking from a real business cycle point of view, given that all these banks failed and that the networks that people had to use to borrow were destroyed and lenders became more cautious probably as a result of all the bank failures, you would think if they don't want to give a role to money, at least they would give a real effect to these network externalities, as they are now called.

Or just considering finance to be part of the production function.
Right. Well that's the network externality. That something was missing that had been there before. So I think that that's a step that is useful in one sense because people do like to work with models, but it's not taking us in the right direction.

Alright. Thanks for that gold standard thing. I'm still chuckling about that.
Yes.

Romer has called the US decision to stay on the gold standard perhaps the biggest policy error of the Depression and calls the Depression a result of failed policy. On the other hand, Temin told me that after 1931 the Fed had "picked their side" and thus their actions should not be construed as policy failures. Their behavior was not a shock or inept but was a continuation of the path they chose to defend the exchange value of the dollar. What side do you come out on in this regard?

Well it's certainly true that they chose to defend the exchange rate of the dollar. Everybody at that time believed that devaluation was a thing to be avoided. But, as I said before, from 1929–1931, until Britain went off gold, we received gold. So what does it mean to say that we were defending the exchange value of the dollar? We were getting more gold. There was no defense necessary, yet they were allowing the money stock to decline. They were not doing enough about the banking failures. I mean, those are mistakes.

OK. So the Federal Reserve was not fettered by gold at any time during the Great Depression, correct?

With the possible exception of November 1931 to January 1932. I mean I'm skeptical about that but I think anyone who wants to make the case can possibly make a coherent case from October/November 1931 to January of 1932. But after the Glass–Steagall Act they certainly can't make that case because they could buy whatever they wanted to buy and didn't have to stop. It was their beliefs that were important at that point. Now you want to give them credit because the open market operations which they engaged in from February of 1932 to about May were the largest up to that time and quite a bit larger than anything they did before. So they really did make an effort.

Temin has said that claiming the Fed should have increased the money supply by what was needed to avert the Depression is a product of ahistorical analysis. There was no credible discussion taken seriously outside of the gold standard mentality. How do you respond to that?

Well we certainly know about the Goldsborough bill and there were other bills in Congress which wanted to do that so that's not quite true. It's also true that Lauchlin Currie wrote a book around that time.

1934, The Supply and Control of Money in the United States.

That's it, yes, pointing out the mistakes of the Fed. I mean his book is quite modern in the sense of Friedman and Schwartz, or my book in terms of the reasons he gave for criticizing the Fed.

Hsieh and Romer (2004) point out, as you did in your book, that the one billion dollar or more open market operation in 1932 had a better chance of working before Britain left gold. It was obviously something they contemplated because they did it. So your colleague and friend Ben McCallum showed in the JME *that something that they actually did wind up doing would have had a very good effect if they had done it earlier on.*

And some of them knew that. That is, I can't remember who it was, it may have been Harrison, it may have been someone else, but who said the initial effect of the expansion is probably offset by the loss of gold. And a lot of the gold that they were losing, of course, was going to France because France was the big predator country at that point. Around May someone there says, "Well now we're rid of the gold, that is the gold problem. All the balances are now gone. So these operations are going to be more effective from here on out than they were before."

Hsieh and Romer (2004) make the point that with the Glass–Steagall Act of 1932 more effective Fed action was a simple legislative change away. If they had passed Glass–Steagall earlier, they could have done that. But would the Fed still have been stuck in their same old mentality?
Yes, they never used Glass–Steagall. They didn't use Glass–Steagall. And they did lose gold but that didn't really hurt them or prevent them from expanding and as far as I know they did not use Glass–Steagall although they renewed it from time to time. They didn't use Glass–Steagall during the 1932–33 period.

Why do you suppose the gold standard was not suspended nor was deposit convertibility during this time, or why the US did not follow the UK's lead in 1931 and leave gold? Is there a simple answer to that?
I don't know the answer to that. I don't know the answer to that. It's a good question. It's certainly true that leaving the gold standard was considered a horrendous act. But why didn't they do it under those circumstances? Did they believe that they could get through it without having to devalue the dollar? I mean, that seems hard to believe after Britain and all the British colonies that devalued against the United States and gold. But I don't know.

Maybe it's one of the things that we'll never know.
Maybe we'll never know. Maybe that's something that you'll find out.

So what's your impression of Figure 2 in Cecchetti (1998) that shows discount behavior by the Fed during the Depression? Does this not show the failure of the Federal Reserve to be lender of last resort?
Oh, absolutely.

And thus should we not let them off the hook so easily? Even if they were on gold as the graph shows, little was done before Britain had left gold when we all agree that the Fed could have done something. And the first and second banking panics passed with discounting barely even registering a pulse.
That's correct. That's correct.

So even though discounting was endogenous...
Yes, the answer the Fed would give you was that it was up to the banks. It isn't up to us to decide whether they discount, it's up to them. Now there's some element of truth to that, but of course changing the discount rate, changing the

acceptance rate so as to push them to discount more rather than to sell acceptances, those are things that you could do, and they were not done.

Charles Calomiris has said that, macroeconomically, bank distress could have been mitigated if the collapse had been avoided, but there was little that could have been done on a microeconomic, lender of last resort level to arrest the bank failures before 1933. Indeed, he then goes on to say that short of a bank bailout not much could have helped on a microeconomic scale, and bailing out failing banks was not part of the thinking of central bankers during this time period. What do you say about that?
I agree with that last part that they didn't think that bailing out failing banks was part of their responsibility. I think the best way to reach an understanding of some of their views comes with the start of what was called the National Monetary Commission, which became the RFC. The examiners would go around from bank to bank and find which parts of the bank's securities, railroad bonds for the most part, were below par or under water. And they couldn't evaluate the loans so they didn't do much about the loans, but they would take the government bonds and they would sell them, dump them on the market and close the bank in order to protect the so-called depositors. And they would go to the next bank and they would find that because they had dumped all these bonds the bonds were even lower in price, so they would dump some more. And this was going on for month after month. That's why President Hoover started the National Monetary Commission. He had a meeting in New York and he got the New York banks to agree to put up a stake to start the National Monetary Commission, to give him capital. And they agreed to do it. They said, "Look, we're not asking for any special help but we're giving you special help, so if we get into trouble because of the money we're putting into the National Monetary Commission we want to be able to discount these National Monetary Commission things with the Federal Reserve Bank." The Federal Reserve Bank said, "No, we can't do that because those are not real bills."

Alright.
So, that's really where the problem arose and Hoover wanted a private market solution and he couldn't get one. That's why we brought in the RFC. Alright then, the RFC wasn't very effective until later. The reason it wasn't very effective was that Congress, probably for political reasons, wanted them to publish the names of the banks that were getting assistance. And of course that was the wrong thing to do because then there would be a run on those banks, but Congress insisted upon that. And they continued to insist upon that through the winter of 1933.

So what about the first part of that statement though, the microeconomic lender of last resort? Would it have done some good?

Of course. This is the same argument I had with the Bank of Japan in the 1990s. They would say to me, "Well the banks won't lend because they have all these bad real estate loans" and I would say, "If you could get the price level to stop falling there wouldn't be quite so many bad real estate loans."

Exactly. What the Japanese needed to see, as Ben Bernanke has told me, was that if you could increase the money supply and not cause inflation you could buy up all the assets in the world. And still they wouldn't listen.
No, that's right. I was the so-called honorary advisor to the Bank of Japan for 16 years and I had many conversations with the previous Governor of the Bank, Governor Hayami, who is a very fine man, but who had a strong set of beliefs.

There's those beliefs again.
He had a strong set of beliefs and one of the things that he believed in very strongly was that the only way monetary policy could work was by getting the banks to expand. The banks were not going to expand until they bailed them out or fixed them up and therefore there was nothing he could do. He rejected all the advice that I gave him and what is very interesting is that Governor Fukui, who took his place, then adopted exactly the proposals that I had made to the Bank.

And what do you know, they're getting out of their mess now, aren't they?
They are getting out of their mess.

Imagine how that works, huh? (laughter). *I mean if they had to bust the windows out of the Bank of Japan in downtown Tokyo and have a money rain then that's what they should have been doing.*
Absolutely.

One of the lessons of the Great Depression Ben Bernanke has pointed out is that fixed exchange rate regimes can be dangerous and destabilizing. Given the experience of the Great Depression and the Asian crisis of the 1990s do you think that fixed exchange rate regimes have much to recommend them?
I think fixed exchange rates have something to recommend them for small countries, mainly because a small country has very little room for an independent monetary policy. What we've learned is that they can make a mess of things in their own country but they can't help it a great deal, so they're better off with a fixed exchange rate. For countries like the US and Japan, the euro, and eventually perhaps the Chinese, floating rates are the way to go.

For small countries, then, that makes their monetary policy endogenous with

respect to the United States, for example.
Right.

OK, great. What are some of the other lessons from the Great Depression that have been learned or need to be relearned? It is interesting that you and Brunner in your 1968 Canadian Journal of Economics *paper blasted the Fed for following the same policy as that of the Fed in the Depression for using interest rate movements as a guide for policy. Is there anything that we still haven't learned or need to relearn?*
Yes, we've done much better. We've learned a lot. We still put too much weight on short-term interest rate movements without looking at what other asset prices are doing. But we are better about that. I would say the other thing that the Federal Reserve needs to do is it has moved a long way toward trying to implement a medium-term strategy, but it has a long way to go. I mean it's still very much caught up with what happened to the unemployment rate today or what was the announcement of the unemployment rate today, what was the announcement of the inflation rate today and so on, and that's not what they should be doing. The great advantage of inflation targeting is that it forces you to have a two-year or three-year horizon and to concentrate on what you are doing to be in the right place two years from now. I think that's a lesson we still have to learn.

I'd like to ask the unofficial historian of the Federal Reserve: what are your ideas on the recent appointment of Ben Bernanke to be Fed chair?
I think it's a good appointment. It may be an excellent appointment but we won't know that for a while, whether it's an excellent appointment or just a good appointment. There are three things that we need to consider when appointing a Fed chairman. The first is does he know enough about monetary economics to be useful and not dangerous? Bernanke certainly passes that test. Second, the job is very much a political job with many, many constituencies. You have the Congress, because the Fed is the agent of Congress. Article I, section eight says Congress coins the money and regulates the value thereof. So the Fed is the agent of Congress and you have to get along with the banking committees of the Congress. He certainly has to be good at getting along with the administration while remaining independent of the administration. He has to be credible as far as Wall Street is concerned as well as foreign financial markets and foreign governments. And then there's the general public. So it's a big political job and it requires somebody with a lot of skill in doing it and Volcker and Greenspan in very different ways were able to do that. So that's the second one and he looks to be pretty good at that. The third one is economic theory never tells you, or often doesn't tell you, what precisely you should do now. Alan Greenspan was very good at making those evaluations, deciding which way the error was likely to be least damaging and doing it.

Right.
We didn't know that 18 years ago when he first came. We don't know that about Bernanke. So that's the one area which will make a very successful Chairman or not, that you make correct judgments. Think about the current policy. Many people in the market are explaining that there is inflation because the CPI is rising. Greenspan and the Fed are avoiding the mistake that they made in the 70s of thinking that that was an inflation that they have to do something about it. This time they're saying, "Well long-term expectations haven't changed, so we're just going to let this pass through." That's correct but that's a judgment, and you get a lot of criticism. So you have to take that criticism and when you come out on the other side people will say, "He was right." And that has been Greenspan's success. That didn't mean that he always was right but you don't have to always be right. You just have to have a pretty good batting average and that establishes it. Now, Greenspan was in a way lucky that there was a big market break two months after he became Chairman and he established his credibility in the way in which he handled that market break. So the market break wasn't good. It was good for establishing his credibility. After that people said, "Well this guy really knows how to do the job, so we can trust him."

Right. OK, two questions I ask everybody. What ended the Great Depression?
The gold inflow and of course ultimately World War II. But the gold inflow pretty much ended the Great Depression. By 1936–37 the economy was almost back to the 1929 level and it would have continued to expand but not as fast, it expanded very rapidly in 1936 because of the bonuses that were given out and the fact that money growth was very high during that period. It ended mainly because the Treasury and the Fed agreed and decided to sterilize the gold inflow in 1937 and that took a very fast money growth rate and turned it around. And then of course WWII came along. It's fantastic to see how the bankers and finance people were haranguing, haranguing, haranguing about deficits, small deficits of the 1930s. So they stopped running to Washington looking for contracts. So when we get to WWII, when the deficits are going to be much, much larger, they stopped worrying about deficits.

Could it happen again, Professor?
The Depression?

Yes sir. Could a depression happen again?
Well you never rule out anything, certainly in economics, you never rule out anything, but I think we know a lot more. We've learned a lot more and politically we're of a very different mindset. So we wouldprobably act more quickly and more effectively.

And have different beliefs too.

Yes that's true (*laughter*). Well you know that I am a strong believer in the idea that you can't know everything and think of everything, so you look at the world through whatever way you have of thinking about the world and you see the things that worked that way and then you tend to push aside the things that are not central to my view of what's happening.

Thanks so much, Professor.

References

Abramovitz, M. (undated), 'The monetary side of long swings in US economic growth', Stanford University Center for Research in Economic Growth, Memorandum No. 146.

Abramovitz, M. (1977), 'Determinants of nominal-income and money-stock growth and the level of the balance of payments: two-country models under a specie standard', unpublished, Stanford University.

Amaral, P. and J. MacGee (2002), 'The Great Depression in Canada and the United States: a neoclassical perspective', *Review of Economic Dynamics*, January.

Anderson, B.L. and J.L. Butkiewicz (1980), 'Money, spending and the Great Depression', *Southern Economic Journal*, October.

Atkeson, A. And L.E. Ohanian (2001), 'Are Phillips curves useful for inflation forecasting?', Federal Reserve Bank of Minneapolis *Quarterly Review*, Winter.

Bagehot, W. (1873), *Lombard Street: A Description of the Money Market*, London: Henry S. King and Company.

Balderston, T., (ed.), (2003), *The World Economy and National Economies in the Interwar Slump*, New York: Palgrave Macmillan.

Balke, N.S. and R.J. Gordon (1986), 'Historical data', in R.J. Gordon (ed.), *The American Business Cycle: Continuity and Change*, Chicago: University of Chicago Press.

Barsky, R. and J.B. DeLong (1990), 'Bull and bear markets in the twentieth century', *Journal of Economic History*, June.

Bayoumi, T. and B. Eichengreen (1996), 'The stability of the gold standard and the evolution of the international monetary system', in T. Bayoumi, B. Eichengreen and M. Taylor (eds), *Modern Perspectives on the Gold Standard*, Cambridge: Cambridge University Press.

Beaudry, P. and F. Portier (2002), 'The French depression in the 1930s', *Review of Economic Dynamics*, January.

242

Bernanke, B. (1983a), 'Nonmonetary effects of the financial crisis in the propagation of the Great Depression', *American Economic Review*, June.

Bernanke, B. (1983b), 'Irreversibility, uncertainty, and cyclical investment', *Quarterly Journal of Economics*, February.

Bernanke, B. (1993a), 'Credit in the macroeconomy', *Federal Reserve Bank of New York Quarterly Review*, Spring.

Bernanke, B. (1993b), 'The world on a cross of gold', *Journal of Monetary Economics*, April.

Bernanke, B. (1995), 'The macroeconomics of the Great Depression: a comparative approach', *Journal of Money, Credit, and Banking*, February.

Bernanke, B. (2000), *Essays on the Great Depression*, Princeton, NJ: Princeton University Press.

Bernanke, B. and H. James (1991), 'The gold standard, deflation, and financial crisis in the Great Depression: an international comparison', in R.G. Hubbard (ed.), *Financial Markets and Financial Crises*, Chicago: University of Chicago Press.

Bernanke, B. and K. Carey (1996), 'Nominal wage stickiness and aggregate supply in the Great Depression', *Quarterly Journal of Economics*, August.

Bernanke, B. and I. Mihov (2000), 'Deflation and monetary contraction in the Great Depression: an analysis by simple ratios', in B.S. Bernanke (ed.), *Essays on the Great Depression*, Princeton: Princeton University Press.

Bernstein, M. (1987), *The Great Depression: Delayed Recovery and Economic Change in America, 1929–39*, Cambridge: Cambridge University Press.

Bordo, M. (1995), 'Is there a good case for a new Bretton Woods international monetary system?', *Papers and Proceedings of the American Economic Association*, May.

Bordo, M. (2003), 'Comment on "The Great Depression and the Friedman–Schwartz hypothesis" by L. Christiano, R. Motto and M. Rostagno', *Journal of Money, Credit, and Banking*, December, Part 2.

Bordo, M., and B. Eichengreen (1998), 'Implications of the Great Depression for the development of the international monetary system', in M. Bordo, C. Goldin and E. White (eds), *The Defining Moment: The Great Depression and the American Economy in the Twentieth Century*, Chicago: University of Chicago Press.

Bordo, M. and F. Kydland (1995), 'The gold standard as a rule: an essay in exploration', *Explorations in Economic History*, October.

Bordo, M. and F. Kydland (1996), 'The gold standard as a commitment mechanism', in T. Bayoumi, B. Eichengreen and M. Taylor (eds), *Modern Perspectives on the Gold Standard*, Cambridge: Cambridge University Press.

Bordo, M. and H. Rockoff (1996), 'The gold standard as a "Good Housekeeping Seal of Approval"', *Journal of Economic History*, June.

Bordo, M., E. Choudhri and A. Schwartz (1995), 'Could stable money have averted the great contraction?', *Economic Inquiry*, July.

Bordo, M., E. Choudhri and A. Schwartz (1999), 'Was expansionary monetary policy feasible during the Great Contraction?', NBER Working Paper 7125.

Bordo, M., E. Choudhri and A. Schwartz (2002), 'Was expansionary monetary policy feasible during the Great Contraction?', *Explorations in Economic History*, January.

Bordo, M., C. Erceg and C. Evans (2000a), 'Comment on "Re-examining the contributions of money and banking shocks to the US Great Depression"', in B.S. Bernanke and K. Rogoff (eds), *NBER Macroeconomics Annual*, Cambridge, MA: The MIT Press.

Bordo, M., C. Erceg and C. Evans (2000b), 'Money, sticky wages and the Great Depression', *American Economic Review*, December.

Bordo, M., C. Goldin and E. White (1998), *The Defining Moment: The Great Depression and the American Economy in the Twentieth Century*, Chicago: University of Chicago Press.

Bresnahan, T. and D. Raff (1991), 'Intra-industry heterogeneity and the Great Depression: the American motor vehicle industry, 1929–1935', *Journal of Economic History*, June.

Brown, E. (1956), 'Fiscal policy in the thirties: a reappraisal', *American Economic Review*, December.

Brown, W.A. (1940), *The International Gold Standard Reinterpreted, 1914–1934*, New York: National Bureau of Economic Research.

Brunner, K. (ed.) (1981), *The Great Depression Revisited*, Boston: Martinus Nijhoff Publishing.

Brunner, K. and A. Meltzer (1968), 'What did we learn from the monetary experience of the United States in the Great Depression?', *The Canadian Journal of Economics*, May.

Butkiewicz, J. (1999), 'The Reconstruction Finance Corporation, the gold standard, and the banking crisis of 1933', *Southern Economic Journal*, October.

Calomiris, C. (1993), 'Financial factors in the Great Depression', *Journal of Economic Perspectives*, Spring.

Calomiris, C. (1995), 'Financial fragility: issues and policy implications', *Journal of Financial Services Research*, December.

Calomiris, C. and J. Mason (1997), 'Contagion and bank failures during the Great Depression: the June 1932 Chicago banking panic', *American Economic Review*, December.

Calomiris, C. and J. Mason (2003a), 'Consequences of US bank distress during the Depression, *American Economic Review*, June.

Calomiris, C. and J. Mason (2003b), 'Fundamentals, panics and bank distress during the Depression, *American Economic Review*, December.

Calomiris, C and D. Wheelock (1998), 'Was the Great Depression a watershed in American monetary policy?' in M. Bordo, C. Goldin and E. White (eds), *The Defining Moment: The Great Depression and the American Economy in the Twentieth Century*, Chicago: University of Chicago Press.

Calvo, G. (1986), 'Temporary stabilization: predetermined exchange rates', *Journal of Political Economy*, December.

Campa, J. (1990), 'Exchange rates and economic recovery in the 1930s: an extension to Latin America', *Journal of Economic History*, September.

Cecchetti, S.G. (1988a), 'The case of the negative nominal interest rates: new estimates of the term structure of interest rates during the Great Depression', *Journal of Political Economy*, December.

Cecchetti, S.G. (1988b), 'Deflation and the Great Depression', manuscript, Ohio State University.

Cecchetti, S.G. (1992), 'Prices during the Great Depression: was the deflation of 1930–32 really anticipated?', *American Economic Review*, March.

Cecchetti, S.G. (1998), 'Understanding the Great Depression: lessons for current policy', in M. Wheeler (ed.), *The Economics of the Great Depression*, Kalamazoo, MI: W.E. Upjohn Institute for Employment Research.

Cecchetti, S.G. (2006), *Money, Banking, and Financial Markets*, New York: McGraw-Hill Irwin.

Cecchetti, S.G. and L. Ball (1988), 'Imperfect information and staggered price setting', *American Economic Review*, December.

Cecchetti, S.G. and G. Karras (1994), 'Sources of output fluctuations during the interwar period: further evidence on the causes of the Great Depression', *Review of Economics and Statistics*, February.

Choudhri, E.U. and L.A. Kochin (1980), 'The exchange rate and the international transmission of business cycle disturbances', *Journal of Money, Credit, and Banking*, November.

Christiano, L., R. Motto and M. Rostagno (2003), 'The Great Depression and the Friedman–Schwartz hypothesis', *Journal of Money, Credit, and Banking*, December, Part 2.

Christiano, L., M. Eichenbaum and C. Evans (2005), 'Nominal rigidities and the dynamic effects of a shock to monetary policy', *Journal of Political Economy*, February.

Clarke, S.V.O. (1967), *Central Bank Cooperation 1924–1931*, New York: Federal Reserve Bank of New York.

Cole, H.L. and L.E. Ohanian (1999), 'The Great Depression in the United States from a neoclassical perspective,' *Federal Reserve Bank of Minneapolis Quarterly Review*, Winter.

Cole, H.L. and L.E. Ohanian (2000), 'Re-examining the contributions of money and banking shocks to the US Great Depression', in B.S. Bernanke and K. Rogoff (eds), *NBER Macroeconomics Annual*, Cambridge, MA: The MIT Press.

Cole, H.L. and L.E. Ohanian (2002), 'The great UK Depression: a puzzle and a possible resolution', *Review of Economic Dynamics*, January.

Cole, H.L. and L.E. Ohanian (2004a), 'New Deal policies and the persistence of the Great Depression: a general equilibrium analysis', *Journal of Political Economy*, August.

Cole, H.L. and L.E. Ohanian (2004b), 'Deflation and the international Great Depression: a productivity puzzle', University of California, Los Angeles, research memo, November.

Cooley, T. and L.E. Ohanian (1997), 'Postwar British economic growth and the legacy of Keynes', *Journal of Political Economy*, June.

Crucini, M. (1994), 'Sources of variation in real tariff rates: the United States, 1900–1940, *American Economic Review*, June.

Currie, L. (1934), *The Supply and Control of Money in the United States*, New York: Russell and Russell.

Dam, K.W. (1982), *The Rules of the Game: Reform and Evolution in the International Monetary System*, Chicago: University of Chicago Press.

DeLong, J.B. and A. Shleifer (1991), 'The stock market bubble of 1929: evidence from closed-end mutual funds', *Journal of Economic History*, September.

Dimand, R. (2003), 'Irving Fisher on the international transmission of booms and depressions through monetary standards', *Journal of Money, Credit and Banking*, February.

Dornbusch, R. (1976), 'Expectations and exchange rate dynamics', *Journal of Political Economy*, December.

Eggertsson, G. (2005), 'Great expectations and the end of the Depression', Federal Reserve Bank of New York Staff Report 234, December.

Eichengreen, B. (1986), 'The Bank of France and the sterilization of gold, 1926–1932', *Explorations in Economic History*, **23**.

Eichengreen, B. (1988), 'Did international forces cause the Great Depression?', *Contemporary Policy Issues*, April.

Eichengreen, B. (1989), 'The political economy of the Smoot–Hawley tariff', *Research in Economic History*, **12**.

Eichengreen, B. (1992), *Golden Fetters: The Gold Standard and the Great Depression, 1919–1939*, New York: Oxford University Press.

Eichengreen, B. (2002), 'Still fettered after all these years', NBER Working Paper 9276.

Eichengreen, B. (2004), 'Viewpoint: understanding the Great Depression', *Canadian Journal of Economics*, February.

Eichengreen, B. and R. Grossman (1997), 'Debt deflation and financial instability: two historical perspectives', in F. Capie and G. Wood (eds), *Asset Prices and the Real Economy*, New York: Palgrave Macmillan.

Eichengreen, B. and K. Mitchener (2004), 'The Great Depression as a credit boom gone wrong', *Research in Economic History*, **22**.

Eichengreen, B. and J. Sachs (1985), 'Exchange rates and economic recovery in the 1930s', *Journal of Economic History*, December.

Eichengreen, B. and J. Sachs (1986), 'Competitive devaluation and the Great Depression', *Economics Letters*, **22**, (1).

Eichengreen, B. and P. Temin (1997), 'The gold standard and the Great Depression', NBER Working Paper 6060.

Eichengreen, B. and P. Temin (2003), 'Afterword: counterfactual histories of the Great Depression', in T. Balderston (ed.), *The World Economy and National Economies in the Interwar Slump*, New York: Palgrave Macmillan.

Einzig, P. (1937), *The Theory of Forward Exchange*, London: Macmillan.

Epstein, G. and T. Ferguson (1984), 'Monetary policy, loan liquidation and industrial conflict: the Federal Reserve open market operation of 1932', *Journal of Economic History*, December.

Evans, M. and P. Wachtel (1993), 'Were price changes during the Great Depression anticipated? Evidence from nominal interest rates', *Journal of Monetary Economics*, October.

Fackler, J. and R. Parker (1994), 'Accounting for the Great Depression: a historical decomposition', *Journal of Macroeconomics*, Spring.

Fackler, J. and R. Parker (2005), 'Was debt deflation operative during the Great Depression?', *Economic Inquiry*, January.

Ferguson, N. (1999), *Virtual History: Alternatives and Counterfactuals*, New York: Basic Books.

Ferguson, T. and P. Temin (2003), 'Made in Germany: the German currency crisis of July 1931', *Research in Economic History*, **21**.

Field, A. (1992), 'Uncontrolled land development and the duration of the Depression in the United States', *Journal of Economic History*, December.

Field, A. (2003), 'The most technologically progressive decade of the century', *American Economic Review*, September.

Fisher, I. (1933), 'The debt–deflation theory of great depressions', *Econometrica*, October.

Fisher, J. and A. Hornstein (2002), 'The role of real wages, productivity, and fiscal policy in Germany's Great Depression 1928–37', *Review of Economic Dynamics*, January.

Flacco, P. and R. Parker (1992), 'Income uncertainty and the onset of the Great Depression', *Economic Inquiry*, January.

Friedman, M. (1969), 'The optimum quantity of money', in M. Friedman (ed.), *The Optimum Quantity of Money and Other Essays*, Chicago: Aldine Publishing Company.

Friedman, M. (2004), 'Reflections on *A Monetary History*', *The Cato Journal*, Winter.

Friedman, M. and A.J. Schwartz (1963), *A Monetary History of the United States, 1867–1960*, Princeton, NJ: Princeton University Press.

Gertler, M. (2000), 'Comment on "Re-examining the contributions of money and banking shocks to the US Great Depression"', in B.S. Bernanke and K. Rogoff (eds), *NBER Macroeconomics Annual*, Cambridge, MA: The MIT Press.

Gordon, C. (1994), *New Deals: Business, Labor and Politics in America, 1920–1935*, New York: Cambridge University Press.

Graham, F.D. and C.R. Whittlesey (1940), *The Golden Avalanche*, Princeton, NJ: Princeton University Press.

Hamilton, J.D. (1987), 'Monetary factors in the Great Depression', *Journal of Monetary Economics*, March.

Hamilton, J.D. (1988), 'Role of the international gold standard in propagating the Great Depression', *Contemporary Policy Issues*, April.

Hamilton, J.D. (1992), 'Was the deflation during the Great Depression anticipated? Evidence from the commodity futures market', *American Economic Review*, March.

Hamilton, J.D. (1994), *Time Series Analysis*, Princeton, NJ: Princeton University Press.

Hayek, F.A. von (1967), *Monetary Theory and the Trade Cycle*, New York: A.M. Kelley.

Hoover, H. (1952), *The Memoirs of Herbert Hoover: The Great Depression 1929–1941*, New York: Macmillan.

Hsieh, C. and C. D. Romer (2004), 'Was the Federal Reserve constrained by the gold standard during the Great Depression? Evidence from the 1932 open market program', University of California Working Paper. This paper has subsequently been published in the *Journal of Economic History*, March, 2006.

Hyman, S. (1976), *Marriner S. Eccles*, Stanford: Stanford University Graduate School of Business.

Johnson, G.G. (1939), *The Treasury and Monetary Policy 1933–1938*, Cambridge: Harvard University Press.

Johnson, H.C. (1997), *Gold, France, and the Great Depression*, New Haven: Yale University Press.

Kennedy, S.E. (1973), *The Banking Crisis of 1933*, Lexington, KY: The University of Kentucky Press.

Keynes, J.M. (1936), *The General Theory of Employment, Interest, and Money*, London: Macmillan.

Kindleberger, C.P. (1986), *The World in Depression 1929–1939*, revised and enlarged edition, Berkeley: University of California Press.

Kitson, M. (2003), 'Slump and recovery: the UK experience', in T. Balderston (ed.), *The World Economy and National Economies in the Interwar Slump*, New York: Palgrave Macmillan.

Klamer, A. (1984), *Conversations with Economists*, Totowa, NJ: Rowman and Allanheld.

Krooss, H.E. (1969), *Documentary History of Banking and Currency in the United States*, New York: Chelsea House Publishers.

Kuhn, T.S. (1962), *The Structure of Scientific Revolutions*, Chicago: University of Chicago Press.

Kydland, F. and E. Prescott (1982), 'Time to build and aggregate fluctuations', *Econometrica*, November.

League of Nations (1933), *Economic Survey 1932/33*, Geneva: League of Nations.

League of Nations (1935), *Economic Survey 1934/35*, Geneva: League of Nations.

League of Nations (1936), *Economic Survey 1935/36*, Geneva: League of Nations.

League of Nations (1937), *Economic Survey 1936/37*, Geneva: League of Nations.

League of Nations (1938), *Economic Survey 1937/38*, Geneva: League of Nations.

Lucas, R. (1981), *Studies in Business-Cycle Theory*, Cambridge, MA: The MIT Press.

Lucas, R. and L. Rapping (1969), 'Real wages, employment and inflation', *Journal of Political Economy*, September/October.

Lucas, R. and L. Rapping (1972), 'Unemployment in the Great Depression: is there a full explanation?', *Journal of Political Economy*, January/February.

Mankiw, N.G., J. Miron and D. Weil (1987), 'The adjustment of expectations to a change in regime: a study of the founding of the Federal Reserve', *American Economic Review*, June.

McCallum, B.T. (1990), 'Could a monetary base rule have prevented the Great Depression?', *Journal of Monetary Economics*, August.

McGrattan, E.R. and E. Prescott (2004), 'The stock market crash of 1929: Irving Fisher was right!', *International Economic Review*, November.

Meltzer, A.H. (1976), 'Monetary and other explanations of the start of the Great Depression', *Journal of Monetary Economics*, November.

Meltzer, A.H. (2003), *A History of the Federal Reserve, Volume I*, Chicago: University of Chicago Press. *Volume II* is currently in production.

Mishkin, F.S. (1978), 'The household balance sheet and the Great Depression', *Journal of Economic History*, December.

Nelson, D.B. (1991), 'Was the deflation of 1929–1930 anticipated? The monetary regime as viewed by the business press', in Roger L. Ransom (ed.), *Research in Economic History*, Greenwich, CT: JAI Press.

Ohanian, L.E. (1998), 'The defining moment: a review essay', *Journal of Political Economy*, February.

Ohanian, L.E. (2000), 'Interview on the Great Depression', *Economic Dynamics*, April.

Ohanian, L.E. (2001), 'Why did productivity fall so much during the Great Depression?', *American Economic Review Papers and Proceedings*, May.

Olney, M. (1991), *Buy Now, Pay Later*, Chapel Hill: The University of North Carolina Press.

Olney, M. (1999), 'Avoiding default: the role of credit in the consumption collapse of 1930', *Quarterly Journal of Economics*, February.

Parker, R.E. (2002), *Reflections on the Great Depression*, Cheltenham, UK and Northampton, MA, USA: Edward Elgar.

Peppers, L. (1973), 'Full employment surplus analysis and structural change: the 1930s', *Explorations in Economic History*, Winter.

Perez, C. (2002), *Technological Revolutions and Financial Capital*, Cheltenham, UK and Northampton, MA, USA: Edward Elgar.

Perri, F. and V. Quadrini (2002), 'The Great Depression in Italy: trade restrictions and real wage rigidities', *Review of Economic Dynamics*, January.

Persons, C.E. (1930), 'Credit expansion, 1920 to 1929 and its lessons', *Quarterly Journal of Economics*, November.

Plosser, C.I. (1989), 'Understanding real business cycles', *Journal of Economic Perspectives*, Summer.

Polenberg, R. (2000), *The Era of Franklin D. Roosevelt, 1933–1945: A Brief History with Documents*, Boston: Bedford/St. Martin's.

Prescott, E. (1999), 'Some observations on the Great Depression', *Federal Reserve Bank of Minneapolis Quarterly Review*, Winter.

Pusey, M. (1974), *Eugene Meyer*, New York: Alfred A. Knopf.

Raynold, P., W.D. McMillin and T.R. Beard (1991), 'The impact of Federal Government expenditures in the 1930s', *Southern Economic Journal*, July.

Rees, A. (1970), 'On equilibrium in labor markets', *Journal of Political Economy*, March/April.

Ritschl, A. (2003), '"Dancing on a volcano": the economic recovery and collapse of Weimar Germany, 1924–33', in T. Balderston (ed.), *The World Economy and National Economies in the Interwar Slump*, New York: Palgrave Macmillan.

Robbins, L. (1934), *The Great Depression*, London: Macmillan.

Romer, C.D. (1988a), 'World War I and the postwar depression: a reappraisal based on alternative estimates of GNP', *Journal of Monetary Economics*, July.

Romer, C.D. (1988b), 'The great crash and the onset of the Great Depression', NBER Working Paper 2639.

Romer, C.D. (1990), 'The great crash and the onset of the Great Depression', *Quarterly Journal of Economics*, August.

Romer, C.D. (1992), 'What ended the Great Depression?', *Journal of Economic History*, December.

Romer, C.D. (1993), 'The nation in depression', *Journal of Economic Perspectives*, Spring.

Romer, C.D. (1994a), 'Remeasuring business cycles', *Journal of Economic History*, September.

Romer, C.D. (1994b), 'The end of economic history?', *Journal of Economic Education*, Winter.

Romer, C.D. (1998), 'Comments on "The causes of American business cycles: an essay in economic historiography", by Peter Temin', in J. Fuhrer and S. Schuh (eds), *Beyond Shocks*, Boston: Federal Reserve Bank, June.

Romer, C.D. (2005), 'The Great Depression', *Encyclopedia Britannica*.

Samuelson, P. (1998), 'Summing up on business cycles; opening address', in J. Fuhrer and S. Schuh (eds), *Beyond Shocks*, Boston: Federal Reserve Bank, June.

Snowdon, B. (2002), *Conversations on Growth, Stability and Trade: An Historical Perspective*, Cheltenham, UK and Northampton, MA, USA: Edward Elgar.

Soule, G. (1947), *Prosperity Decade, From War to Depression: 1917–1929 (The Economic History of the United States, Vol. VIII)*, New York: Rinehart and Co., Inc.

Taylor, J.B. (1999), 'An historical analysis of monetary policy rules', in J.B. Taylor (ed.), *Monetary Policy Rules*, Chicago: University of Chicago Press.

Temin, P. (1976a), *Did Monetary Forces Cause the Great Depression?*, New York: W.W. Norton.

Temin, P. (1976b), 'Lessons for the present from the Great Depression', *American Economic Review*, May.

Temin, P. (1981), 'Notes on the causes of the Great Depression', in K. Brunner (ed.), *The Great Depression Revisited*, Boston: Martinus Nijhoff Publishing.

Temin, P. (1989), *Lessons from the Great Depression*, Cambridge, MA: MIT Press.

Temin, P. (1998) 'The causes of American business cycles: an essay in economic historiography', in J. Fuhrer and S. Schuh (eds), *Beyond Shocks*, Boston: Federal Reserve Bank, June.

Temin, P. (2002), 'Moses Abramovitz and open economy macro', presentation at the meetings of the American Economic Association.

Temin, P. and B. Wigmore (1990), 'The end of one big deflation', *Explorations in Economic History*, October.

Weinstein, M. (1980), *Recovery and Redistribution under the NIRA*, the Netherlands: North-Holland Publishing.

Weinstein, M. (1981), 'Some macroeconomic impacts of the National Industrial Recovery Act, 1933–1935', in Brunner, K. (ed.), *The Great Depression Revisited*, Boston: Martinus Nijhoff Publishing.

Wheelock, D. (1987), 'The strategy and consistency of Federal Reserve monetary policy, 1919–1933', unpublished dissertation, University of Illinois at Urbana.

Wheelock, D. (1991), *The Strategy and Consistency of Federal Reserve Monetary Policy, 1924–1933*, Cambridge: Cambridge University Press.

White, E. (1990), 'The stock market boom and crash of 1929 revisited', *Journal of Economic Perspectives*, Spring.

Whitehouse, M. (1989), 'Paul Warburg's crusade to establish a central bank in the United States', *The Region*, Federal Reserve Bank of Minneapolis, May.

Wicker, E. (1965), 'Federal reserve monetary policy, 1922–33: a reinterpretation', *Journal of Political Economy*, August.

Wicker, E. (1966), *Federal Reserve Policy 1917–1933*, New York: Random House.

Wicker, E. (1996), *The Banking Panics of the Great Depression*, New York: Cambridge University Press.

Wigmore, B, (1987), 'Was the bank holiday of 1933 caused by a run on the dollar?', *Journal of Economic History*, September.

Index

arbiter of security prices 4, 85, 149
Austrian school 10, 69, 148
autonomous consumption 12, 126
Bagehot's rule 199, 215–6
balance of payments 21, 193
bank holiday 9, 25, 61, 179–80, 207
Banking Act of 1935 183–6, 188
banking panics 7–8, 21, 61–2, 78, 104, 112, 162, 194, 201, 205, 217, 236
binding nominal floor 220
boom 4, 9, 47, 49, 69, 73, 148, 199, 207–9
broker loans 5
bubbles 4, 6, 63, 85, 148, 156–60, 177, 199, 207
Civil Works Administration 25
classical gold standard 191–2
clearing houses 7, 62, 128, 168
consumer durables 2, 6, 134, 178
cost of credit intermediation 17, 173
Council of Economic Advisers 52
crash 6, 12, 89, 124, 126–7, 137, 139, 156–8, 164
credit boom 9, 47, 148
currency board 171, 205
currency–deposit ratio 9
debt deflation 15–16, 23, 35, 53, 64–5, 82–3, 91, 108, 110, 153–4, 160–1, 172, 174, 203–5, 220
deposit insurance 7, 26, 66, 189, 215
deposits-to-output ratio 23, 172

discount rate 5, 39, 49, 73, 110, 181–2, 200, 208, 227, 237
distribution of income 99
DSGE 14, 22–4, 27, 52, 80–1, 107, 109, 112, 117, 120
expectations hypothesis 17
Federal Deposit Insurance Corporation 189
Federal Emergency Relief Administration 25
Federal Reserve Act 3, 5, 11, 62, 196, 226, 229
financial orthodoxy 194–5, 199
free gold 13, 131, 146, 151, 183–6, 192, 232
Glass–Steagall Act 25, 131, 184, 187, 189, 232, 235–6
Goldsborough bill 11, 76, 100, 129, 188–9, 228–9, 232, 235
gold standard hypothesis 3, 12, 18, 27, 162
gold standard mentalité 15, 59, 75, 93, 128, 145, 147, 152, 194
great contraction 13, 64, 92, 190
great inflation 91, 125, 167, 220, 225–6, 229–31
Harberger triangles 140
high-powered money 6, 8–9, 27
hyperinflation 41, 80, 156
inflation targeting 65, 101, 125, 209, 231, 239
installment credit 2, 12
international commitment 18
international cooperation 18, 21

international transmission of deflation 4, 18

Kredit-anstalt 8

lender of last resort 7–8, 13, 15, 61, 146, 158, 162, 165, 168, 171, 197, 201, 212–3, 215–6, 227, 236–7

lessons of the Great Depression 47, 64, 204, 218, 238

liquidationists 10, 147

liquidity trap 83–4, 166

London Economic Conference 200

M1 6, 8–9, 14, 27, 73, 76, 78

M2 9

Main Street 6

McFadden Act 7

monetary base 6–7, 13–15, 27, 38, 73, 83, 100, 161, 165–6, 198

monetary hypothesis 12–13, 15, 17

money multiplier 7–9, 13, 27, 76, 161

NAIRU 125

National Industrial Recovery Act 22, 25, 27–8, 54, 66, 105, 123, 125, 197, 207

National Recovery Administration 90, 93–4, 100, 106–7

National War Labor Board 123

neoclassical growth theory 22, 27

New Deal 25–6, 28, 80, 90–1, 94, 98, 104–5, 107, 123, 197, 207–8

Nobel Prize in Economics 88

nonmonetary/financial theory 12, 15–17

nonmonetary/nonfinancial theory 12

oil price shocks 60, 68, 209

Okun's gap 140

overinvestment 9, 47, 69, 148

panic of 1907 7, 75, 168

Phillips curve 120

poverty 99

pre-war parity 33, 60, 94

price-specie-flow mechanism 18–19, 72

price stability 11, 18, 59–61, 66–7, 77, 91–2, 125, 143, 148, 167, 193, 204, 220, 225, 230

productivity shocks 23–4, 51, 55–7, 80–1, 95–6, 104, 113, 115–8, 129, 173

Public Works Administration 25

rational expectations 88, 204

real bills doctrine 5, 11, 15, 101, 152, 164, 184, 189, 194, 199, 207–8, 214, 226–7, 231, 233

real business cycle hypothesis 12, 21, 24

recession of 1920–21 3–5, 7, 23, 109–10, 197

Reconstruction Finance Corporation 25, 178–81, 184, 187, 189, 202, 213, 215–6, 237

reserve–deposit ratio 9

Riefler–Burgess doctrine 147, 152, 201

Say's Law 9, 11, 97

Securities Exchange Act of 1934 25

Social Security Act 25

Strong bill 11, 228

supply shocks 2, 125, 221

suspending deposit convertibility 13

Taft–Hartley Act 123

Tennessee Valley Authority 25

total factor productivity 23–4

transmission mechanism 15, 23–4, 52–53, 82, 134, 170, 203

tyranny of zero 230

uncertainty hypothesis 12

velocity 119, 206

Wagner Act 25, 123, 197

Wall Street 6, 84, 122, 208, 226, 239

Works Progress Administration 25

World Economic Conference 200

zero bound 65